RELIGION, POLITICS, and RATIONALITY

RELIGION, POLITICS, and RATIONALITY
in a Philippine Community

RAUL PERTIERRA

 UNIVERSITY OF HAWAII PRESS
HONOLULU, HAWAII

Published in North America by
University of Hawaii Press
2840 Kolowalu Street
Honolulu, Hawaii 96822

First published in the Philippines by
Ateneo De Manila University Press
Bellarmine Hall, Loyola Heights, Quezon City
P.O. Box 154, Manila

Library of Congress Cataloging-in-Publication Data

Pertierra, Raul, 1941–
    Religion, politics, and rationality in a Philippine community
    Raul Pertierra.
        p.   cm.
    Bibliography: p.
    Includes index.
    ISBN 0–8248–1212–3 (pbk.)
    1. Ilocos Sur (Philippines)—Religious life and customs.
    2. Ilocos Sur (Philippines)—History.   I. Title.
    BR1261.I56P47 1988
    306'.6'095991—dc19   88–18873
                                                    CIP

Cover design by Visual Schemes, Inc.
Book design by Esther M. Pacheco

Printed in the Philippines

Preface

Like other human products, this study is the result of a collective effort. Chandra Jayawardena and Ken Maddock taught me social anthropology, colleagues at the University of New South Wales (Australia) have forced me to reassess anthropological theory in the light of contemporary sociology, the people of Zamora patiently explained to me the features of their society, members of my family shared the time in the field and, since then, have endured periods of neglect, while I unraveled the rich but initially incoherent experiences incorporated in this work.

Following an established convention, I have changed the name of the municipality where I conducted fieldwork. The fictitious name is Zamora. This was done both to protect people's privacy and to indicate to the reader that my analysis is a theoretical product several steps removed from "raw experience." Another investigator might have reshaped her experience of Zamora differently.

The major portion of the research (1975-76) was financially supported by Macquarie University and an Australian Commonwealth postgraduate scholarship. Several trips to Zamora since then were made possible by The University of New South Wales. Filipinists in Australia, by readily sharing their knowledge, have given me a broader and less idiosyncratic understanding of the country. Despite certain misgivings, the Ateneo de Manila University Press patiently agreed to retain what at times is a highly theoretical style of this study. While I regret the difficulty this may cause some readers, my position is that both theoretical and practical work often require considerable effort and perseverance. Moreover, since domination has both ideological and material aspects, emancipation consequently requires a theoretical as well as a practical critique.

Philippine society is currently undergoing significant structural changes, the end product of which, at least to me, is unpredictable. I claim it is unpredictable not because I hold a particular social theory; rather, it acknowledges the fact that people create the social world out of counterfactuals. Filipinos are presently reconstituting their range of social possibilities through contestation and struggle. I hope that the outcome will better represent their general interest than what has so far been the case. With its divergent range of individual and collective interests, this study of Zamora should dispel any illusions regarding the difficulty of determining the general good. It is to be hoped, however, that this difficulty can impel rather than prevent us from redoubling our efforts to so determine the general good.

Contents

Introduction

This study examines the relationship of religion—viewed as an ideological system—to the wider social structure of which it is a part. Specifically, I explain why religion in Zamora, Ilocos Sur, has taken the forms that it has from the 1820s, when Catholicism was first introduced, to the relative success, for a few decades, of Protestantism early this century, and finally to the present role of radical and separatist denominations. These patterns of conversion are linked to the municipality's economic and political vicissitudes as well as to certain relatively invariant aspects of the local cultural tradition. The interplay of economic, political and cultural factors explain why religion in Zamora has undergone certain transformations while, at the same time, retaining invariant features. Thus, while Christianity has taken over most areas of public life, private-domestic rituals retain much of their indigenous orientation. More generally, this study explores how the processes of modernization are unevenly adopted and adapted. For example, while Zamorans successfully exploit new economic opportunities, such as the growing of Virginia tobacco and cotton, they

1

reject the new rice varieties in favor of traditional species. At the cultural level Zamorans, like most Filipinos, are extremely interested in pop music, modern dress styles, and stories of romantic love but, on most occasions, voluntarily conform to the exigencies of village life which, in many of its principles, is diametrically opposed to Western values.

The examples above indicate the complex and variegated relationship between consciousness and its associated material interests and practices. I explore this relationship using the classical sociological tradition established by Marx, Durkheim, and Weber.

Theoretical Orientation

Following this sociological tradition, I treat religion as a system of beliefs and practices that reflects the social structure of which it is a part while simultaneously contributing to the constitution of this structure. In other words, I see religion as having ideological and practical functions; it is both a view of the world as well as a position in the world. It is for this reason that Marx claimed (Schaff 1973) that while bourgeois society could provide a conceptually valid critique of religion, it is unable to eliminate its practice since this would require a radical revolution in social relations. For Marx, the fundamental contradiction of bourgeois society is indicated by this society's valid theoretical critique of religion while necessarily preserving its practice.

Religion constitutes a more essential element of social life for Durkheim than it does for Marx. While both agree on the social origins of religion, they disagree on the fundamental role it plays. For Marx, religion arises out of the hitherto inevitable contradictions in society. When these contradictions are resolved, the need for religion will disappear. Durkheim, however, sees religion as the moral expression of significant social relations and consequently all societies will express these relations in a religious form. Durkheim emphasized the importance of religious symbolism in expressing the unconscious yet intimate relations that members of a society have with one another.

Weber is not as concerned in examining the origin and ultimate basis of religion as are Marx and Durkheim. In Weber's view, religion is primarily concerned with the quest for meaning and order which has consequences (intended and unintended) for the organization and constitution of social life. For Weber (as for Marx and Durkheim), "not ideas, but material and ideal interests directly govern men's conduct" (1970:280). Weber's main quarrel with Marx was directed primarily at Marxists who refused to recognize that ideal (read *moral* for Durkheim) interests often moved people to alter their material conditions. Weber was not arguing for the total autonomy of the ideological order from its material base but was simply pointing out that a person's image or conception of the world affects his response to it. Moreover, this image is not, in Weber's view, only determined by material interests since material interests are themselves seen and expressed in ideal terms. Marx, Durkheim and Weber all agree that a person's position in the world (i.e., material interests) structures his conception of the world (i.e., ideology) which in turn shapes his responses to the world (i.e., conscious, purposive activity). They differ simply in the emphasis given to each of these three modes.

The theoretical model used in this study draws from the above tradition and views society as a system of culturally constructed material practices reproduced through communicative exchanges. This model sees culture and structure on the one hand, and ideology and practice on the other, as constituting one reality. Thus, attempts to separate meaning from organization or the ideological aspects of practice from the practical aspects of ideology are ultimately futile.

The emancipatory potential of critical reason has been a major theme of this classical sociological tradition and more recently, Jürgen Habermas has continued this interest in exploring how the structures of rationality constitute and organize social life. I use Habermas's work to investigate the notion of modernization in Zamora while recognizing that a critical consciousness and practical action proceed from different aspects of the social structure. Using the theoretical model indicated, I examine the problem of rationality and its relationship to the rationalization of social life in a society whose institutions have diverse power structures. Using Habermas's concept of communicative rationality, I show that Filipino peasants are as concerned to maintain conditions of unrestricted and rational discourse as they are to retain normative standards or to pursue strategic goals. Unrestricted discourse allows Zamorans to articulate values that underlie their normative expectations and constrain their strategic pursuits.

The possibilities for rational action in peasant societies obviously depend on both internal and external structures which control choices. These structures are neither uniformly constraining nor equally constraining on all aspects of actions. Thus choice may be constrained at the extradomestic level but open at the intradomestic level, or it may apply mainly to instrumental aspects (e.g., market exchange) and not to communicative or expressive aspects of action (e.g., religious practice).

The difficulty that social theory has had in conceptualizing the relationship between consciousness and structure (e.g., Giddens 1976, Tourraine 1973) is often due to the conflation of aspects of actions with their corresponding structures. Reason and its embodiment in structure (i.e., the process of rationalization) is, to use a mathematical metaphor, neither homogenous nor continuous. A major problem in social theory is to investigate the functional relationship between individual and social consciousness, and the nature of its discontinuity. It may be the case, as

Habermas indicates, that certain discontinuities are nonremovable, thus practical rationality does not generate structures because its institutional embodiment is undefinable. The rationalization of social life, as Weber understood it, is an attempt to remove these discontinuities. However, the persistence of practical-moral schemes of action like religion and other aspects of civil life shows that the gap between individual and collective rationality remains unbridgeable.

Society and Religion in Zamora

Although Christianity was first introduced in Zamora over 150 years ago and has, since then, exercised a considerable influence, certain aspects of the religious experience of its people have been relatively unaffected by it. The shortage of priests and the variable extent of colonial control only partially explain why some areas of religion have largely retained their indigenous characteristics. Essential features of Christianity like a supreme and ethical deity, an emphasis on spiritual merit and the transcendent, have remarkably little influence on people's religious practices and beliefs. In cases where Christian influence is strong, adherents are often those who have rejected more orthodox Christian denominations in favor of radical and separatist ones.

These features of religion in Zamora should be seen in an economic and political context characterized by shifting and diverse sources of patronage, the lack of an effective universal legal code with its agencies of implementation, and the necessity of maintaining a complex network of political alliances through a system of reciprocal and normative exchange based primarily on pragmatic and contingent considerations.

I argue that although these economic and political factors do not directly determine religious ideology, they favor and facilitate certain ideologies over others. People in Zamora who reject the dominant religious ideology are often those whose position within the traditional economic and political system has become increasingly more difficult and hopeless. While they are usually unable to alter their material conditions significantly, their new religious commitment offers them a satisfactory explanation for their poor situation in life.

The principal aim of this study is to show how religious practice and belief are firmly rooted in social relations. These relations often arise out of economic and political interests, but they are often defined in ideal or moral terms. Thus, although I agree with Marx (1976:38) when he says that "this state, this society produce religion," I disagree with its implication that its product (i.e., religion) must necessarily constitute "an inverted world consciousness." Marx's observations may be more applicable to societies with developed state institutions and whose religions stress spiritual merit and the transcendent order (Hinduism, Buddhism, Christianity, and Islam, for example) than in a case like Zamora where political processes are comparably accessible and whose religious practice stresses contractual ties and an orientation to the present life.

Following Durkheim, I regard religion as a more essential component of social reality than what Marx implied. And like Weber, I believe that religion, among other things, satisfies the human quest for meaning and order at the level of nature and the cosmos. In Zamora, this quest for order has undergone several significant changes, in line with the economic and political fortunes of the municipality. Many of the forces of change affecting Zamora originate outside of it. Much of the local economy, local politics and even local religion are simply responses and adaptations to these external forces. As a consequence, the local ideological structure must be seen in relation to the wider structure, of which it is a part, to fully comprehend it.

However, despite the acceptance of Christianity in its several variants, essential features of the indigenous religious ideology have remained basically unchanged, e.g., the importance of ancestors and seniors, the emphasis on contractual relations, and the multiple sources of supernatural patronage.

This study discusses and explains why some indigenous religious elements like domestic rites have persisted, while others like public and communal rites have not. It also explains the varying degrees of success encountered by the Christian denominations in Zamora.

My immediate purpose is to show the links between religious ideology and its social substructure, i.e., make explicit the relations of inequality and exploitation that underlie much of the religious practice and belief. A second purpose is to contribute to the understanding of the substructure itself. In the words of Marx (1976:39),

> Once the holy form of human self-estrangement has been unmasked, the task is to unmask self-estrangement in its unholy forms—thus the criticism of heaven turns into the criticism of earth, the criticism of religion into the criticism of law and the criticism of theology into the criticism of politics.

Institutionalized religion has been a major feature of Philippine lowland society since the arrival of the first Catholic friars in the sixteenth century. The formal and close links between Church and State existed throughout the Spanish colonial period from 1568 to 1896. These links were manifested at the level of the economy through Church control of the vast friar-estates (Roth 1977); at the level of the polity, through the institution of the *patronato real*, or the privilege exercised by the Spanish Crown to appoint Church officials in exchange for support of Church activities; and at the level of ideological formation, through the Church's control of educational institutions.

The close articulation of Church and State interests had been so highly developed during the colonial period that even during the Revolution of 1896, the practical expediency of retaining these links was advocated by otherwise fervent anticlericalists (Majul 1967:137-59). The eventual intervention of American colonialism imposed the separation of Church and State and finally broke the formal nexus between religious and secular interests. In its place, the Americans supported the notion of religious pluralism so long as the religious order recognized and accepted the authority of the State in national security. Catholicism quickly adapted to the new political conditions while a host of Protestant and nationalist sects spread throughout the country. Most of these latter denominations were accepted by the secular authorities, while those mainly of peasant origin were suppressed (Sturtevant 1976) because they often combined religious fervor with subversive secular ideals.

The close links between rebellion and religious dissatisfaction experienced throughout the Spanish colonial period were maintained well into the present century (Ileto 1975, Covar 1975, Shoesmith 1978, Pertierra 1983) and still characterize much of the discourse and rhetoric of radical and revolutionary movements.

However, beyond noting the historical, political and cultural significance of religion in the Philippines, there has been little systematic study of its role in the daily lives of ordinary Filipinos.

Earlier studies of religion in the Philippines have been marked by both methodological and theoretical weaknesses. These studies were often polemical justifications for a particular religion (e.g., Achutegui and Bernad 1961, Braganza 1965, Bulatao and Gorospe 1966, and Alonso et al. 1968), or they were conducted without a clearly articulated theoretical framework (e.g., Carroll 1970, Magannon 1972, Claver et al. 1973 and Lynch 1975). More recent studies have overcome some of these difficulties (e.g., Covar 1975, Ileto 1975, Sturtevant 1976, Love 1977, and Gonzalez 1985); these have shown the significant and complex links between religion and politics. My study of Zamora shows how religious practice at one level reflects and at another supports the secular order.

Writers such as Santa Romana (1955), Ellwood (1969), Lynch (1975), Covar (1975), and Love (1977) have discussed in other contexts some of the matters that I raise in this study, like the variable influence of orthodox Catholicism on ordinary rural Filipinos; the limited success of Protestant conversion, and the present role of radical and separatist sects. These writers, however, do not attempt to situate religion explicitly within a social structure wider than the community of believers. For them, religion consists of beliefs and practices with a life and character of their own, a phenomena *sui generis.* I do not accord the religious life such a degree of autonomy and for this reason, I discuss religious practice in Zamora after I have described the major economic and political parameters that shape and limit its expression. This approach would only be complete if one situates Zamora within the national and international economic-political framework significantly affecting it. I shall only be able to indicate briefly some of these external factors: the role of external capital, the urban political bias, the importance of education, the growth of a national bureaucracy, the effects of migration.

For the immediate purpose of this study, I have imposed analytic boundaries limiting my choice and treatment of religion. These boundaries explain the emphasis and focus on local interpretations of religious orthodoxy and their links with elements of the local economy and polity. It is therefore not so much a study of village religion as it is of religion manifested at the village level.

Fieldwork

My treatment of religion has concentrated on aspects that are accepted and understood by a large majority of people—example of these aspects are the main calendric rites, healing rituals, life-crises rites—rather than present an account of religion as practised and understood by religious virtuosi, such as indigenous practitioners, local ministers, and/or theologically educated Catholics.

My interest in the external and accessible areas of religious life stems both from methodological and theoretical considerations. The limited time of fieldwork (sixteen months) and the practical difficulties of gaining acceptance into the community prevented me from acquiring the linguistic competence in Itneg, Kankanai and Iloko necessary to evaluate the highly abstract systems expounded by religious specialists. In addition to these methodological problems, my theoretical framework considers religion to be primarily a social phenomenon expressing collective ideas and practices rather than something expressing only an individual's theoretical reflections on the natural and transcendent orders. For these reasons, the more private and edifying aspects of religious experience in Zamora are not described in any detail.

The main period of fieldwork was from May 1975 to June 1976. An earlier visit of one month and a subsequent one lasting two months brought the total time in the field to just over sixteen months. Apart from short stays (one or two months) in the barrios of Ambugat, Dayanki and Macaoayan, most of the time was spent in Luna. This barrio is centrally located and allows easy walking access to most other barrios in Zamora.

To gain acceptance into the community, my wife and I helped teach

English and mathematics (part-time) at the local private secondary school; we also took a general interest in other aspects of education. However, the event that most facilitated our acceptance into the community was the birth of our first child. Many people saw this event as a confirmation of the strong ties we had developed in the municipality.

Our initial contacts with the community were mostly with its elite members —municipal and barrio officials, teachers and other professionals—but gradually, we established friendships with ordinary people in the local neighborhood and the barrio.

I began my research using both English and Tagalog but after a few months, made increasing use of Iloko. My understanding of Itneg and Kankanai was never more than rudimentary but most informants in the barrios where these are spoken are also fluent in Iloko.

Rationality and Social Change

In my fieldwork, like many anthropologists, I was struck by the uneven pace of social, political and economic change that affected the village. Certain areas of social life seemed remarkably resistant to outside influences, but other areas not only yielded to change: change was actively anticipated and promoted there. To give some examples: Catholicism as a religious ideology was available to most villages since the early 1800s, some accepted at least a nominal version of this religion while others doggedly resisted conversion to it well into the 1930s. And even then, they rejected Catholicism in favor of the recently introduced Protestantism. Among Catholics, certain areas of life like public rituals are heavily impregnated with Catholic practice while others like private-domestic rituals still retain much of their pre-Catholic orientation. In the sphere of politics, there is a similar incongruity: local or village politics appears to follow externally imposed forms—barrio captains, barrio meetings, etc.—but it often operates according to traditional lines: elders, ritual specialists, etc. However, in extravillage matters, people are highly attuned to the most recent political practices. They make extensive use of urban-based relationships and even anticipate radical political programs. In the sphere of production, a crop like rice is treated with extreme interest and concern: change and innovation in its production are not rejected but are subjected to great critical examination since it is the major subsistence crop. Other crops such as tobacco, maize, and cotton, however, are accepted or rejected with the equanimity and interest of a capitalist entrepreneur. In the legal and regulative spheres of village life similar discrepancies are encountered. The national law is applied under certain circumstances and ignored in others. Certain disputes are settled along customary lines while others are brought before the courts. The procedure preferred is determined by normative and strategic factors.

In the area of culture, a very large degree of acculturation is found in the villages. Gone are most of the traditional arts and crafts; radio and television sets are eagerly purchased whenever possible and people are aware of the latest city fashions in clothes and music. Yet even in apparently superficial matters like learning the latest dance steps, external influences are not simply being arbitrarily imposed on village culture. Selective forces are at work accepting certain behavioral modes, rejecting others, or adjusting them to suit local requirements. Barrio children, for instance, spend a considerable amount of their time at school learning the latest dance steps, but display their newly learned skills only under specific conditions like school programs. The latest dance steps are not integrated with the dancing repertory of adolescents or adults who retain the more traditional and modest demeanor expected at public dances. In other words, while a new behavioral orientation has been readily and willingly learnt—in the form, say, of a religion like Catholicism, or of new political affiliations, national legal norms, new productive techniques, or the latest cultural fashions—it is recontextualized to meet local conditions. The extent of this behavioral recontextualization depends on the degree of articulation between internal village structures and external forces at the provincial, national and international levels. It is this varying degree of articulation between village and external structures that explains the variable response of peasants to the technical, normative and strategic choices available to them. These typical observations lead many anthropologists to dispute theories of modernization that portray peasant society as static, conservative, and xenophobic or theories that fail to appreciate the variable response of the peasantry to forces and influences that seek a fundamental overthrow of the traditional order.

Within anthropology, there are two main approaches to the study of peasant societies: (1) moral economy (e.g., Scott 1976) and (2) political economy (e.g., Popkin 1979) approaches. Moral economists view peasants as largely homogenous, moral communities concerned with maintaining minimal subsistence levels for all their members. They see peasant traditions as adaptations to technological and environmental limitations; any threats to these traditions challenge the very existence of peasant life. The political economists, on the other hand, point out the heterogeneity and the self-interest found among peasants. In this view, peasants take risks if the calculated returns appear promising despite the existence of norms to the contrary. Political economists also point out that significant divisions characterize peasant society and the survival of the individual is not always the concern of the village community as a whole, that market forces and technical innovations that threaten traditional relations do not always have adverse effects for all peasants, and that poor peasants are often disenchanted with traditional village society because the traditional order did not meet their legitimate expectations, not because their position has been worsened by the impact of a cash economy. In such cases, the movement from the village to the town may reflect not only the attractions of a modern economy but also the failure of the traditional economy.

Both of these approaches to peasant society have their merits. While peasants, like everyone else, often pursue their strategic interests, they also defend their deeply felt moral values. Purposive-rationality and value-rationality characterize peasant social life. What I wish to explore, however, is how these rationalities are responsible for the differential responses to social and technological forces currently acting on peasant society. To do this, I shall first examine the idea of rationality to see how it applies to cognitive structures, social relationships, and expressive states. Rejecting the more naive and simplistic aspects of modernization theory, social anthropologists have fallen back either on normative models like those advocated by the moral economists or on the strategic models by the political economists. This dichotomy, however, rests on a specific and restricted notion of rationality. The first unduly emphasizes value-rational action; the second considers only purposive-rational conduct. For this reason, I am attracted by the not yet fully developed concept of communicative rationality suggested by Habermas in his latest work, *Theory of Communicative Action* (1984). I am not claiming that peasant societies exemplify Habermas's concept of communicative rationality better than other societies. My present concern is to use this concept to examine the differential response to change in a peasant society and to supplement the existing concepts of peasant rationality.

Initial studies of the peasantry often portrayed village life as culturally and intellectually inferior to town life. Peasants were described as naturally conservative, inward-looking, and irrational. Judged by urban standards, peasant life was seen as changeless, archaic, and inefficient. Social change had to be imposed on the village and the response to drastic change varied from anomic resignation to violent, if usually ineffective, resistance. Modernization theories pointed out the distinctiveness of urban structures and their technical, moral, and rational superiorities (Weiner 1966). Peasants have to be "infected" with the need for achievement (McClelland 1966), this latter always being defined in instrumental terms. Institutions like formal schooling (Anderson 1966) and Western style of jurisprudence (Galanter 1966) are seen as typical examples of rationalized urban-based structures that have to be imposed on the less rationalized and by implication, the less rational village institutions. This rationalization of social institutions is seen as a necessary precondition for the adoption of technology and hence, a more efficient economy. The replacement of this urban perspective by one more sympathetic to village values challenged many of the earlier views on the peasantry. The moral economists have established that peasants act rationally within their strongly held normative beliefs—beliefs which in themselves are their adequate adaptations to the constraints of subsistence economies. What appear as their innate compliance with their exploiters turns out to be their long-term insurance against bad harvests. Their reluctance to enter a cash economy is based on a rational assessment of the insecurities of a market whose exchange relationships are uncontrolled by village norms.

Taking for granted the normative rationality of peasants, the political economists point out the existence of diverse and often irreconcilable interests within village society (i.e., incommensurable moral principles). In their view peasants are not mainly moral actors but strategic ones. While against ascribing irrationality to the peasantry, the moral economists conceded peasant rationality to the normative order. The political economists extended this rationality to include both instrumental and strategic behavior. They pointed out that social change is keenly accepted or strongly rejected according to the strategic interests of the distinct sectors of peasant society. Many anthropologists accept the political economists' view of the peasantry as a complex and at times diverse society whose members, while subscribing to a rationalized system of technical action and normative control, nevertheless pursue individual interests. However, the political economists must recognize that these individual pursuits, which ensure the dynamism and flexibility of peasant society, are not exclusively strategic in their goal but also refer to specific normative and communicative expectations. Moreover, while the impetus for change may be introduced from outside, peasant social structure may itself intensify or promote such change rather than attempt to absorb it within traditional modes (Fegan 1982). This expanded political economist model of village life, despite its being an improvement over earlier views, still does not operate outside the earlier mentioned restricted model of rational action. Its concern still lies mainly within the normative and strategic aspects of action and denies its communicative aspects. An examination of these communicative aspects enables one to expand rationality beyond the technical, normative and strategic modes conceded by this existing model.

As Habermas (1979) has pointed out, Weber's discussion of occidental rationalism includes a confusing range of phenomena starting from mathematized modern science, harmonic music, perspective in painting, a systematized legal system, a developed bureaucracy, the capitalist enterprise with rationalized accounting, employing labor as a commodity and using technological production, and finally, what Weber calls "the capability and disposition of men to practical-rational modes of life."

According to Habermas, "Weber uses the expressions 'rational' and 'rationalization' first of all to characterize utterances, opinions, and actions for which reasons can be given" (p. 187). Hence such activities as modern empirical science are rational to the extent that their knowledge claims are sustained by systematic appraisal and correction. Similarly, normative activities are rational to the extent that they are consciously guided by general and discursively redeemable ethical principles.

Habermas noted that for Weber rationalization is linked not only to formal properties of thought but also to their substantive contents. Hence, "not only the cognitive but also the socially integrative components of world views are rationalized, that is, on the one hand, empirical knowledge of external nature and, on the other, moral-political knowledge of the society in which one lives and even aesthetic-practical knowledge of one's own subjectivity or of inner nature" (1979:189). It is for these reasons that Weber is able to link world domination through science and technology, with the domination of social relations under capitalism that emerged as a result of an earlier methodic domination of the inner world found in Protestantism. In other words, the objectivization and domination of nature is posited on the objectivization of society manifested in the treatment of social relations as commodities, which in its turn is preceded by the objectivization of spiritual life through the Protestant denial of individually gained religious merit. However, this conjunction between social actions and their corre-sponding structures is, as mentioned earlier, theoretically problematic.

Habermas (1984) argues that the inability to link social actions to their corresponding structures is the reason why social systems theorists such as Parsons do not relate the rationality of acting subjects to the rationality of social systems, this latter being defined exclusively in the system's capacity to adapt to changing environments in order to maintain itself. For anthro-pologists, this problem is illustrated by Malinowski's unsuccessful attempt to reduce culture to individual and psychological needs; by Radcliffe-Brown's inability to go beyond the observation of regular and constant interactions and to relate social structures to any system of meaningful actions; and more recently in Levi-Strauss's failure to include a consciously acting subject in his concept of structure.

In his latest work, Habermas (1984) has been concerned to clarify and extend Weber's concept of rational action. Weber's model takes the view that the rational actor is primarily oriented to achieving his goal, having previously defined his ends or purposes and calculated all the other consequences of his action as secondary conditions of success. Success is defined as the effective intervention in a state-of-affairs through conscious goal-directed action. Such an action is instrumental when we consider it from the aspect of following technical rules and evaluate it in terms of the efficacy of the intervention into a physical state-of-affairs. In contrast, strategic action, while also oriented to success, is primarily concerned with the application of rules or maxims and is evaluated in terms of its efficacy in influencing the decisions of rational opponents. While an instrumental action may be connected with social interaction, a strategic action is social action.

Strategic action is primarily oriented toward obtaining success, while communicative action is oriented toward reaching an understanding. This understanding is based on mutually recognized and discursively redeemable validity claims. A forced agreement cannot be counted subjectively as agreement or understanding. Habermas derived the concept of communicative action from the model of speech; to him, one of the intrinsic ends of speech is understanding. Communicative action, however, need not necessarily be linguistic in form, nor is all linguistic communication necessarily an instance of communicative action. In some situations, media other than language may constitute communicative action, although ultimately, validity claims related to constative speech have to be invoked.

Whenever linguistic utterances are used to coerce or instrumentalize alter for ego's end, such uses of language do not constitute communicative action. In order to be communicative, an action must bring into play notions of propositional truth, normative rightness, and subjective truthfulness. In contrast, a strategic action, while based on the truth of propositional statements, temporarily suspends claims to subjective truthfulness and normative rightness since these latter claims are not constitutive of the social relationship.

Communicative actions may be judged according to their propositional content (i.e., whether they are true or false), their normative rightness (i.e., whether the action conforms or breaches mutually acceptable norms), and their expressive truthfulness (i.e., whether the speaker's claims to private feelings are seen as truthful or authentic). Various theories of social action have stressed one of these types to the exclusion of others (i.e., instrumental-technical, strategic-normative, expressive-dramaturgical).

At this stage, I should point out that I see some fundamental difficulties in Habermas's analysis and in his suggestion for reconstituting rationally motivated activity. In particular, the lack of an extended discussion of power as a separate dimension structuring and defining social relationships raises serious questions for anthropologists interested in the effects of culture and structure on discourse in societies with weak centers of power (e.g., Clastres 1977, Rosaldo 1980). Moreover, Habermas's solution for breaking the spell of culture is to undermine its objectivity by continually subjecting it to reflective criticism, a process that is itself constitutive of a cultural tradition. A similar predicament was clearly recognized by Durkheim (1915) when he linked a future science of religion with the necessity of first turning science into a religion (i.e., by elevating the practice of systematic inquiry into a dogma). For Habermas, a culture must first accept the cult of reason or reflective criticism in order to expose itself to rational critique. However, these technical difficulties (recognized by Habermas) do not immediately concern this study. Its primary aim is to examine religious ideology and its relationship to the rationality of peasant life.

Chapters 1-3 deal with the historical background of Zamora, its local economy and system of stratification, and discuss the dispute between political factions concerning the proper site for the *poblacion*, the administrative, cultural and market center. Significant aspects of religion in Zamora, including denominational membership, are influenced by factors like class and status, and by the relations between the main political factions. The lack of a developed poblacion has affected the nature of political competition, with important consequences in the religious sphere.

Chapter 4 analyzes the kinship structure and its relation to political alliances and access to land. Zamora kinship terminology follows the general Ilocano pattern but marriage and residence preferences differ significantly among barrios. These differences are related to political and economic factors. Patterns of residence have had considerable effects in maintaining the cultural distinctions existing in Zamora and have consolidated various political and religious interests in its barrios.

Chapter 5 describes the main transition rites and the social changes they signify. The importance of feasting to indicate these transitions may be compared with similar practices which Geertz (1960) observed in Indonesia. Like the *slametan*, feasting expresses a range of relations with the natural and supernatural orders. All significant events in Zamora are marked by feasting, the extent depending on the event's importance and on the family's resources. In addition to expressing social ties, rites of passage also manifest and create spheres of interest appropriate to each sex and age. Birth and death are areas of concern appropriate to women, while marriage negotiations are the concern of men.

Chapter 6 discusses indigenous and folk religious practices, and relates these to the Christian tradition. The use of indigenous and folk rites occurs principally in the private and domestic sphere, an area less affected by Christianity and traditionally associated with women. However, even in areas significantly affected by Christianity, the predominant moral attitude is closer to indigenous moral notions than it is to orthodox Christianity. This moral attitude views human beings as inherently and potentially good and considers evil to be an existential feature of the world rather than an inevitable result of human nature.

Chapter 7 describes the role of elites in defining and practicing what is accepted as local religious orthodoxy. The extension of domination in the religious sphere is exemplified by members of the elite through their control of most Catholic organizations. This control often results in the exclusion of nonelites from participating in many Catholic activities, except during the main calendric rites. Others join separatist and radical denominations that challenge the prevailing notions of religious orthodoxy.

CHAPTER I

History and Geography

Zamora is an interior municipality in the province of Ilocos Sur, on the western coastline of northern Luzon. It is about seven kilometers southeast of San Jose, the main coastal town linking it to the national highway and to the other major towns on the Ilocos coast.

The people of Zamora frequently travel the unsealed road to San Jose to go to market, visit friends and relatives, attend school, or to make connections with the buses that pass through San Jose on their way to other parts of the province and to other provinces.

Zamora may be described as a satellite of a larger and more important center which provides it with the services and facilities that small inland municipalities lack. This situation resembles that of the thirteen other interior municipalities in Ilocos Sur. The facilities these large coastal centers offer to the interior municipalities are substantial, ranging from regular markets to tertiary education, hospitals, entertainment, and information.

While it may give an impression to a visitor of being a small municipality, Zamora in 1975 had a population of nearly 8,000 in 26 barrios, ranging from

15

99 in Lesseb to 836 in Luna. Most barrios or villages in Zamora have between 250 to 450 people.

Following the common Philippine rural pattern, people in Zamora live in barrios which are separated from one another by ricefields. The barrios are strung along the river that winds down from the foothills of the Cordillera and passes through the municipality and on to the coast. The river is the main source of water for irrigation; it yields significant quantities of fish, prawns, and other foods. It is used as the reference line when people refer to themselves as living east or west. Barrios are located on land with access to the main river or to one of its tributaries.

Zamora is in a narrow valley between a small coastal range and the foothills of the central Cordillera. Several trails link Zamora to the main highland communities on its eastern side. These communities form part of the Tinggian, Bontoc-Sagada and Kankanai culture areas. Apart from the main road to San Jose, there are narrow tracks over the western range to adjacent coastal municipalities. During the late eighteenth century—when raids were regularly carried out by highland headhunters against outlying lowland villages—the topography of the Zamora valley would have made the establishment of lowland communities unsafe. The valley remained sparsely populated until the midnineteenth century, and most of its established villages were culturally and politically related to the highland groups mentioned. These villages conducted trade with the large coastal towns, providing them with gold, honey, and forest products.

Zamora was formed in 1919 by combining parts of the adjoining coastal municipalities south of San Jose and wedged between the Ilocos coast and the mountains of Abra. Zamora links many of the more interior municipalities to San Jose and the coast. There is a regular movement of people through Zamora on their way to the markets held in the large coastal towns. This movement has created a wide network of kinship and friendship, linking Zamora to both interior and coastal municipalities.

The trip from San Jose takes about twenty-five minutes to cover the 10 kilometers to the barrio of Luna, including the various stops along the road to allow the people to alight and disentangle their belongings from the packed jeepneys which ply this route. One passes several barrios before arriving at Bato, the present *poblacion* (administrative center) of the municipality. A number of passengers usually get off at Bato to visit the municipal hall or to take the narrow tracks that lead to other barrios situated on the western side of the main river. The jeepney, its load considerably reduced, proceeds to Luna, three kilometers down this road. About 100 meters down from the poblacion, the road crosses the main river which has had a bridge since 1967. This bridge often needs repairs, and as a consequence, jeepneys sometimes have to ford the river.

During the rainy season, from early May to late October, when the river

Zamora Municipality

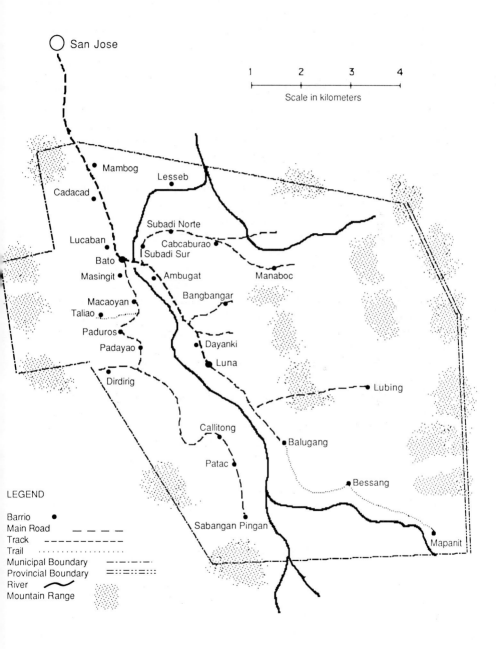

San Jose

Scale in kilometers

| 1 | 2 | 3 | 4 |

Mambog
Lesseb
Cadacad
Subadi Norte
Lucaban
Cabcaburao
Bato
Subadi Sur
Masingit
Ambugat
Manaboc
Macaoyan
Bangbangar
Taliao
Paduros
Padayao
Dayanki
Luna
Dirdirig
Lubing
Callitong
Balugang
Patac
Bessang
Sabangan Pingan
Mapanit

LEGEND

Barrio   ●
Main Road   ─ ─ ─ ─
Track   ─ ─ ─ ─ ─ ─ ─ ─ ─
Trail   . . . .
Municipal Boundary   ─ ·· ─ ·· ─ ·· ─ ·
Provincial Boundary   ═ ∷ ═ ∷ ═ ∷ ═ ∷
River   〜
Mountain Range

level rises, one may have to cross the bridge on foot and take another jeepney to Luna. This last part of the trip runs parallel to the river, and cultivated fields lie on each side of the road as the jeepney crosses the main plain of the municipality. Various barrios and isolated settlements (*sitios*) can be seen lying several kilometers on each side of the road. Access to them is by narrow track or trail.

Luna is not very impressive although it is by far the largest barrio of Zamora. From Luna, the main road narrows considerably but during the dry season, jeepneys are able to reach several other barrios two or three kilometers farther south. The map of the area shows the road going from Luna to adjoining interior municipalities. While it is possible to travel by four-wheel-drive vehicle to the respective administrative centers of these interior municipalities, the slightest rise in the river level makes such a trip dangerous and almost impossible.

There is also a narrow road veering east from Luna to the Abra border via Lubing, the highest barrio in Zamora, at an altitude of about 1,500 feet above the valley. This road is impassable after heavy rains, but during the dry season, jeeps and trucks use it to transport tobacco and other produce from the highland barrios of Abra province.

The generally poor roads do not prevent a constant movement of people from highland barrios across the Abra border to San Jose and other coastal towns. Many of these people pass through Luna on their way to the coast, and for this reason, Luna has always claimed to be the most important barrio in the municipality. The original and founding families of Luna claim that their ancestors came from the highland communities to the east around the beginning of the nineteenth century and they relate complex genealogies to prove it. Old people tell the story of how their ancestors planted a mango tree to mark the site of the original settlement, northwest of the present barrio. Whenever this tree bore fruit, all the descendants of the original settlers—most of whom had settled in the barrios of Luna, Macaoayan, and Lucaban—gathered to share the harvest. As each descendant was given his share, the old men recited the list of ancestors (usually no farther than four to five generations above ego) entitling him or her to receive it. Shares ranged from a dozen fruit to half or quarter of a single fruit, depending on closeness and the line of descent to the original settlers (Reinante-Dilem 1976).

Historical Background

Historical references to the area which is now Zamora begin around the 1830s. Foronda and Foronda (1974:24) mention the establishment of the township in 1831 after missionary activities by Fr. Bernardino Lago. This zealous Augustinian used the town of San Jose, founded toward the middle of the previous century, as a base from which to venture into the mountain-ous interior to christianize the "wild" tribes. Keesing (1962:138), making use of Buzeta's investigations carried out in 1818 and 1848, writes:

> San Jose had off to the southeast the mission of Coveta, near which there were three rancherias of infidels: this in modern times has become the municipal district of Zamora. Many rancherias to the east also adhered to it (i.e., Nueva Coveta), Buzeta says, before the province of Abra was created. The local people mined some gold in the Mt. Pingsal area.

In a local document, reference is made to several petitions referring to the boundaries of the township of Zamora. This document, written around 1832, affirmed the rights to the ownership of land of its non-Christian inhabitants. Some of these petitions refer to the encroachment by Christ-ians from San Jose and other adjoining municipalities upon the lands mentioned and ask the provincial governor to prohibit these encroach-ments. A map was enclosed showing the area that is now Zamora and including parts of the adjoining interior municipalities.

Historical records about Zamora are few soon after the formation of Nueva Coveta as a *rancheria* (non-Christian township) in 1831, until the end of the century. Apart from birth and baptismal records kept at the church at San Jose which occasionally mention residents of Nueva Coveta, there are no significant documents describing life in this township during the remain-der of the century.

By the middle of the last century, the area around Zamora was sufficiently pacified for Ilocanos from the coast to establish various barrios in what is now the municipality. Many of the Ilocanos came as tenants of the local inhabitants but intermarriage and the introduction of a money economy later enabled Ilocanos to acquire land.

Soon after the American invasion and occupation of the Philippines, several investigatory missions were sent north to examine the situation of the predominantly non-Christian townships. In 1904, M. Miller, an American official, investigated the political aspirations and intentions of the interior municipalities near Zamora. Nueva Coveta is not mentioned but non-Christian townships to the south of it were visited and it was recommended that these be integrated within the provincial and national systems. The inhabitants of these townships, being non-Christians, had been exempted from paying taxes by the Spanish authorities. But according to M. Miller, they were willing to forego this privilege in return for retaining their traditional political structures rather than come under the domination of coastal Ilocanos.

The center of the township of Nueva Coveta, later to be known as Luna, was the focus of much of the interaction between coastal Ilocanos and Nueva Coveta's non-Christian inhabitants. Other indigenous settlements such as Macaoayan, Lucaban, Masingit, and Mambog retained much of their non-Ilocano identity well into this century.

Religious Conversion

Despite the zealous activity of Fr. Bernardino Lago in the 1830s and his equally determined Augustinian successors, the penetration of Catholicism among the highland groups around San Jose was not as impressive as the rapid conversion of coastal Ilocanos.[1] Scott (1974) describes the nature of much of the historical contact between the lowland peoples, under the leadership of their colonial masters, and the fiercely independent highland communities. Since much of this contact was hostile and aimed at the reduction of these highland groups, it was not surprising that they equated conversion to Catholicism with political and cultural subordination. Ironically, when the Spaniards—having realized the disadvantages of a military policy (search and destroy operations) of political conquest—replaced it with peaceful inducements like tax exemption for non-Christians willing to acknowledge Spanish political sovereignty, other reasons for rejecting religious conversion were inadvertently introduced. Partly for this reason, non-Christian barrios in Zamora preserved their religious traditions, with the accompanying sociopolitical structures, almost halfway into the present century. When the inhabitants of these barrios were eventually converted, the majority of them became Protestants rather than Catholics. The reason for this pattern of conversion is a major interest of this study.

While the non-Christian inhabitants of the township of Nueva Coveta enjoyed their tax exemptions and control of much of their village lands, an increasing number of Christian Ilocano settlers from the adjacent coastal municipalities migrated into the area. By the beginning of the present century, most of the inhabitants of Zamora were Christians. By this time, apart from the non-Ilocano barrios mentioned (i.e., Macaoayan, Lucaban, Mambog, and Masingit), and to some extent the barrio of Luna, the other barrios in the municipality retained very few indigenous non-Christian religious and political institutions. The people of the latter barrios called themselves Ilocanos, professed to be baptized Christians and distinguished themselves from the inhabitants of the other barrios whom they called *paganos* (pagans) or *infieles* (infidels). While many of these self-identified

1. The Augustinians were one of the major Catholic religious orders responsible for the Christianization of the Philippines. They arrived in Ilocos in 1575 and proselytized along the coast and in the adjoining mountain areas until their expulsion in 1898 (*Ilocos Review*, vol. 3, 1971).

Christians were undoubtedly coastal immigrants with a long history of Christian experience, others were new converts who saw little advantage in resisting conversion particularly in a political climate that increasingly favored Christians. These recent converts were referred to as *bago* (new Christians) by their more experienced coastal brethren.

The barrios of Macaoayan, Lucaban, Masingit, and Mambog are characterized by the retention of many pre-Christian political institutions. These institutions were closely associated with the religious life of these communities, both politics and religion having been under the control of old men (*panglakayen*). This group of senior men adjudicated disputes, both within their barrios and between barrios, whenever one of their members was involved. They were also responsible for performing the main communal religious rites. Their control of ritual was an aspect of the ideological hegemony exercised by senior men. They also dominate other aspects of the normative and moral order such as kinship obligations, duties to ancestors, and the belief in supernatural entities.

The combination of political and religious control by elders in the barrios mentioned made religious conversion more difficult there than in those barrios whose religious structures were more loosely integrated with specific political interests. This would have been so in barrios with a Catholic Ilocano majority. Here, political leadership is exercised by individuals who have no special claims to religious privilege or merit while religious leadership rests with the priest or his assistants. This separation of the profane and sacred spheres was far less marked in barrios that resisted conversion to Christianity.

Political leadership in Macaoayan, Lucaban, Masingit, and Mambog was, until recently, centered on the *dap-ay* (men's hut), the meeting place for the barrio's leaders. The *panglakayen* were also responsible for the community's ritual activities like praying for rain, performing rites to mark the opening of the planting and harvesting seasons, warding off illnesses and other evils threatening the community, and preparing the dead for its trip to the next world. Old women were allowed to participate in some of these activities, and even to initiate some, but most ritual activities of communal significance were controlled by senior men. While this group of senior men effectively controlled the barrio's political affairs, they refused to relinquish control over its ritual affairs. Loss of religious control is especially marked in conversion to Roman Catholicism, with its emphasis on ordained Western-educated specialists belonging to a foreign-controlled bureaucracy. In contrast, conversion to some Protestant denominations did not result in complete loss of control over the barrio's religious life. The pattern of religious conversion in the predominantly non-Christian municipalities near Zamora in favor of fundamentalist and evangelical Protestantism contrasts sharply with the success of conversion to Catholicism among coastal Ilocanos. However, the lukewarm reception to these same Protestant sects in the coastal urban centers such as Vigan, Narvacan, and Candon, indicates a fundamental difference in response to religious conversion by the inhabitants of large coastal urban centers. Part of the explanation of this pattern lies in the structure of lowland political organization, with its emphasis on urban centers of control, presided over by the poblacion-residing elite. A similar hierarchic structure characterizes the Catholic Church, and close links between the Church and the local government structures have existed in both colonial and postcolonial times. In contrast, evangelical Protestantism allows each congregation considerable autonomy in its own affairs, enabling the elders to keep their dominant position in a politicoreligious structure found in the formerly non-Christian barrios.

The process of conversion to Protestantism began in Luna. The Mision Cristiana (Christian Mission) was the first sect to proselytize and by 1913, a small congregation was established in this barrio. Its members included some of the most prominent local families. It was this initial success of Protestantism that prompted the Catholic authorities, following several appeals by Roman Catholics in the barrios of Luna, Dayanki, and Balugang, to establish a parish, with a resident priest, in Zamora. The priest was installed in Luna in 1932 and the new parish was dedicated to the Santo Niño de Praga, a religious image popular throughout the Philippines (Tenazas 1965).

In the meantime, the main non-Christian barrios of Macaoayan, Lucaban, Masingit, and Mambog were becoming increasingly more interested in Protestantism. Apart from the Christian Mission and the Methodists, the Pentecostalists gained a large following in these barrios. These Protestant denominations strongly opposed Roman Catholicism. Their elders maintained the tradition of local autonomy for each congregation, i.e., interpretation of the Bible, performance of services, etc.

Several factors were responsible for the final conversion to Christianity of these barrios. The increasing political and economic integration of interior municipalities, such as Zamora, into provincial and national structures made it necessary for their inhabitants to participate in these wider spheres as full citizens. It became increasingly difficult for them to do so while they were pejoratively referred to as *paganos* or *infieles* if they remained non-Christian. By converting to Catholicism, they were patronized by coastal Ilocanos as *bago*. But many of these inhabitants of interior municipalities wished to differentiate themselves from the coastal Ilocanos. Protestantism offered a partial solution to both requirements: political participation and cultural distinction. The prestige of American missionaries suited their need to raise the status of their religious activities in order to deal with the coastal Ilocano Catholics as equals. In addition, the organizational autonomy of Protestant congregations allowed them to retain considerable control over their own affairs.

Political and economic integration into the wider structures occurred in

Zamora soon after the American occupation. By 1905, elementary schools, using English as the medium of instruction, had been established in Luna and Bato. Literacy was soon after expected of aspirants for political office.

Between 1903 and 1916, political officials were chosen to represent the area that is now Zamora. One set of officials were chosen for the northern barrios and another set to represent the southern barrios. Most of the officials came from the predominantly non-Catholic barrios, including Luna, a barrio with both Catholics and non-Catholics. The political domination by the non-Catholic minority was achieved through their control of much of the land in the municipality and the resulting political disenfranchisement of the largely tenant Catholic Ilocano majority. However, even in those early days, certain affluent Catholic Ilocano families were able to achieve political prominence.

Political domination by members of the predominantly Protestant, non-Ilocano barrios lasted until the outbreak of the Second World War. The changes in the political consciousness brought about by the war, and the movement for political independence soon after, significantly altered the political status of the Ilocano majority. When this was combined with the introduction of Virginia tobacco as a major cash crop, and its concomitant attraction of external capital, in addition to the integration of Zamora into the national and provincial political party structures, the earlier domination by the Protestant non-Ilocano minority was much weakened. In the present political climate, a non-Catholic candidate is at a significant disadvantage and for this reason, the political elite, which still includes the leading families of the formerly non-Catholic barrios, consists mostly of active Catholics.

Who is an Ilocano?

Wernstedt and Spencer (1967:332) describe the Ilocos provinces as having "one of the most homogenous ethnolinguistic populations of any Philippine region." Lewis (1971:20), quoting the 1960 census, lists Ilocos Sur as 97.5 percent Ilocano. A map issued in 1974 by the National Museum of the Philippines (Fox and Flory) purporting to show the differentiation and distribution of Philippine linguistic, cultural and racial groups shows the area around Zamora as totally Christian Ilocano. The 1970 census shows almost all the people of Zamora and other interior municipalities around it (i.e., Zamora 99.5 percent) to have Iloko as their mother tongue.

One soon becomes aware, however, of the complexity of cultural affinities and linguistic competencies in a municipality like Zamora. The barrios of Macaoayan, Lucaban, Masingit and Mambog—with a total population of 1,268 (16.5 percent of the 1975 population)—are still considered, both by themselves and the other barrios, as non-Ilocano. Their inhabitants speak

Igorot, in the case of Macaoayan and Lucaban (793 speakers), and Itneg or Tinggian, in the case of Masingit and Mambog (475 speakers). However, most of the people of these barrios are also fluent in Iloko and use this language outside their own barrio. To most outsiders, and for census purposes, they would classify themselves as Ilocanos and claim Iloko as their mother tongue. It is in this limited sense that I would agree with Lewis (1974:20) when he says that "when mountain people become Christian, they called themselves Ilocanos. Ilocanos call them *bago* (i.e., new Christians)." There is a certain ambiguity and looseness in the use of the term *Ilocano*, which is not surprising, since it spans distinct political and cultural levels.

Several anthropologists, including Cole (1945:149), Keesing (1962:326), and H. Lewis (1971:20) who have worked in the Ilocos region, suggest that the interior populations are descended from Ilocanos who left the coast as runaways, political refugees, or migrants searching for new opportunities after Spanish rule was imposed toward the end of the sixteenth century. Little evidence is given for these conjectures beyond some similarities in economic and political structures between certain groups near the coast (i.e., Zamora) and those living farther inland (Keesing 1962:113-43). These similarities could just as easily be explained by postulating that some highland groups established themselves in coastal valleys allowing them to conduct trade with the comparatively large Ilocano coastal towns.

The hypothesis suggested by Cole (1945:149) and Keesing (1962:326) about the lowland origins of highland groups such as the Tinggian, Bontoc-Sagada, and Kankanai is not supported by evidence from Zamora, particularly when the occupation of the highlands is seen as having resulted from the pressures of Spanish colonization. Ethnohistorical evidence and historical sources describing the fierce and dogged resistance of highland groups to Spanish encroachment (Scott 1974) and the daring raids highlanders made on coastal centers such as Vigan, Narvacan, Candon, and Tagudin (Routledge 1979) make it unlikely that the highlanders were simply coastal Ilocanos escaping from Spanish domination. It is likelier that despite the hostilities, the regular trade between the highlands and the coast encouraged some highland groups to establish settlements near the coastal centers (Scott 1974:21).

Many highland groups were assimilated into the coastal Ilocano communities and towns, particularly after accepting Catholicism. In this respect, H. Lewis's (1971:20) comments about highlanders calling themselves Ilocano once they accepted Christianity is correct. However, Lewis's remark was made in the context of highlanders calling themselves Ilocano following the heavy penetration of many of the highland regions by coastal Ilocanos early this century. Although I agree with Lewis's observation, I disagree with the implication that this example of assimilation by highlanders into Ilocano society is proof that all highlanders were originally coastal Ilocanos.

The question of the origins of these highland groups is complicated by the use of the term *Ilocano* to cover a range of incommensurable qualities. For a census taker, an Ilocano is someone born in the Ilocos region, of Ilocano parents, and one who has lived in the province and speaks its language. Most people in Zamora would accept this usage for that purpose, but they would also point out that Ilocanos are associated with a long experience of Christianity (Catholicism) that is not shared by most of the inhabitants of barrios such as Macaoayan, Lucaban, Masingit, and Mambog. Further, the people in these barrios practice marriage, death, sickness, birth and other rites that distinguish them from their coastal neighbors. Finally, the people of these barrios speak a language that is incomprehensible (for the most part) to their neighbors. For all these reasons, people in the other barrios of Zamora do not consider the inhabitants of Macaoayan, Lucaban, Masingit, and Mambog (some would include Luna) to be true Ilocanos. For their part, the people in the barrios mentioned concur in this judgment and refer to themselves as Igorots or Itnegs, a distinction which in certain contexts they are proud to make.

These distinctions are ignored in census statistics, which also fail to record that nearly one-sixth of Zamora people do not principally speak Iloko at home, even though they become fluent in this language at an early age.

For these reasons, one must reexamine statements made by writers such as Wernstedt and Spencer (1967), Lewis (1971), and Fox and Flory (1974) describing the Ilocos region as a culturally and linguistically homogenous area.

In Ilocos Sur, fourteen out of the thirty-four municipalities in the province are classified as interior and all fourteen exemplify the cultural diversity found in Zamora. To talk about cultural and linguistic homogeneity in such a context is obviously misleading, unless one means by this that most people in these municipalities are Iloko-speaking Christians who have given up their "savage" practices. According to the 1903 census, Ilocos Sur had 13,576 Igorots, of whom two were classified as "civilized" and the rest "wild" (Keesing 1962:115). By the 1948 census, the category "wild" was no longer used and in its place, 4,208 people were described as Igorot speakers and 476 as Tinggian or Itneg speakers. During the intervening years, the process of political and cultural annexation had been completed. In the 1970 census, Igorot was no longer a linguistic classification and Kankanai—of which there were 4,047 speakers—was used in its place. In this same year, there were 2,200 Itneg speakers. The Iloko-speaking population in 1970 was 375,554 in a total population of 385,139. In other words, 97.5 percent claimed Iloko as their mother tongue. This is presumably the criterion used by Lewis (1971:20) when he claimed that the province of Ilocos Sur was 97.5 percent Ilocano. However, if Zamora is any indication of ethnic affiliation—and there is reason to believe that non-Ilocano ethnic affiliation in other interior municipalities is much higher—then about thirty to forty thousand people, or 10 percent of the 1970 population, do not consider themselves, nor are considered by others, as Ilocanos in the contexts previously described.

Ten percent may not be a large proportion of the total population, but this cultural minority is well represented in 41 percent of the province's municipalities embracing about half the land area of Ilocos Sur. It is within this perspective that the cultural and linguistic homogeneity of the province should be reexamined. A map purporting to show the ethnolinguistic groups in the Philippines, done by Fox and Flory (1974), which shows all of Ilocos Sur in one color, thereby implying that the area is occupied by only one ethnolinguistic group, should be revised.

Social Dislocation and the Emergence of an Ilocano Municipality

The Second World War brought to Zamora considerable social disloca-tion, as throughout most of the rest of the Philippines. The polarization of the community by years of Japanese occupation created problems of greater significance than the physical ravages of war. Steinberg (1967), in his study of Philippine collaboration during the Second World War, distinguishes what he sees as collaboration with the Japanese on the part of the country's political elite on the one hand, and on the other, the continued resistance to Japanese rule by the majority of the Filipinos. He explains this apparently divergent response to the Japanese as an historically consistent attempt by the elite to retain effective control, while accommodating themselves to new colonial masters. (The native elite or *principalia* had done much the same in relation to the Spaniards and later, the Americans.) Steinberg argues that in the years between Spanish domination and the Japanese invasion, a feeling of national self-consciousness developed in the Filipino masses that led them to see the response of the political elite as betraying the nation.

As far as I could ascertain, the situation in Zamora was not so simple. Some members of the political elite appeared to accept Japanese rule, while others opposed it by becoming guerrillas. Most people simply wished to pursue their traditional occupations. For them, the change of colonial masters was not their primary concern. However, the split within the elite soon produced serious divisions throughout the municipality because of the strong ties binding members of the elite to their followers. The dilemma of dual allegiance created by the demands of the Japanese and the Americans was compounded by the strong ties binding members of the elite and their supporters. In wartime, with normal constraints suspended, these divisions had devastating results. Old feuds were revived and harsh retribution became commonplace. Several executions took place in Luna and in other barrios during the Japanese occupation, and these atrocities escalated toward the end of the war. On most accounts, the guerrillas were seen to be as destructive as the Japanese and their collaborators. Many people in Zamora relate how difficult it was to dissociate themselves both from the collaborators and the guerrillas. One of the strongest memories people have is of the depredations caused by a guerrilla unit, led by several Americans, that terrorized the local population toward the end of the war.

In such circumstances, it is difficult to agree with Steinberg's assessment that "a large percentage of the populations sensed what was expected of them . . ." (1967:174), implying thereby that the majority of Filipinos supported the guerrillas and actively opposed the Japanese.

The final result of the war as it affected Zamora was the intensification of preexisting tensions between competing factions and their immediate families. These tensions resulted in many unsolved killings in the immediate postwar period whose consequences are still deeply felt.

The intensity associated with Ilocos politics (Lewis 1971), to which Zamora is no exception, can partly be explained by the enmity generated by the Second World War.

The end of the war marked a significant change in the political and economic development of Zamora. When the Americans granted political independence to the Philippines in 1946, a new phase of political mobilization was introduced. Political parties were reorganized and followers were recruited throughout the provinces and municipalities. An immediate effect was to lessen the importance of the earlier political distinction between the people of Ilocano and non-Ilocano barrios. The mobilization of party ties created an increasing dependence on national and provincial political structures, with a corresponding decrease in the importance of local political distinctions. At about the same time, Virginia tobacco was introduced into the district creating a more affluent cash-oriented local economy and linking Zamora into a wider national and international market.

For these reasons, the end of the Second World War marked an increase in the rate of the Ilocanization of Zamora. While it was still seen as an interior, and to some extent a culturally different municipality by members of the urban-coastal elite, its own inhabitants were beginning to emphasize their Ilocano cultural links and to identify their own interests in Ilocano terms.

The Barrios of Luna and Macaoayan

Luna and Macaoayan are two of the biggest and most important barrios of Zamora. Luna has always considered itself the political and religious center of the municipality. But this claim has been challenged by a coalition of northern barrios, to which Macaoyan belongs. While Luna is indisputably the most important in the coalition of southern barrios, the coalition of northern barrios has chosen Bato, until recently a relatively undeveloped barrio, as the focus of its political claims. The opposition between these northern and southern factions is discussed later, but let me give a brief description of Luna and Macaoayan.

Luna

The barrio of Luna consists of clusters of houses along the main provincial road and across a set of intersecting roads, making up a grid system. There are no specific boundaries except for the roads that divide the community into sections or districts, but the people in Luna refer to the northern, southern, western and eastern parts when directions are asked for or when details are given as to one's destination or point of departure. When asked where he is going, a person might answer that he is going north (*idiay amianan*) or south (*idiay abagatan*), by which is meant that the person is heading for the northern or southern parts of the barrio. In this sense, Luna may be said to be divided into named sections. According to the 1975 census, Luna has a population of 836 from among 154 households.

In Luna, as in many other Philippine barrios, the church-plaza and the school form a central complex in which the main public activities take place. Apart from the Catholic Church that dominates the plaza, Methodists and the Church of Christ have prominent churches in this central complex. The plaza and its surrounding area consist of a cemented basketball court, an all-purpose cement pavement used on Sundays as a tennis court by members of the municipality's elite, and the old municipal hall (dating from the days when Luna was a poblacion) that is at present being used as a storage shed, a preschool, and the place for barrio meetings. Next to the old hall are two elevated concrete stages, one belonging to the barrio council and the other, to the Catholic Church, used for school, religious and social functions.

Houses in Luna are built along certain patterns. A group of siblings often builds houses close to one another, forming a compound or neighborhood, where passage from one houselot to another is open and frequent. Houses with fences around them are relatively few, but when they occur, they indicate the high status of their owners. A cluster of houses is often separated from another cluster by a fence, indicating the kin orientation and closeness of its residents. Luna's roads also act as boundaries and dividers, separating one compound from another.

While there is a strong feeling of belonging to Luna, as against belonging to another barrio, there are at most only weak feelings about belonging to a section of Luna. Occasionally there are sporting competitions pitting one half of the barrio against the other, but these are not characterized by the tensions present when Luna competes against another barrio. There are several mutual aid organizations (*saranay*) that give financial and other help in times of serious illness or death; they are based on a section or a cluster of local compounds. In October, the Catholics divide the barrio into several areas, each area being responsible for carrying out the devotion of the rosary in the homes of Catholics in its jurisdiction. Although the members of the various religious denominations are found throughout the barrio, common kinship and religious affiliation create pockets of heavier concentration of members belonging to a particular denomination. There is a higher proportion of non-Catholics in the southern and western sections, while Catholics predominate in the northern and eastern sections.

Membership of the different status categories (to be discussed in chapter 2) is not the main determinant of the pattern of residence. People of high status tend to remain within the compound of close kinsmen but adopt certain architectural styles and materials, together with the appropriate lifestyle, to indicate their status. It is this lifestyle, with its pattern of consumption and economic resources, which entitles a person (but not necessarily his kinsmen) to a particular status. Affluent families do, however, prefer to live near the main plaza or at least, on the main road. Those who live in the fringes and periphery of the barrio tend to be poor and are thought of as being socially disadvantaged.

Several factors, whose significance dates from the beginning of the present century, have transformed Luna from a barrio that used to be considered non-Ilocano to one which, within the municipality, is now considered almost completely Ilocano. Intermarriage particularly between coastal Ilocano men and daughters of affluent Luna families resulted in uxorilocal residence and the consequent inclusion of these coastal Ilocano men into their wives' political community. This pattern has distinguished Luna since the beginning of this century from a barrio like Macaoayan. In earlier days, both barrios shared the same cultural origins.

The role of the Ilocanos in local politics became more significant after the formation of Zamora. Men like Don Cleto Principe, Don Quintin Vilor, and Don Hermogenes Tino were coastal immigrants who, as young men, married into non-Ilocano families and settled in Luna in the early 1900s. By the 1920s and 1930s, these men were influential in local politics. However, unlike them, their sons married locally, thus reinforcing their existing matrilateral links with affinal and later, with cognatic ties to Luna's leading families. The effects of uxorilocal residence of coastal Ilocano men paradoxically led to the transformation of Luna, in the following generation, into a barrio where marriages were predominantly between fellow barrio residents. This change in pattern of marriage and residence should be seen in the context of the availability of land. The uxorilocal residence formerly found in Luna and still practiced in Macaoayan assumed a husband's access to his wife's land, either in preference to his own land or because he depended on her. Ilocano men who married into Luna had little land of their own and consequently depended on their wife's land. The children of such marriages had only their mother's land to inherit and the resulting preference for intrabarrio marriages reflects the limited availability of such lands.

The increase in political activity, which marked the emergence of Zamora, first in the American-designed political order and later, after political independence, had important consequences for Luna. Much of the activity centered on this barrio and brought with it an expansion in the range and nature of relations with the rapidly increasing Ilocano majority in the municipality.

This increasing political exposure attracted various families from Ilocano barrios allied to Luna who had, in the meantime, become prosperous and politically important. They have since become established residents of this barrio.

The progressive Ilocanization of Luna has changed the barrio's cultural orientation and very few traces of its highland origins remain. Except for some old people who still speak Kankanai, Iloko is the language of the household and the barrio. The institution of the dap-ay which started to fall into disuse before the last war, has not been reinstated. Birth, marriage and mortuary rites and practices are now similar to those in other Ilocano barrios. Most importantly, a significant change in self-perception has occurred. Luna's inhabitants now see themselves as differing culturally and ethnically from the people of Macaoayan, Lucaban, Masingit, and Mambog, despite the protests of some older folk who still insist on the cultural and ethnic affinities of Luna with Macaoayan and Lucaban.

Hand in hand with the Ilocanization of Luna, the authority and control formerly exercised by the group of male seniors has been considerably reduced. Old men and women still wield considerable authority in some of Luna's Protestant denominations, but the increasing integration of the barrio into the provincial and national political structures exposes its inhabitants to a society that demands ever higher levels of formal education and wider political experiences from its leaders.

Macaoayan

This barrio is often referred to as "the rice granary of Zamora." The ricefields surrounding it and the large wooden houses of its inhabitants are evidence of its prosperity. Macaoayan lies west of the river, not far from the hills separating Zamora from the coastal municipality of San Rafael. A large irrigation canal (*pay-as*) passes along its eastern side to provide its fields with water, which is particularly crucial during the early period of tobacco planting (January-February) when the rains have ended. According to the

1975 census, Macaoayan has a population of 480 from among 104 house-holds.

The barrio does not give one the impression of being planned, in the sense that Luna does. A road joining Macaoayan to Bato and to the barrios south passes along the eastern boundary, but several tracks wide enough for a jeepney wind their way through the barrio itself. In Macaoayan many houses are larger and more substantial than most of those in other barrios. These houses are usually built of wood and are progressively enlarged by attaching more rooms to the central structure. The ground floor is used for storing tools and for sheltering chickens and pigs, but a portion of it is often used for gatherings in the late afternoon, when the rest of the house is still warm from the day's heat. The upper story contains a large living room with very little furniture, except in some cases for a large television set, an appliance which has become more common since the introduction of electricity in 1976. Usually two small rooms, each with a large wooden bed and wardrobe, lead into the living room. Blankets, pillows, and the house-hold's valuables are kept in these rooms, access to which is allowed only to members of the household and their close kinsmen and friends. A large kitchen leads to the living room through a passageway or connecting hall. It is in this hall or in the kitchen that most entertaining takes place, the living room being used only for special or formal occasions.

It is not unusual for people to sleep on the ground floor (on a bamboo bed), the hallway or the living room floor in preference to using the beds in the bedrooms. People are often hesitant to sleep in basically private as against public quarters. They often express a fear about sleeping in a bedroom if they are alone, but not about sleeping on a kitchen floor or on the ground floor.

The house plan described does not differ in any essential way in other barrios, but Macaoayan houses are generally much larger and made of more durable materials.

Macaoayan is divided into two sections. One is referred to as *amianan* (north) and the other as *abagatan* (south). Unlike in Luna, these sections constitute important political and social units. The boundary separating them begins at the men's hut, which is in the center of the barrio, runs between the clusters of houses, and ends on the hill overlooking the entire barrio. The hill was formerly the site of the main communal sacrifices (*patpatayen*). The dap-ay is the focus of much of Macaoayan's political life and still serves as the sleeping quarters of adolescent boys and the occasional drunken elder. The barrio's increasing prosperity is seen in the construction materials used in the dap-ay. It has a galvanized iron roof built over a cement foundation with a slightly elevated bamboo floor that serves as the communal bed. Outside, there are heavy flat stones which once were used as tables and stools during the major sacrificial offerings (*bignas*). Men use the dap-ay whenever they wish to discuss important affairs in the absence of women. Public meetings are also held in people's houses, and on these occasions, men usually sit in a circle in the middle of the living room while women and children crowd around the stairs or in the hallway. This arrangement does not prevent senior women from taking an active part in these proceedings.

The village gongs and drum, used to summon the elders and the rest of the community whenever the occasion requires, are kept in the dap-ay. On its wall is posted a list of the names of people responsible for maintaining a general watch and supervision over the village at times when most of its adult members are working in the fields. Two men are posted in the dap-ay to make sure that cooking and other fires do not get out of control and to ensure the protection of the barrio. The care taken to see that each section has its own guard, with the implication that a man only ensures the protection of his section, indicates some of the tensions and hostility existing between them. In the past, each section was responsible for a specific ritual role during the main religious celebrations but conversion to Christianity in the 1920s and 1930s ended most of this ritual complementarity. At present, the most important ritual role associated with each section has to do with the preparation and serving of food during mortuary rites. Members of the deceased's section, usually his close kinsmen, wash and prepare the corpse for burial while members of the opposite section cook and serve food to the many guests expected during the period of mourning prior to the burial.

These examples illustrate the manner in which sections constitute ritual and political units. Old people in Macaoayan claim that in the past these sections were opposed and occasionally engaged in ritual combat. Some elders point to certain fields with names such as *kin-gab-bo* (the place where they wrestled) and *makaremkem* (the place where they bit one another) where this ritual combat is said to have taken place.

Compounds of close kin are less common in Macaoayan than in Luna. While kinsmen may live next to one another, patterns of visiting between them do not differ from those between neighbors who are less closely related. Occasionally parents and their children live in different sections and siblings do not express the preference for living next to one another— something that siblings still prefer to do in Luna. Macaoayan people maintain that since almost everyone in the barrio is related to everyone else, it is not important to delineate close kin.

Parents in Macaoayan state a preference for their sons to marry into other barrios sharing the same cultural background as Macaoayan's. Since there are many such barrios in the municipalities in the southern and interior parts of the province, a wide network of kinship has been established throughout these parts of Ilocos Sur. This marriage preference is often accompanied by uxorilocal residence with the result that many of the leading men come from other barrios and these men, in turn, encourage their sons to marry back into their own (i.e., the fathers') natal barrios. A consequence is that the land owned by a pair of spouses is usually scattered over several barrios in different municipalities.

The affluence of most people in Macaoayan is based on the ownership of land. They work some of the lands themselves and have tenants work the rest. There are several barrios such as Taliao, whose inhabitants mainly work as tenants of Macaoayan families. It is the ownership of much land and the resultant relationships with tenants that has enabled this barrio to play an important part in local politics since the formation of Nueva Coveta in 1831. Families from the barrio have provided Zamora with much of its political leadership from the earliest days of its history. However, unlike Luna, Macaoayan itself has not been the focus of much political activity, and instead, most of it has been focused on Bato, the present site of the poblacion.

The factors responsible for the Ilocanization of Luna have been less important in Macaoayan.

The practice of marrying their daughters to coastal Ilocanos still does not appeal to many Macaoayan families, but the increasing emancipation of the younger generation and their wider social contacts make such marriages inevitable.

Christianity was not significant in this barrio, until after the war. Since then, Catholicism has become a major force, although Macaoayan is still predominantly Protestant.

Macaoayan's affluence has had a generally conservative effect in the past, but this same factor is also the main reason for its rapid integration into the wider social and political spheres. Affluence had, in the past, enabled many of its families to preserve and defend many of its political and cultural interests without having to adopt a subservient attitude to the municipality's Ilocano majority. Access to land was a sufficient guarantee of high status and of a secure economic and political position. The present situation has changed considerably. While the ownership of land is still the most important element in determining social, political and economic status, ownership must now be validated in consumption patterns including formal education, modern housing, and other practices resulting from the barrio's increasing exposure to urban lifestyles. Because of their secure economic base, many families in Macaoayan have been able to afford a private education for their children, larger and more expensive houses, and investments in commercial enterprises. All this has turned Macaoayan from a barrio where people are said to have lived in small, unpretentious huts before the war, to one where large houses, a university education, and travel abroad are more often enjoyed by its inhabitants than by the people of the much poorer Ilocano barrios of Zamora. The latter, despite their poverty, had always seen themselves as culturally superior to the Igorots of Macaoayan.

Such a transition, from a conservative barrio cherishing its ancestral customs and religion to being one where the signs of modernity are most apparent, should not be understood in terms of the values or other psychological traits of its inhabitants but in terms of a more primary factor. Macaoayan's position in the system of production, particularly its control of land and labor resources, has given it a greater chance to prosper socially and politically than the other barrios have had. Luna had a similar opportunity but exploited it in a different way.

CHAPTER 2

The Economy, Division of Labor, and System of Stratification

The economy of Zamora revolves around the growing of rice and Virginia tobacco. Other crops are grown but these are not as significant for subsistence needs or as an income source, as are rice and tobacco. The system of stratification is based on land ownership and access to other economic and social resources. Rice is the basic subsistence crop and is associated with traditional notions of wealth and status while Virginia tobacco provides farmers with a cash income.

Zamora may therefore be described as a society with coexisting modes of production: (1) a traditional mode based on the cultivation of rice for domestic consumption, and (2) a capitalist mode based on the sale of Virginia tobacco to an external market. These modes involve distinct relations to land, require a different organization and evaluation of labor, entail particular attitudes to profits and capital accumulation, and activate specific links with the national economy and polity.

Let us examine how these coexisting modes of production affect social

35

classes and status hierarchies. In particular, I shall comment on the position of women under these changing conditions.

The Rice Economy

Farmers in Zamora plant both traditional and high-yielding rice varieties. The traditional varieties consist of ordinary, nonglutinous species (*magu-prad*) and special glutinous species (*diket*). For example, *ginorio* is an ordinary nonglutinous variety chosen for its hardiness while *ginundo* is a glutinous species used on special occasions for making rice cakes (*sinuman*) and rice wine (*tapuy*). Despite the low yields of glutinous varieties, most farmers feel obliged to plant a small quantity of *diket*, to meet important ritual obligations. Rice cakes are essential in all festive activities, and glutinous rice is always included in ritual offerings (*atang*) to ancestral and environmental spirits.

High-yielding varieties such as IR 36 and IR 45 are also planted by most farmers. While recognizing the higher yields of the new varieties, many farmers prefer the traditional species. Qualities such as the possibility of storing unthreshed grain in bundles, little deterioration during storage, and its taste and consistency are the major reasons given for favoring the traditional species. However, because farmers obtain credit from the local rural bank only on condition that they plant high-yielding varieties, they are forced to make increasing use of them. The move to new varieties brings with it a change in technology and an increasing dependence on national bodies, especially the rural banks, the Department of Agriculture and the National Irrigation Administration.

The Ilocos provinces have a rice-yield per hectare that is among the highest in the Philippines (Rice Production Manual 1970:4). The average in Ilocos in 1968 was about 37 cavans of paddy rice per hectare. The yields in Zamora of some varieties are often higher, for example, 50-60 cavans, but the lower-yielding glutinous varieties bring the average closer to the provincial figure.

Most farmers grow only one kind of rice crop a year because of the shortage of water, but some, using the new varieties and irrigation, manage two crops. Precise figures for average yields are difficult to obtain, since they vary from one field to the next, and from one farmer to another. A yield of 35-45 cavans (one cavan = 44 kilograms of unhusked paddy) per hectare would be considered good. Although the average yield per hectare is made difficult to estimate by the varying sizes of fields, the different varieties planted in the same field, and the storing of many varieties in bundles instead of cavans, a farmer has a good idea of the yield of each of his own fields and often of his neighbors' yields, too.

Most people in Zamora realize that their rice yields could be improved by more use of fertilizers, pesticides, and the new varieties, but they will often justify their traditional practices on the ground that in the long run, the results are more certain and predictable. Farmers are willing to be as experimental and innovative as their resources allow, but to grow rice calls for more than economic rationality. Different varieties of rice are associated with different cultural and nutritive values, and in addition, social and religious factors must be considered. Small quantities of certain varieties are needed to make rice wine and rice cakes which are served to guests on special occasions. Offerings to ancestral and house spirits require particular rice varieties: *killaban, makaraniag, arikuykuy.* There are traditional obligations regarding planting and harvesting schedules. Ecological responsibilities such as not killing the small fish, frogs, and other semiaquatic organisms living in the wet ricefields (through the use of pesticides) are observed because these resources are considered common property. It is within this complex of aesthetic, social, religious and ecological factors that decisions regarding the species and methods of cultivation are made. It is, therefore, not unusual for an outsider, who sees rice as nothing more than a commodity crop, to interpret the farmer's traditionalism as a result of innate stubbornness or stupidity (Barnett 1967, Lynch 1972).

Farmers in Zamora claim to be willing to increase their rice yields if this can be done on equitable conditions. Often, however. increases require unfamiliar varieties and a different technology to be used. Reliable access to fertilizers and pesticides, and the high costs of transport and seedlings usually necessitate capital loans, which involve the farmer in unfamiliar formal transactions, where the organizational bias benefits urban economic and political interests, i.e., local politicians, buyers, Chinese exporters. The whole process frequently ends with the farmer having to sell his tobacco crop to pay for the costs of his higher rice yields.

The proportion of people who grow sufficient rice for their own needs varies considerably from one barrio to another. In a prosperous barrio like Macaoayan or Luna, 25 to 30 percent (estimates made by several reliable informants, including agricultural extension officers) of households have to supplement their own rice harvest, whereas in a less affluent barrio like Bangbangar or Taliao this rises to 50 to 60 percent. Purchases are paid for from the tobacco crop or occasionally by exchanging labor for rice.

While rice has always been the main crop, other crops have, in the past, been grown to supplement household resources. Aside from small quantities of fruits and vegetables, various cash crops have been grown in the municipality. In the nineteenth century, indigo was grown and during the first decades of this century, cotton was a significant cash crop. The indigo industry collapsed as a result of the increasing use of chemical dyes, and cotton-growing was discouraged by the importation of cheap textiles. These fluctuations in the local and international markets are not thoroughly understood by the average farmer, but he is broadly aware of the implications of dependence on a market economy, particularly of its uncertainties. It is in this frame of mind that farmers accept the introduction of cash crops. As long as the new crops do not interfere too much with the growing of rice, which he sees as his main activity, the farmer is willing to invest his limited resources in other crops. If the new crop is profitable, farmers need not be persuaded much to cultivate it. Virginia tobacco is an example.

Farm labor in Zamora comes mainly from within the household, except that at times of peak activity, outsiders are hired to help.

Ricefields are prepared by men, either on their own or by labor exchange (*ammoyo*) usually with kinsmen and neighbors. (*Ammoyo* refers to a group of people who work in each other's land.) Occasionally a farmer has his land ploughed, for which he usually pays cash. Several of the more prosperous farmers own small tractors which they hire out for ploughing, but most of this work is still performed by carabaos or cattle, usually owned by the farmer himself.

Once the field has been prepared, all members of the household and some outsiders help in planting. Weeding is done by both men and women, and when the crop has matured, young children protect the fields from marauding birds with a system of strings to which are attached tins and cans that make a noise when the strings are pulled.

The rice harvest usually requires extra labor. This is generally paid in kind: one bundle out of every nine harvested. Women will often work as hired labor on occasion, particularly when their own families' harvests are insufficient for household needs. While men, too, are willing to perform this labor, they are more likely to hire out their services for a fixed wage of about ₱5 (US $0.70) for seven or eight hours work a day. Most people give their paid laborers a midday meal, but those who are paid in kind bring their own food.

The traditional varieties of rice are harvested using a finger-knife (*rakem*), but the new varieties are cut with a sickle (*kompay*). The stalks are stored in bundles, in the case of traditional varieties, or threshed, in the case of new varieties. The former can be stored, with a minimum of drying, in specially constructed granaries (*agamang*) or even kept in the fields in covered piles. In contrast, the newer varieties must be properly dried after threshing and before storing.

The Tobacco Economy

Virginia tobacco (Torres:1982) was introduced to Zamora in the late 1950s. It is planted in January-February and harvested in April-May. Despite the heavy labor input of the initial phases of growth, and later in harvesting and drying, Virginia tobacco may be a very profitable crop for farmers, particularly when its prices are high. However, tobacco prices are difficult to predict, as they result from factors determined by the government, private investors, and foreign buyers. Prices vary considerably from one year to the next, despite government measures for price stabilization. Local and foreign buyers can control the price by simply varying the amounts bought from farmers at any given time. This advantage is compounded by heavy indebtedness of farmers to buyers. Moreover, such practices as loans at high interest rates (up to 100 percent per annum), deduction of part of the weight to allow for shrinkage, deliberately low assessment of leaf quality, and costs of transport to warehouses—all these reduce the farmer's profits. However, despite these disadvantages, a good tobacco crop provides the only significant cash income for most farmers and tobacco has, over the years, given Ilocano farmers, particularly in municipalities like Zamora, one of the highest per capita incomes in the Philippines. Ilocanos often refer to the relative affluence of their province and Zamora farmers justly point out that Virginia tobacco has enabled many of them to build houses, provide education for their children—in short, their material standards have improved considerably.

Unlike many of the traditional varieties of rice, Virginia tobacco is far more dependent on the regular use of fertilizers and pesticides. These chemicals must be bought before the tobacco season, and seedlings often have to be bought. Moreover, harvesting, spiking and drying the leaf require considerable labor and fuel. The drying kiln, if built of durable materials, is a considerable capital investment, requiring several good seasons to recoup its cost. Many of the expenses mentioned are often partly or entirely covered by loans advanced by the buyers, who then deduct part of the final tobacco payment to the farmer. Some loans carry a high interest rate but others do not, the interest charged depending on the relationship between the buyer and the farmer. In some cases, no interest is charged on the loan; the buyer then downgrades the assessed leaf quality to a greater extent than usual and, in addition, expects the indebted farmer to act as his agent in buying more tobacco.

During the 1975 season, tobacco prices rose sharply, with the highest quality leaves selling for ₱10-15 a kilogram (US $1.50-2.00), whereas in the previous year, the same quality had brought only ₱2.00-2.50 a kilogram. The low prices in 1974 had discouraged many farmers from planting in 1975, thus contributing to the high prices in that year. In 1976, after pressure by farmers' associations on the government, President Marcos issued a decree setting the price of high quality leaf at ₱7.00-7.50 a kilogram. However, as there exists no mechanism to enforce this decree, e.g., impartial government assessors, very few buyers in Zamora actually paid these prices, thereby providing yet another example that presidential decrees are often only observed in the breach. In the preceding twelve months, (1975-76), inflation had raised the prices of fertilizers, pesticides, gasoline and wood by 20 to 25 percent. As the previous year had been a good one, many farmers in Zamora and elsewhere had planted, in 1976, a larger crop than usual, creating a glut on the local market and contributing to the collapse in prices. Despite the presidential decree and the preceding high rate of inflation, tobacco prices in 1976 seldom rose above ₱6.50 a kilogram for high grade leaf, and often fetched much lower prices.

In 1977, the government attempted to enforce a minimum price for specific grades of leaf by appointing government inspectors and licensing major buyers. As a consequence of the close links in Ilocos Sur between economic and political interests, and the fact that these links favor urban entrepreneurs rather than rural farmers, the effects of these government measures were at best marginal. Those responsible for implementing the decree establishing the minimum prices were often the major buyers. Many local buyers who might have sympathized with the farmers were themselves squeezed by price ceilings controlled by foreign interests. For all these reasons, farmers in Zamora barely managed for the second consecutive year to cover their expenses in relation to tobacco.

Even if farmers in Zamora were able to acquire the capital required for investment and technical innovation, experiences like those described above create an economic climate totally unconducive to doing so. It should be noted that Virginia tobacco has none of the noneconomic aspects associated with the growing of rice, being viewed purely commercially. However, there exists a range of constraints in the economic and political structures effectively blocking significant economic gains on the part of the ordinary farmer. These economic and political constraints are effective despite psychological and individual predispositions to work and personal gain. The Ilocano's predisposition to work is indeed widely recognized in the Philippines as second to none. None of these favorable psychological and individual qualities can be effective in the face of the entrenched economic and social interests of certain classes and political factions.

The months from January to May are exceptionally busy in Zamora. Tobacco seedlings are germinated in special beds and after five to seven weeks are transferred to the main fields. The seedlings need to be watered regularly, with consequent expenditure of gasoline for the small water-pumps which are now commonly used. Farmers who do not have a pump hire or borrow one from a neighbor or a kinsman. There were very few pumps five or six years ago and therefore the quantity of tobacco grown locally was limited.

Virginia tobacco is a labor intensive crop and its success in Zamora results partly from its period of growth being in the slack months after the rice harvest. Some farmers could extend their rice season by using longer maturing varieties or by double cropping, but such alternatives are believed to be less profitable than Virginia tobacco.

A week or two after transplanting, the tobacco plants have become established and have to be watered only once or twice a week. This period lasts five or six weeks and allows the farmer some leisure. The first leaves are ready for picking by late March and the arduous task of spiking the leaves with bamboo sticks and placing them in rows to be dried in the kilns begins. Much of this work is done by members of the household, including young children, but often additional help must be found. The leaves are spiked by young children, adolescents of both sexes, the elderly, and in general, anyone with nothing else to do. Workers are paid by the number of leaves spiked. Drying requires skillful control of heat in the kiln and many farmers employ someone who has proved his competence in this task, rather than do it themselves. The quality of the dried leaf, and hence the value of the crop depends largely on the drying. This process takes between three and five days, depending on the leaf-quality and kiln efficiency. The men employed to regulate the kilns are usually local farmers able to spare a few days from their own harvests. A man can earn a substantial income if he proves to be specially competent in this work.

Since 1975, several Japanese firms have been trying to convince local farmers to use fuel-oil in their kiln instead of firewood. The rapid deforestation and the resulting rise of firewood prices in the last few years have forced farmers to consider alternative fuels. But by using fuel-oil they will add even more to their growing dependence on the external and often uncontrollable factors that generally work against their interests. The cost, supply, and distribution of fuel-oil may be expected to come under the control of urban interests, thus reinforcing the already existing close links with other capital interests (urban and elite interests) in the tobacco industry. Furthermore, while an ecological gain can be expected from conserving forests, it is unlikely that any significant gain in efficiency will result from a switch to synthetic sources of energy. Any potential gain would probably go to the urban elite. Finally, there has been a total failure to provide the means necessary for the reliable and efficient supply and distribution of the new fuels.

In April and May, when the tobacco is ready to be sold, Zamora is a hive of activity with buyers coming from the coastal trading centers. There are several buying firms and each has several agents with large warehouses in the main coastal towns like Candon, Narvacan, and Vigan. The agents come in jeeps and trucks to take tobacco from the municipality to their warehouses. They first visit farmers who are indebted to them to recover their debts, usually in tobacco, and often buy the farmers' remaining stocks. Then they visit other barrios accompanied by their local contacts to buy what tobacco is still available. In a year (e.g., 1975) of temporary shortage, something approaching a free market is created by competition among buyers. Even in such conditions however, the ordinary farmer, having already committed most of his crop to a buyer under less competitive conditions, stands to gain comparatively little. Much more commonly the buying, and consequently the price, is controlled by the buyers who have previously established firm obligations on the part of most farmers. Under these conditions, the farmer must sell at the buyer's price regardless of his own costs. His only alternative is to take his tobacco to one of the major trading centers on the coast, where he may deal directly with the bulk-buying, and consequently the price, is controlled by the buyers who have previously established firm obligations on the part of most farmers. Under quality assessed fairly in unfamiliar and often daunting conditions, and the very dangerous possibility of being confronted by the rebuffed middlemen. Anyone familiar with the violence chronic in Ilocos Sur will realize the dangers faced by ordinary farmers.

The sale of tobacco is one of the major links between a farmer and his urban resident patron. Such a patron-broker may provide the farmer with required contacts when he needs help or assistance from government bureaucracies, or when he needs a loan for hospital or education expenses. For these reasons, many farmers prefer to sell their tobacco to buyers who are also their patrons, even if this means a lower price for the crop. The importance of developing ties with an element of altruism, however paternalistic, shows how economic relations are embedded within the political, social and ideological orders. Such is the case because the nature of production is not autonomously determined by its own logic or goals as in advanced capitalist production; it is still embedded in other nonproductive economic interests like status, religion, kinship, etc.

The local Chinese, many of whom are Filipino citizens, are often blamed by the media as the cause of the exploitation and the state of indebtedness of Ilocano farmers. There are no Chinese residents in Zamora, but Chinese buyers do visit the municipality during the tobacco season. They do not seem to offer conditions less favorable than other buyers. In fact, some farmers prefer to deal with Chinese buyers on the grounds that these do not expect the services that are often attached to equivalent relationships with Ilocano buyers, e.g., electoral support, personal services, and regular gifts. But the Chinese, while having considerable economic wealth which may be tapped by their regular clients, usually have less influence in helping them with powerful government bureaucracies. On the other hand, Ilocano patrons, many of whom belong to the province's leading political families, can easily offer their clients political contacts and influence.

The Sexual Division of Labor

The comparatively favorable position of women in Southeast Asia has been noted by numerous writers (Geertz 1961, Ward 1963, Owen 1978).

Throughout this region, women often control domestic property and exercise considerable autonomy over their personal lives and those of their dependents. However, despite their private and domestic autonomy, Southeast Asian women, like their counterparts elsewhere, are underrepresented in the wider political sphere. The basis of the transformation of women's domestic autonomy into their subordinate position in political institutions is a major problem in the social sciences. In addition, the imposition of colonial structures (e.g., cash and wage labor, international markets, introduced technology) and the introduction of capitalist relations have further complicated the links between the traditional society and modern structures of class and status. Owen (1978) has explored some of the consequences of Western economic forces for the status of women in Southeast Asia in the nineteenth century, arguing that the introduction of cheap textiles diminished the importance of women's contribution to domestic production and hence led to a lowering of their status. The coexistence of a cash and a subsistence economy and its relation to the social organization of labor and intersexual relations has been examined by Jayawardena (1977). Jayawardena argued that cash and a subsistence economy have a logic and rationale of their own and hence are differently related to their respective sociocultural structures. However, the basic problem remains: Why do men control public affairs in Southeast Asia despite the considerable autonomy possessed by women in crucial areas of the economy and in central institutions of society (i.e., the household and domestic group)? I do not attempt to provide an answer to this question. I simply raise the suggestion that the organization and ideologization of sexual domains has consequences in other levels of the social structure, ultimately resulting in public and political institutions dominated by men. I am not arguing that the organization of sexual domains, or the way in which the construction of gender identity is related to other social-cultural spheres (e.g., organization of the family, division of labor, political roles, etc.), creates male-dominated political structures (although this may be so in particular societies, where gender relations are generated by kinship relations), but rather the reverse—that political and economic institutions lead to particular notions of gender. However, because of the central role played by the family in social reproduction, the ideology supporting economic and political institutions is often modeled on domestic relations and on the allocation of gender roles (Rutten 1983).

The division of roles in the domestic sphere reproduces the wider structure of authority in society. It is these wider structures which determine domestic relations. Family roles and the inequalities between its members often provide useful models for viewing the wider society of which the family is a part. In Zamora, family roles provide a model for extrafamilial relations, e.g., pseudoparentation is extended to all Ilocano speakers through the use of kin terms, political discourse uses a kinship idiom to express relations of subordination—superordination, notions of honor are specifically related to sexual and generational domains.

In Zamora, the organization of sexual domains generates a fundamental disjunction between the economic role of women (and hence their class position) and their political role. As the municipality is progressively drawn into a cash economy, and capital becomes the crucial component for the allocation of power and status, the existing tension and contradiction in intersexual relations may be expected to increase.

Zamora kinship follows the cognatic model found throughout Southeast Asia. In terms of descent (traced bilaterally) and inheritance, male and female links are given jural equivalence. The nuclear family is the basis of most households. However, a three-generational household, or one containing members (e.g., cognates or affines) outside the nuclear core, is common and accepted. All the members of a household except young children and old people contribute to its maintenance. Men, women, and older children work in the fields, tend the animals, and carry out the activities associated with subsistence and cash farming. There are very few tasks which are seen as the exclusive responsibility of one sex or age. Men generally do the ploughing and repair the irrigation canals, women do much of the weeding, and children guard the ripening grain from marauding birds.

Many household tasks, such as looking after children, are shared, but the routine cooking and cleaning is done by women. They also have a special responsibility for looking after the rice surplus. Access to the family granary is controlled by senior women and they seldom, if ever, delegate this right to others.

While men and women are equally involved in production, the use of family surplus is determined by the concerns of each sex. Men tend to direct surplus outside the household, reflecting their interest in establishing links with the wider community. Women prefer to reinvest surplus within the household to ensure the viability of all its members. These different interests are seen as complementary, one (male) concerned with establishing political and social ties with other households, the other (female) ensuring that household members are adequately provided for. Women are expected to supervise and contribute to the household's resources, thereby allowing men to use part of the surplus to build political links with the wider community. Women are more concerned with immediate or direct "use value" in production, while men produce largely with "exchange value" in mind (Engels 1972). However, both activities are seen as essential and in their respective domain each sex exercises considerable autonomy.

The cultivation of political ties requires qualities defined in terms of social honor and public standing. Hence activities like lavish feasting, contributions toward public or civic projects, excessive generosity and the use of indirect and elaborate speech modes are all important and all these qualities are closely identified with and controlled by men. Political ties ultimately revolve around the threat and control of physical violence, as a consequence of which elaborate stratagems are employed to minimize uncontrolled agonistic encounters. In contrast, domestic relations occur in an essentially private and nonviolent context, and hence do not require elaborate safeguards against agonistic encounters. Violent disputes between spouses is regarded as a valid ground for separation and the physical chastisement of children is strongly disapproved.

Class Structure and the System of Stratification

A number of social scientists have written about Philippine social structure. Following their North American outlook, most of them (Fox 1956, Hollnsteiner 1963, Lynch 1959, 1965; Eder 1974, Arce 1973, Claver 1973) define social structure in terms of the perceived social categories on the part of native informants. This usually results in a two-tiered structure (Lynch 1959, 1965; Arce 1973) such as rich-poor, big people-little people, leader-followers, but sometimes more than two social categories are reported (Eder 1974, Claver 1973). A useful critique amd summary of these approaches is provided by Turner (1978).

For my purposes, I distinguish ranked and locally perceived social categories (i.e., status) from analytic categories, such as class, whose purpose is to explain the social forces responsible for a historically given social structure. I shall therefore distinguish conscious models of what I call status from models—of which native informants may be unaware—of specific positions in relation to a system of production, which I call class. Status always includes aspects of class, but I shall try to explore some of the differences between the two and explain their divergence.

Lenin's (1960) concept of class (i.e., the relationship to the means of production and the position in the social organization of labor) is useful for analyzing Zamora social structure (where the concept of private property and a market economy play significant but not totally dominant roles) if one keeps in mind the limited extent to which the process of capital formation shapes the social structure.

Class

A class in its most basic sense is a group of persons who occupy a similar or equivalent position in a system of production. The elements constituting a class consist of the smallest corporate units whose members enjoy reciprocal rights of access to the corporation's resources. In Zamora, this is usually the nuclear family, all of whose members participate in a common estate. However, in the case of unmarried adults or childless couples, the

Table 1. Estimates of status composition of the households in Luna, Macaoayan and Bangbangar

Status[1]	Macaoayan		Luna		Bangbangar	
	No.	%	No.	%	No.	%
Nabaknang[2]	12	(10)	18	(12)	1	(5)
Kalkalaingan	56	(53)	78	(51)	8	(38)
Napanglaw[3]	36	(37)	55	(37)	12	(57)
No. of households	104		151		21	

NOTES
1. Several key informants were asked to classify the status positions of each of the households in their barrio.
2. A *nabaknang* household has a cash-income of between P6,000-25,000 a year in addition to owning sufficient land for its rice needs (i.e., between 4-12 hectares).
3. A *napanglaw* household has a cash-income below P3,000 a year before purchasing part of its rice needs.

Table 2. Estimates of class composition of the households in Luna, Macaoayan and Bangbangar

Class	Macaoayan		Luna		Bangbangar	
	No.	%	No.	%	No.	%
Owners	52	(50)	60	(39)	4	(19)
Tenants	32	(30)	50	(33)	11	(52)
Agricultural Laborers	10	(10)	25	(16)	5	(24)
White-collar Workers	6	(6)	8	(6)	1	(5)
Craftsmen-Entrepreneurs	4	(4)	8	(6)	–	
Total households	104		151		21	

NOTE
    Each household was classified into one of the five given classes. Most households could have been put in more than one class, particularly when the full range of activities of all its adult members was considered, but the main economic activity of the household head was used to determine its class position. Multiple class membership in these barrios is therefore considerably simplified in the data given. My use of major and minor classes is related to, but does not correspond exactly with Lenin's division of the Russian peasantry (Lenin 1960:172-87; Galeski 1972:110-11).

corporate unit may consist of a single individual, a group of cognates, or a group of affines. A description of a class structure is simultaneously an analysis of the social relations responsible for maintaining and reproducing a given social structure. While this description may initially begin at the economic level, it must eventually encompass juridical and ideological structures for the description to constitute an analysis (Terray 1972).

In an agricultural municipality like Zamora, the landowner has greater control over the system of production (in this case, the growing of rice and Virginia tobacco) than the agricultural laborer, since the latter is dependent on the goodwill and favor of the former for access to land. However, the link between landowner and agricultural laborer encompasses juridical and ritual relations as well as specific ties to the land. Political support, ritual preeminence, and status position are embedded within the dyad landowner: agricultural laborer. The position of one class can be seen only in relation to and in the context of the other class or classes.

The existence of classes in the widest sense of this term does not assume a developed market situation, where labor is a commodity, but it assumes a system of production and a social organization of labor with different positions exercising varying degrees of control (Galeski 1972:107). Structural inequality in Zamora is becoming increasingly more affected by market conditions, as the municipality enters into a highly monetized economy. In this sense, Weber's notion (1970:182) of class as ultimately a market situation becomes more applicable.

Although my definition of class assumes structural inequality, and with it the possibility of conflicts of interest, it does not assume the necessity of overt conflict. Moreover, it does not assume that people are conscious of their class or that any collective action necessarily results from the belief in common class interests. Classes in Zamora overlap in membership, instead of consisting of discrete social groups, and so class consciousness and class activity are relatively undeveloped compared to other areas of the Philippines like central Luzon (van den Muijzenberg 1973, Wolters 1983).

Even in Zamora, the system of production means more than the exploitation of land. This exploitation involves the use of buffalos, implements, seed, irrigation systems, some machinery and patterns of labor exchange. Besides land exploitation, such capital investments as rice mills, retail stores and passenger vehicles constitute part of the system of production. The services of craftsmen, domestic helpers, religious specialists, and government employees are also a part of the economic system. Finally, it should be noted that the system of production in Zamora is part of a much wider productive system. Many economic activities in Zamora can only be fully understood in relation to external links. The role of outside capital in the tobacco economy and the external bases of government bureaucracies constantly impinge on the local economic system, much of the structure of which results from its response to these external forces.

Class Structure

There are three major classes and two minor ones. Most of them have important internal subdivisions. The major classes are landowners, tenants, and agricultural laborers. The minor classes are white-collar employees and small-scale entrepreneurs.

Landowners. The land-owning class is subdivided into (1) those who rarely work their own land but have it worked by others whose product they expropriate, and (2) those who mainly work their own land. Most Zamora landowners belong to the second subdivision. Thus a class, one of whose chief characteristics is leisure (Wild 1975:112), is not significant. The leisure class is significant in some large towns with an urban-residing elite. In Zamora, the few families of leisured landowners (composed mainly of unmarried female siblings) are characterized by their religious interests and activities. They support the Church generously and spend most of their leisure at Church activities.

Most members of the land-owning class in Zamora are owner-cultivators; they cultivate their own holdings, rather than employ others to do so. Members of this class mainly grow rice, which is used primarily for their own needs. Any surplus is sold. They grow Virginia tobacco as their main source of cash. They are free to sell or mortgage (*salda*) their land, but do so only for special reasons, e.g., illness, educational expenses, or important ritual expenses. Some members of this class invest their surplus in capital equipment and improvement but the majority use surplus to validate their status position. Women have equal rights of inheritance and retain control of paraphernal property. Hence, they are as likely to be landowners as men. Associated with the practice of matrilocality in some barrios is the fact that more local land is owned by women than by men.

Tenants. The second major class consists of tenants. They have limited access to land, guaranteed by both local custom and national law. This access is only guaranteed for the main rice crop, however, and does not extend to other crops. Most tenants in Zamora are sharecroppers. Normally, 50 percent of the rice harvest, after deduction of agreed upon expenses, is kept by the tenant and the rest goes to the owner. Other arrangements are possible, such as paying a fixed rent or dividing the harvest in different proportions, depending on the particular agreement between the tenant and the owner. Very few tenants in Zamora take advantage of their legal rights to 75 percent of the harvest. Some tenants have challenged the traditional apportionment but with little success. Government officials are reluctant to enforce the law about harvest shares in Zamora lest they alienate the comparatively large number of small landowners. Only those tenants who are not landowners themselves stand to gain from enforcement of the law, and although they may be numerous, their political influence at the local and national levels is, at present, too small to achieve this end.

This second class may be divided into two categories: (1) tenants who have sufficient land for their rice needs and regular access to land to grow cash crops like tobacco; and (2) tenants with marginal and insufficient land.

Members of the first category enjoy a security approaching that of some landowners. In good years, when tobacco prices are high, they can accumulate savings which may be invested in land. They often buy land (*salda-gatang*) from landowners unable to repay loans. Members of the second category are in a much more difficult position. They have to take employment to supplement their income, and do so at the peak period of labor demand. They also engage regularly in hunting, fishing and petty trading.

Although men and women may hold tenancies separately, it is more common for men to hold a right to a tenancy. The political ties between landowners and tenants favor the choice of men, rather than women, as tenants. This relation is often expressed in terms of superordination-subordination and, whenever possible, is used to achieve political ends. Since competition for public goals is seen preeminently as the concern of men, a male tenant facilitates the conversion of an economic tie to a political one. In this case, the notion of sexual domain and the pattern of domestic authority affect the membership of the class of tenants.

Agricultural laborers. The third main class is composed of agricultural laborers. Members of this class do not have special skills and do not own sufficient land or have secure rights of tenancy. They take employment on a daily basis, or exchange their services for payment in kind. Members of this class have no regular income, having only temporary and insecure employment. For these reasons, agricultural laborers seek to establish ties of patronage with or support from wealthy landowners or established tenants. Even at times of peak labor demand, their wages or harvest shares are barely adequate to cover their ordinary needs. As a consequence, they are often permanently indebted to their patron or employer and must perform domestic or other services for him. Men as well as women often enter domestic service, there being no domestic chores seen as the prerogatives of one sex.

Although the members of this class sell their labor, the economy of Zamora does not create conditions approaching a "pure" market situation, where labor is treated as a commodity. Thus, under Marx's and Weber's definitions, they constitute proto-classes. Since much of class theory has developed in the study of advanced capitalist economies (Giddens 1973), where production is geared to the maximization of profits in a large market economy, in which labor itself is an item of exchange, this theory often does not fit class formations in undeveloped economies. This class theory assumes structural conditions resulting in more exclusiveness in class affiliation than is the case in Zamora. Many Marxist theories of class have taken as their point of departure Lenin's definition of class. This arose largely out of an analysis of capitalist structures, including examples of rapidly changing rural societies, e.g., Lenin's studies of the Russian peasantry. However, the adequacy of using a notion of class referring essentially to the process of capital formation in the case of undeveloped economies has not yet been sufficiently investigated. Early studies of the peasantry (Thomas and Znaniecki 1919, Lenin 1960, Chayanov 1967) were limited to Western examples (i.e., Europe and America). More recent studies have been marked by their atheoretical and descriptive nature rather than by their attempt to apply general theoretical concepts (Wolf 1966, Bock 1969, Shanin 1971, Scott 1976). Marxist contributors to peasant studies (Galeski 1972, Terray 1972, Bock 1969, Godelier 1977, Hindess and Hirst 1975) have so far only been schematic and suggestive.

White-collar workers. The class of white-collar workers in Zamora is small (less than 5 percent of the total workforce) but significant. It consists of teachers (55), agricultural officers (10), policemen (8), administrative employees (12), salaried employees of private companies (30), and one independent professional (a dentist). The members of this class usually have special skills or training, often in an administrative capacity that allow them to join such government departments as Education, Health, Agriculture, Local Governments, or private companies. They draw regular salaries and enjoy relatively secure employment. The main subdivision of this class results from differences in seniority: (1) upper bureaucrats, e.g., school principals or head teachers, office managers, and other senior administrators who supervise the work of others, earn considerable salaries (₱450-800 a month) and are mostly university graduates; (2) lower bureaucrats, e.g., administrative assistants, junior clerks, mailmen, and policemen who do not supervise the work of others and whose salaries (₱200-300 a month) and educational qualifications are much lower.

Members of the first category often act as brokers for ordinary barrio members who have to deal with government bureaucracies. Although lacking the power themselves to allocate government services, they facilitate transactions between their clients and the appropriate government officials. There are more women than men in this class (60 female, 55 male) and women are better represented in senior positions (16 female, 14 male). Education is highly valued in Zamora (as it is in the rest of the country), and women are given as many opportunities as men to pursue advanced studies. For this and other reasons, women are well represented in all government departments and are achieving parity with men in the private sector.

While members of this class essentially sell their labor, they do so under conditions significantly different from agricultural laborers. It is the position in the social organization of labor rather than the relation to the means of production that differentiates white-collar workers from agricultural laborers. The former enjoy a regular, above-subsistence wage which enables them to participate in the market sector of the economy and in the national polity. The latter are oriented primarily to the traditional subsistence economy (often being paid in kind) and to the local polity.

The penetration of a monetized economy creates opportunities for white-collar workers but simultaneously threatens the viability of the traditional bonds affecting members of the class of agricultural laborers.

As might be expected, white-collar workers are recruited mainly from the class of landowners or well-to-do tenants. The practice of partible inheritance (dividing property among heirs before death of owner) has forced some families to convert their decreasing holdings into another asset, such as education, leading to a process of depeasantization (Lenin 1960:173). In this sense, the class of white-collar workers may be considered a subclass of the land-owning class, brought about by the introduction of a capitalist economy. There are a number of religious specialists in Zamora in charge of the different denominations. Some of them including the Catholic priest and the Methodist, Church of Christ and Iglesia ni Kristo ministers, are full-time accredited members of professional and national organizations. Others, including the ministers of the Pentecostalists, Jehovah's Witnesses and Christ Jesus' Holy Church are part-time and are chosen by their congregations. The former group of religious specialists enjoy many of the privileges and advantages of membership in professional associations which are part of developed organizations. The latter are closer to the category of craftsmen who, while exercising a special skill, depend on the need of their congregations for their services. They do not enjoy the advantages of regular and secure employment.

In addition to the religious specialists mentioned, there are others working within the indigenous, pre-Christian tradition. Unlike their Christian counterparts, these practitioners do not have a regular congregation to whom they offer their services. Instead, like members of a craft or of the independent professions, they cater to all those who ask for their services.

The incomes of religious practitioners differ significantly. They range from someone like the Catholic priest, whose income would be one of the highest in the municipality, to someone like the Methodist minister, who has to supplement his income by fishing. The traditional practitioners seldom accept monetary payment, preferring payment in kind or the remains of the ritual offerings. However, all religious specialists are shown deference and consequently enjoy high status. In this case, it is the moral rather than the economic dimension which is emphasized.

Craftsmen and entrepreneurs. The final class consists of craftsmen and small-scale entrepreneurs. They are essentially self-employed and their members provide a skilled service, e.g., carpentry, photography; buy and sell produce, e.g., rice, tobacco or manufactured goods; or provide public transport. Characteristically, they invest moderate amounts of capital, since labor is often contributed by members of the household, in a situation where competition between individuals or enterprises is shared. Internal subdivisions in this class have to do with the nature of the service and the scale of the enterprise. Thus, relatively large investments, e.g., rice mills, bread ovens and jeepneys, are to be distinguished from small retail stores (*sari-sari*), which require low capital investment and give a bare subsistence return. Factors of competition, efficiency, technology and labor assume different meanings in each of these subdivisions. For example, small retail stores are not concerned with labor time, since labor is provided by household members but are more concerned with the volume of trade, since this determines the viability of the enterprise. On the other hand, the owner-operator of a jeepney must consider not only labor costs but must ensure that his takings cover repairs, spare parts, and depreciation.

Unlike agricultural laborers, the majority of these craftsmen are well-paid and at times of peak demand, can earn relatively high incomes. However, unlike white-collar workers, craftsmen are not assured of a regular wage but must seek work themselves. Craftsmen are not members of unions and have none of the fringe benefits, e.g., pensions, special loans, and allowances, enjoyed by salaried workers. There are very few women who earn a significant income through practicing a craft, although many supplement their income by weaving straw mats, hats and baskets. Most women engaged in craft are dressmakers, including a few who service and maintain the sewing machines used in the municipality. Women, however, are much more active in trading than men. Most of the retail trading and market vending is done by women, and they often control large investments such as rice mills and bakeries. In addition, all the local moneylenders are women. Members of this class are characterized by their ability to participate in both modes of production, or shift from one to the other as the opportunity offers. This class is, however, becoming more dependent on the market economy rather than on the traditional rice economy.

Conscious Models

The model of class structure I have suggested is not held by people in Zamora as a conscious model of their society. People realize that there is a hierarchy of social categories, related to an economic and moral base, but they do not relate these categories to the system of production and the organization of labor. It would be wrong, however, to assume that there is no awareness of the class categories mentioned. Native (Ilocano) concepts corresponding to landowner (*akinkukua ti daga*), tenant (*katalon*), and laborer (*mangmanged*) exist but are generally subsumed in a status model of local society, i.e., the model is based as much on evaluative as on analytic concepts. In other words, ideological aspects of the social structure are seen as directly responsible, in a causal and explanatory sense, for the social divisions present in Zamora.

Status

I use the term *status* to refer to social esteem. Status is therefore an evaluative term, whereas class, in the sense in which I use it, does not imply a moral evaluation. A particular status group is associated with a complex of interests and orientations that usually generate a feeling of community among its members—often expressed in rites of commensality, expressions of familiarity, habits of dress and speech and the possession and use of certain items of wealth (Weber 1970:186). The concepts of status and class are closely related, since to lead a particular lifestyle requires a certain level of economic resources. However, membership in a status category rests on the conscious perception by members and by nonmembers of the appropriate status of a given category; whereas class membership may not be accompanied by a similar degree of consciousness. Strictly speaking, classes are not ranked but differentiated in relation to the economic base and the degree of control that the class wields within it. Status categories are always ranked by both economic and noneconomic criteria. To describe a status is to enumerate a range of values shared by those who belong to it. To describe a class is to allocate the level of control and power that that class has in relation to other classes in the same system of production.

Social esteem has several dimensions. To gain it, one must possess certain qualities like wealth, civic spirit, rank, industry and a desire to help others. One must have a particular lifestyle that is, for instance, associated with higher education and the trappings of urbanity. Status is allocated in proportion to the possession of these qualities and the exercise of this lifestyle.

The differentiation of sex roles affects the allocation of status. The activities and interests appropriate to each sex determine the possibility of achieving social esteem. Thus, high status requires the use of part of a person's resources for the benefit of the wider community, e.g., by giving elaborate feasts or supporting collective rites or activities. This use of household resources is often opposed by women, who see it to be in conflict with their primary responsibility to members of their household. A woman's sphere of activity and interest is seen as being essentially private and domestic, rather than public and civic. A person wishing to enjoy high status must actively establish a favorable pool of public opinion, an area more within the proper interests of men.

Gender involves the classification of a sphere of activity and interest appropriate to each sex. These spheres of activity and interest have consequences for the system of production and the attainment of social ideals. In Zamora, the significance of social roles affects various levels of the social structure. Economic, political and ritual competence are partly defined by one's sex. These competencies are relatively uncontrasted in some areas, like the economic, where men and women are allowed equal scope, but contrasted more in others like politics, a sphere seen as more appropriate to men, or in ritual, where communal rites are performed by men and domestic rites by women.

While both class and status assume the ontologically prior division of sex roles, this division in Zamora occurs at a different level of the social structure. Class and status essentially express power relations involving positions in the system of production and prestige, while gender concerns the allocation of roles in a given unit of production or within a given status unit. In Zamora, the household or domestic group is the most common unit of production and is the basic unit of the social stratum. However, while sex roles affect various levels of Zamora society, like the economy, religion, and politics, relations between classes and those between status groups are not structured solely out of the prior division of sex roles. In a sense, sex roles often reflect the relations between classes and status groups such as when a woman of high status is allowed the privileges of a man in her dealings with status inferiors.

Status Categories

When people in Zamora are asked to describe the social divisions (*kasasaad*) or categories in the municipality or in their barrio, they answer in terms of three main divisions. These are (1) *nabaknang* (wealthy or prominent), (2) *kalkalaingan* (moderate or middle), and (3) *napanglaw* (poor or marginal). When pressed to make finer distinctions, people subdivide the *nabaknang* category into *kabaknangan* (fairly rich or prominent) and *kababaknangan* (the richest or most prominent) and the *napanglaw* category into *kapanglawan* (fairly poor or marginal) and *kapapanglawan* (the poorest or extremely marginal).

Although these categories are clearly related to an economic base, they are also meant to indicate an assessment of social worth or value. Thus, to be called *nabaknang* means not only that a person is wealthy, but that his wealth enables him to lead a socially approved lifestyle. For a person to be described as *napanglaw* connotes that he has undesirable traits, such as laziness and irresponsibility, as much as that he is poor.

The way in which people in Zamora rank social categories follows the general Filipino pattern. Essentially, there are three main categories, two of which are subdivided. These distinctions can be made to fit the two-category system reported by Lynch (1959, 1965) and Arce (1973) in which social rank is seen primarily as the opposition between the *nabaknang* and the *napanglaw* categories—in other words, between the prominent, wealthy, and politically active and the marginal, poor, and politically passive. This opposition is not conceived of in class terms (i.e., as a conflict out of which new structural alignments develop) but in terms of social or political estates, all of whose final interests lie in a common good. It is a model of society that assumes social but not class differentiation. On the other hand, using the finer distinctions given, one could as well argue for five or six social categories, as do Eder (1974) and Claver (1973).

Those who belong to the *kababaknangan* category are accorded respect and deference, but they must validate this status by giving lavish feasts, particularly at weddings and funerals. On these occasions, they are expected not to rely on the contributions from neighbors, kinsmen, and friends by which less wealthy families are helped to bear such expenses.

The concept of social honor (*rebbeng* or *dayaw*) is highly developed in Zamora. People who aspire to it or who claim it must have, in addition to material resources, the social virtues of generosity, industry, and readiness to help others in the community. Political office or high educational attainment is usually the confirmation of a person's social honor. People who have achieved a significant political rank will often use the honorific title *Don* for men and *Doña* for women to indicate their high status. At present, a common alternative to the use of these honorifics is to mention the highest political office held, or the education attained by a person whenever he is referred to or addressed in public or in a formal gathering, for example, Ex-Mayor Juan Principe, Attorney Pedro Gracia or Doctora Josefina Reyes.

Relations between men are often constrained by public notions of honor (*dayaw*) and duty (*rebbeng*) or by shame (*bain*) and deference (*raem*), making purely commercial or monetary transactions awkward and difficult. Women are not as publicly constrained by these roles. As a result, they may engage in economic transactions with greater ease and facility. An activity such as money-lending imposes a considerable strain on a man's need to maintain good public relations. Since women are not perceived to be as concerned with maintaining this same public image, an activity such as money-lending comes under their competence. The political roles of men prevent them from extracting certain specific economic benefits in a relationship. A woman's nonpolitical interests allow her to maximize economic gains without lowering her public standing.

Political activity and success require a level of economic resources. These resources can only be assured given a strong political position. Hence, the complementation of sex roles may be seen to result from structural forces generated outside the family—and to facilitate the accumulation of honor by certain high status families.

The achievement of social honor is associated with a corresponding lifestyle expressed in a variety of ways. Apart from the high value put on education—dress, bearing, food, housing, and patterns of visiting and entertaining indicate a person's status. Patterns of seating and serving during private and public functions indicate status boundaries. At many functions, such as public dances, people holding the highest status often monopolize the occasion, making it awkward and embarrassing for members of the lower statuses to share even the same dancefloor. In addition, in public interactions, gender also regulates behavior. Intersexual behavior in public is usually restrained and formal; displays of affection between members of the opposite sex are strongly disapproved even in the case of spouses. In contrast, members of the same sex may display their affection for one another. However, the normal restraint between members of opposite sexes is relaxed on the part of high status women in their interactions with lower status men. In all public interactions, status takes precedence over the other main constituents of the conscious model of Zamora society (i.e., generation and gender), and women of high status are largely free of the constraints of their sex and their age.

To be classed as *nabaknang*, one must generally own land, but not all landowners belong to this category. *Nabaknang* have at least enough land to provide for their own rice needs, including the requirements for major feasts. The *napanglaw* category may include members who own small parcels of land but whose large families and unfortunate lifestyles (i.e., "uncooperative," "often drunk," "quarrelsome," "idle") are seen as surpassing the capacity of their land to provide them with an adequate living. Members of this category usually explain their situation in terms of fate or luck (*gasat*) rather than in terms of the difficult conditions and limited opportunities of their position. The epithets used by the well-to-do to describe less fortunate members of the community constitute one of the many nascent forms of class consciousness in Zamora. The latter, at least publicly, accept some of these accusations but disclaim moral responsibility for their situation.

Nabaknang, *kalkalaingan*, and *napanglaw* are status terms that have evolved in a predominantly agricultural community. All are closely linked to land, the principal resource in the local economy, but they express more than landownership. These terms also express the exploitation and use of land along socially approved lines. To be *nabaknang* means to be generous, hospitable, and active in community affairs. To be *napanglaw* is not simply to be poor but to deserve poverty for not having a sense of social responsibility. Implicit in these terms is the view that wealth and social prominence accrue to the deserving, while poverty is the desert of those who neglect their responsibilities. This view may have been well-founded when a resource like land was readily available to most people, and when the political system was comparatively egalitarian in its opportunities. Of course, even under these conditions, people recognized that personal differences often explained the differences in life careers. Families with foresight, who not only worked hard and provided for the future, but planned proper marriages for their children, became *nabaknang*. They then not only enjoyed social prominence but had the resources to satisfy important ritual obligations and thus, to ensure the protection of their ancestors. This concatenation of economic, political and moral advantages was the envy of the less fortunate.

Conditions affecting the availability of land changed significantly in the course of the present century. Other factors, including the increased exposure to urban lifestyles, the spread of education, and the rapid monetization of the economy, have altered the predominantly agricultural and subsistence orientation of the municipality. Nowadays, although land is still the ultimate basis, such factors as formal education and certain patterns of consumption also determine status.

Class, Status, and Gender

As Zamora becomes more integrated into a money economy, and market forces generate conditions of inequality resulting directly from the control of property, one can expect the present emphasis on and consciousness of social honor (status) to be replaced by a consciousness of class interests. This change in consciousness will bring with it a change from the struggle for status (Weber 1970:185) to a conflict between classes. These changes are becoming apparent in Zamora.

Although there is a considerable overlap in the range of activities of both sexes, much of the orientation and purpose of an activity differs between sexes. Women are seen as closely involved with household responsibilities and orient their activities to this end. Their participation in production and in ritual is intended primarily for the benefit and security of household members. Women with fewer domestic responsibilities (i.e., single, childless, or rich) devote their time and interests to business, professional or religious activities, rather than civic affairs. Men are not expected to be as closely bound to immediate household responsibilities and often develop interests outside this area, resulting in their control of most public and community matters.

While women play an active and significant role in the local economy, they are underrepresented in politics. The political arena is seen as more appropriate for men, although success in politics depends largely on economic support provided by women, for a man's time away from productive activity is supplemented by his wife. The existing ideology, however, masks the importance of women in enabling men to engage in politics. The exclusion of women from politics must be seen in the context of native theories regarding gender and the control of public violence since the political domain is seen as ultimately involving the possibility of agonistic encounters. These encounters are controlled through the notions of social honor, public standing, and the use of special speech modes. The cultivation of these skills is seen as a prerogative of men and it is they who control access to political institutions. Their control is reinforced in the ritual domain and in the structure of authority within the family.

Some of the wealthiest people in Zamora are women. Their wealth comes from landownership or from profitable retail, milling, transport, or money-lending enterprises. These women generally manage their own business affairs without the supervision or assistance of men. There is a higher proportion of women in the professions, e.g., in education, health and administration. Although Zamora's wealthy women are referred to as *nabak-nang*, people often complain that many of them are only interested in accumulating wealth, rather than in carrying out the obligations of this status. This charge is less often made against rich men.

In so far as both status and gender refer to a conscious set of norms and values, they articulate a model justifying aspects of social inequality. This ideology has implications for the system of production, allocating and legitimating class positions. Unlike the notions of status and gender, which lead to a more or less conscious model of society, class relations have consequences not frequently examined. Because class is not a major constituent of the conscious model of Zamora society, the discrepancy between the economic and political position of women is unresolved. This discrepancy has generated an elaborate ideology resulting in intersexual relations often marked by tension and contradiction. For example, the notion of female subordination and of romantic love coexist with the belief that women control household expenditure because they have greater self-control and are more reliable in such matters than men.

The internalization, maintenance, and reproduction of Zamora's social structure occurs at several levels. At one level domestic roles encapsulate, reflect, and re-create structural forces acting at wider areas of Zamora society. At another level, access to economic, political and ritual activity is a function of class and status, and these factors determine public and private role expectations. Notions of gender arise out of the differential participation in and orientation of each sex in relation to economic, political, and ritual institutions. These institutions are undergoing change following the introduction of a commodity economy and the growing importance of a national bureaucracy. These changes affect both intersexual relations (i.e., the status of men and women as categories) and relations between corporate units that make up distinct classes and status groups. As the private accumulation of capital and control over the social organization of labor increasingly come to characterize the social structure, the traditional complementation of sex roles and the former bases of status may be expected to come into conflict with the realities of class. The progressive monetization of the economy has generated more opportunities for wage-labor, a field favored by men. Women's traditional autonomy in the subsistence sphere and in other areas of the economy is coming under increasing pressure as men decide that their political interests require control over production.

CHAPTER 3

Political and Religious Mobilization and Factionalism

Zamora was formed into a municipality in 1919. Even before this time, it had been divided into two main factions.

This factional division is manifested at two structurally separate levels: one level involves a coalition of barrios and the other, the elite families who determine the political affairs of the municipality. These families live in the municipality's principal barrios. While they determine the final configuration of personal alliances that will ultimately make up these factions, the coalition of barrios exercises constraints on the range and stability of their choices. Alliances between local elites and their links with patrons outside the municipality constitute local politics. The coalition of barrios, on the other hand, focuses local political activity along certain geographic and ethnic directions.

One of the main issues of contention between the factions in Zamora is the site of the *poblacion* or administrative center. Its location has symbolic and material consequences. Proximity to the poblacion is an important determinant of status; it affects the availability of government services and personnel. Access to and use of national and provincial pork-barrel funds, and the allocation of government licenses and franchises primarily benefit poblacion residents and so, its location is keenly contested by members of the two factions. These symbolic and material rewards are the main reasons why people in Zamora engage in politics. Success in politics has significant consequences in economics and religion.

Bato and Luna

Bato is the center of the northern faction which includes the linguistically and to some extent, culturally distinct non-Ilocano barrios of Macaoayan, Lucaban, Masingit, and Mambog. Luna is the center of the southern faction; the constituent barrios of this faction, except Luna, are exclusively Ilocano. Before becoming the municipal center Bato was an uninhabited stretch of land between the Itneg barrio of Masingit and the Igorot barrio of Lucaban. Some old people in these barrios say that in the past, this area was important for the performance of ritual. Its rocky and hilly topography, typical of sacrificial sites, bears out what they say.

Zamorans can no longer recall the precise reasons for Bato being the initial site for the poblacion in the context of Luna's claims of being the more appropriate municipal center. Even though Macaoayan recognized important kinship links with Luna, its closer ties to Lucaban led it to support the northern (Bato) faction.

However, these characteristics of north-south and non-Ilocano-Ilocano do not constitute precise divisions between the factions in Zamora. Each of the twenty-six barrios composing the municipality sees itself, to some extent, as an autonomous unit against all the others. But each barrio has ties of varying strength with other barrios. These ties lead to interbarrio alliances expressed in religious congregations, political parties, and ethnic affiliations that ultimately culminate in the two major factions. Finally, all of these ties between barrios depend, to some degree, on the personalities of the leaders of such alliances. All these factors create the complex and shifting boundaries between the two factions.

The Bato faction includes barrios like Macaoayan and Lucaban. Their inhabitants describe themselves as Igorot speakers, and they possess some cultural traits different from the lowland, coastal Ilocanos. This faction also includes the barrios of Masingit and Mambog whose members call themselves Itneg or Tinggian speakers and, like the previous barrios' inhabitants, they also differ in certain respects from Ilocanos. And yet, this faction also includes barrios like Ambugat, Lesseb, and Cadacad whose inhabitants regard themselves as Ilocanos.

None of the barrios generally aligned with Luna has linguistically and culturally distinct non-Ilocano communities. While the Bato faction includes barrios whose inhabitants consciously differentiate themselves from Iloca-nos, the Luna faction is composed only of barrios whose inhabitants refer to themselves as Ilocanos.

The present geographical division between the northern and southern factions goes back to the time before the municipality of Zamora was formed. In those days, the northern faction was part of the municipality of San Jose while the southern faction was within the municipality of San Rafael. During the years immediately before Zamora's formation as a municipality, the leaders of each faction disagreed considerably about the proper location of the poblacion. The Luna faction succeeded initially and as a consequence, this barrio—then called Nueva Coveta—became the poblacion of the new municipality. This lasted until 1923 when a man from the Bato faction gained office (as mayor) and transferred the municipal center to Bato, where it stayed until 1928. From 1929 to 1934, the poblacion was once again in Luna. But in 1935, the Bato faction gained political control and relocated the poblacion at their end of the municipality. In 1960 the Luna faction was back in power and consequently, Luna became the administrative center until 1966. That was when the Bato faction managed to transfer the poblacion again. It has remained in Bato since then.

When the Luna faction came into power in 1960, it immediately set into motion the political machinery that enabled it to transfer the poblacion. A change of poblacion requires the approval of the President of the Republic and an appropriate Act of Congress. The political contacts of the Luna faction allowed it to carry out this complex procedure. Its members trans-ported the old municipal building from Bato to Luna!

In the election of 1963, the mayoral candidate belonging to the Bato faction promised his supporters in Bato that he would build a new and permanent building to be used as a municipal hall. This same candidate, when campaigning in Luna and its allied barrios, assured the people that he would not remove the building that was, at that time, being used as the municipal hall in Luna. When he won the elections, he kept both promises.

He used his party contacts and obtained the approval of the Office of the President to reestablish the poblacion in Bato. Using both national and local funds, he constructed a large cemented building that is presently used as the administrative center. As he promised, he did not remove the large former municipal hall in Luna. That building has since been used at different times as a school, a warehouse, and as the barrio's meeting hall.

People in Luna have not altogether given up on the idea of making their barrio the poblacion once more. They maintain that the last transfer of the poblacion in 1966 was achieved without the proper legislative procedures. On several occasions in the last few years, official mail from the Office of the President has been sent, mistakenly, to Luna. Such events merely confirm the belief of members of the Luna faction that Luna is still the proper poblacion.

Party Politics

The dispute concerning the site of the poblacion is not the only manifestation of the coalition of barrios that make up the main factions in Zamora.

Since the end of the Second World War and the rise of the Nacionalista and Liberal parties, until the local elections held in 1967, the factions in Zamora followed party divisions. The Bato faction voted for the Liberal Party while the Luna faction supported the Nacionalistas. Prior to 1942-46, local politics reflected the split within the Nacionalista Party. During the decade of the thirties, Zamora supported both the Democratas and the Nacionalistas; Luna supported the Democratas, while Bato voted for the Nacionalistas. From 1942 to 1946, the war and the Japanese occupation interrupted the normal channels of political support. Elections were not held in Zamora during these years. From 1946 to 1967, the Liberal and Nacionalista parties alternated in power, each party drawing its leaders and supporters from the appropriate faction. However, in 1967, the neat division according to party affiliations became confused as a result of the mass changeover in party membership by local and provincial leaders who followed the example of Ferdinand Marcos. When Ferdinand Marcos left the Liberal Party in 1964 to join the Nacionalistas, and gained the presidency the year after as a Nacionalista, many of his supporters at the provincial and municipal levels decided to switch loyalties from the Liberal to the Nacionalista Party. In the local elections held in 1963, Liberal Party candidates (mayor and vice-mayor), both of whom were from the Bato faction, won. In the next local elections (1967), the mayor, who had by then changed from the Liberal to the Nacionalista Party, chose a man from Luna as his vice-mayoral candidate. This was the first time that a party had chosen candidates coming from traditionally opposed barrios. In the past, each party chose its candidate only from among allied barrios.

While the two-party system coincided with the factional division in Zamora until 1967, the change of party membership among the local elite in this year made it difficult for this division to continue to be reflected along traditional party lines. Since political parties in the Philippines consist essentially of personal alliances among elite politicians (Agpalo 1972, Hollnsteiner 1963, Lande 1964) rather than reflect an ideology held at the mass base, the change of party loyalties in 1967 was arbitrarily imposed on the structure of local politics. As a result, the Nacionalistas in 1967—which now come from opposed barrios—included members who would normally have been expected to draw their support from Liberal Party members.

The structure of local politics in Zamora is a consequence both of indigenous factors (local alliances, kinship links, etc.) and external forces. While external political forces are often reinterpreted in local terms, the final political outcome is ultimately dependent on provincial and national alliances and factors.

The strategy of the mayor, who is a member of the Bato faction, in choosing a Luna-based vice-mayoral candidate in 1967, succeeded. In 1971, the same strategy worked although this time, the mayor chose another Luna-based candidate for vice-mayor when tensions in the previous coalition developed. At these elections, the Liberal Party resorted to the same strategy and the very close results showed that each combination attracted almost equal support.

The present mayor's use of party affiliations and knowledge of local loyalties has enabled him to retain his position since 1964, a total of twelve years. This is a considerable accomplishment in the light of both local and national political trends. But this success has blurred the former party divisions that characterized the major factions in Zamora until 1967. After 1967, the political parties no longer reflected in the same way the two factional divisions in Zamora.

Local Politics after Martial Law

When martial law was declared in September 1972, and political parties were effectively dismantled, factional rivalry in Zamora no longer manifested itself in political party labels. Instances of this division may instead be seen in activities like the Flores de Mayo fund-raising competition held by Catholics, the feast of the patron saint of Luna and the segmented congregations of the more established Protestant denominations and in the membership of civic and religious associations.

In Zamora, as in other parts of the Philippines, political parties do not constitute the primary structure on which political activity is based. Instead, personal alliances between local elites and their political patrons outside Zamora together with local barrio rivalries and ethnic affinities shape much of local political activity.

In December 1975, in line with President Marcos's directions regarding the creation of new legislative bodies, elections were held in Zamora for the Sangguniang Bayan, or the municipal legislative chamber.[2] The Sanggunian

---

2. The precise function and constitution of the Sangguniang Bayan had not been fully decided from 1975 to 1976. Only five out of the fourteen members were elected in 1975; the rest automatically assumed their seats in this body following their previous positions (i.e., seven councilors and the mayor).

is meant to represent the capitalist, industrial, agricultural and professional sectors of the municipality, as well as the youth sector (*kabataan*) and the association of barrio captains (*capitans*). The municipal mayor and the former municipal councilors (elected in 1971 and whose terms would normally have expired at the end of 1975) automatically became members of the Sangguniang Bayan, at least until the precise nature of its functions and method of recruitment were finally decided.

In other words, in a principally agricultural municipality like Zamora, the capitalist, industrial and professional sectors of the community are not representative of the large majority of the local population. But representatives from these sectors were elected to complete the membership of the Sangguniang Bayan.

Due to the present distribution of political power which is heavily in favor of the Bato faction, representatives from barrios allied to it were elected to constitute the Sangguniang Bayan. The traditional rivalry between the two factions—this time no longer seen in terms of Liberal-Nacionalista Party affiliations—has led to the usual result in which one faction monopolizes the senior elective positions. In 1976, the three most crucial positions in local politics (chairman of the Sanggunian, head of the barrio captains, municipal delegate to the Sangguniang Panlalawigan) were occupied by members of the Bato faction. Ironically, the new political order brought about by President Marcos's martial law regime has redrawn the political divisions in Zamora along traditional factional lines.

Between 1968 and September 1972, the political party structure no longer reflected in a simple and direct way the traditional political division between Bato and Luna. The mayor, who belongs to the Bato faction, successfully ran for reelection twice with the support of certain people from Luna because he had chosen a Luna-based candidate for vice-mayor. The astute manipulation of a political division closely tied previously to traditionally opposed camps has so far benefited the present mayor. His success is partly due to the disarray he created (following President Marcos's lead) in the previously neat political dichotomization of the municipality. But the new political system, instituted through President Marcos's decrees, dismantled the former structure of local politics and replaced it with a new and different structure.

In the process of transition from the old to the new system, following an old and well-established pattern in Philippine politics, persons in power took advantage of this transition to install their supporters or members of their faction into the newly created offices. The direct links between party and factional membership in Zamora, disrupted from 1967 to 1975, following President Marcos's party defection in 1964, were reestablished in the local elections of December 1975, as a consequence of President Marcos's latest political maneuvers. The elections of December 1975 indicated once more that the major basis of political support lies, not in the loyalty to a particular party, but in the firm obligations to members of one's faction.

In 1976, the political power structure in Zamora resembled the structure before 1968. Members from Bato presently occupy the senior political positions, and Luna is clearly underrepresented in the structure of local government. According to the old pattern, if regular elections were to be held shortly (the elections held in December 1975 were not "typical"), the Luna faction would replace Bato and the political pendulum would swing from one extreme to the other. However, in the absence of regular elections and because of the introduction of certain significant new elements in the structure of local government, it is impossible to predict the future of the relationship between the traditional political rivalry of Bato and Luna and its reflection in the formal political structure. For a more recent discussion of these links see Pertierra (1987).

Barrio Identity

While loyalty to one's barrio is felt strongly by people in Zamora, other ties compete for the individual's loyalties. These ties often extend beyond the barrio and create a network spanning several barrios inside and often outside the municipality. In many cases, this network is directed more strongly in certain directions than in others. Thus barrios like Macaoayan and Lucaban, on the one hand, and Mambog and Masingit, on the other, have particularly strong personal networks linking many of their inhabitants. Aside from sharing strong cultural affinities, members of these barrios have close kinship ties. Macaoayan also has close economic ties with its neighboring barrio of Taliao, many of whose members are tenants of Macaoayan families. Barrios like Luna and Dayanki, partly on account of their proximity, have close ties of friendship between their inhabitants, while Luna and Balugang have a strong common interest in the activities of the Catholic Church.

While all the barrios of Zamora have a strong sense of community, particular barrios manifest this feeling in different ways. For example, Dirdirig, a southern barrio of Zamora, is noted for its religious homogeneity since almost all of its members belong to the Christ Jesus' Holy Church. And barrios like Macaoayan and Masingit have cultural traits that differentiate them from the surrounding predominantly Ilocano barrios. Finally, a barrio like Luna, despite being religiously heterogenous, articulates a strong feeling of solidarity through the annual celebration of its fiesta. While the Santo Niño de Praga is, strictly speaking, meaningful in religious terms only to Roman Catholics, many members of other religious denominations in Luna support the fiesta held in its honor.

In Zamora, there exists a range of situations that indicate a person's loyalty to his barrio. Aside from the various fund-raising competitions held yearly, which pit barrio against barrio, there are other occasions like public dances (dances are often held as part of fund-raising competitions), during which the feeling of belonging to one barrio as against another is comparatively high. Girls who attend these dances are escorted to them by young men from the same barrio. Fights often occur when young men from other barrios are suspected of molesting or insulting the girls of one's barrio. In public dances, participation in each dance is announced by barrio, thus preventing young men from different barrios from sharing the same dance-floor and competing for the girls' favor.

Basketball matches and other competitions are often arranged between barrios, during which heavy betting occurs with the attendant risk of violent confrontations. At these matches, barrio loyalties become clearly delineated.

The composition of *barkada* (gangs of young men) seldom includes members of different barrios. These gangs attend social functions as groups, and the presence of several barkada is often the cause of fights.

Although serious feuds between barrios in Zamora no longer occur, a state of latent hostility between certain barrios is still present among the young men who form the barkada. However, only a generation or two ago, these hostilities included adult men. During a period of social turmoil such as the years 1942-46, these hostilities reached considerable proportions. At the present time, only male adolescents conduct organized raids against other barrios. While their elders deplore this activity, particularly when serious injuries occur, little is done by them to discourage this behavior. The pattern of such hostilities is more complex than the division between Bato and Luna previously discussed, but this division also expresses the most bitter confrontations between barkada belonging to the coalition of barrios within each faction. Thus, the young men of Macaoayan, a barrio that belongs to the Bato faction, are on particularly hostile relations with the young men of Padayao, a barrio aligned with Luna.

Local Religion

The traditional division in Zamora is expressed in ways other than the attempts to relocate the poblacion, or in voting patterns and the election to political office of the members of each faction. The dichotomization of the municipality is also reproduced in its religious congregations.

Roman Catholics constitute about 75 percent of the population of the municipality (1970 census estimate). Since 1932, when Zamora obtained its first resident priest, Luna has been the center of the parish. The establishment of the parish was achieved mainly through the efforts of Catholics in the barrios of Dayanki, Luna, and Balugang. Since its establishment, the parish center has remained in Luna despite the repeated transfer of the poblacion. Catholics belonging to the Bato faction have tried to have it transferred to Bato, but the opposition of the Catholics in Luna and the difficulty associated with its transfer has so far frustrated them. While the main church and priest's residence have remained in Luna, the Catholics in the Bato faction have built a church (technically it's only a chapel) in Bato, and they continuously attempt to persuade the priest to accord their church equal religious status.

During the month of May, Catholics in Zamora hold a fund-raising competition to celebrate the Flores de Mayo. In 1975, as in previous years, both Bato and Luna held separate competitions. Each faction refused to pool its resources with the other, despite the fact that belonging to a single parish technically assumes a consolidation of funds. Instead, each faction used its proceeds separately.

Every fifteenth of January, Luna celebrates the feast of the Santo Niño de Praga, the Catholic patron of Zamora. Although this day is theoretically significant for all Catholics in the municipality, it is Luna that takes a special pride in celebrating the fiesta. Even non-Catholics in Luna are prepared to help and contribute funds toward its success. This sense of obligation is shown in the words of the Methodist minister: "We are all members of Luna and therefore, we should all do our share to help celebrate its fiesta."

The members of the Bato faction attempt to underplay its importance. They argue that it is important only to Luna and to its allied barrios.

In its turn, Bato celebrates the feast of St. Joseph, its patron, but this celebration has not attained the importance of the feast of the Santo Niño de Praga. The support of senior members of the Catholic hierarchy would be needed for the feast in honor of St. Joseph to attain greater religious significance. Such support is unlikely to be given while the Church continues to recognize the present parish center in Luna. The Catholic Church represents a more consolidated set of interests than do political parties, thereby making partisan demands much less likely to succeed. Furthermore, the hierarchical and ideological structure of the Church creates links with its municipal adherents that are of a significantly different nature to the links a political party has with its local supporters.

To further complicate matters, Zamora also celebrates a fiesta in honor of Father Zamora, the martyr-priest after whom the municipality was named. However, this celebration is a state affair. Even if it were supported by Catholic authorities, non-Catholic ministers would have to be invited to take part in it, thereby neutralizing the religious significance of the occasion. Interdenominational activities like the celebration of the fiesta in honor of

Father Zamora is not perceived as religiously significant by most people. This is not to deny that most people operate in an eclectic religious field, drawing elements freely from different religious traditions to suit specific needs. This eclecticism derives from conditions that are quite different from those giving rise to interdenominationalism or ecumenism.

It would not be to Bato's advantage to antagonize and divide its non-Catholic supporters by attempting to convert a secular or state occasion into a religious one—one designed to compete with the fiesta held in Luna in honor of the Santo Niño de Praga.

While Bato currently has the advantages of having the resources of the municipal administration, its attempts at legitimating its position through the use of religious symbolism have not been successful. This lack of success is partly due to the inherently difficult task of converting secular resources into religious merit in a political system that acknowledges pluralism. The formal separation of Church and State, with their reliance on different ideological, bureaucratic and power bases, has made more difficult the conversion of merit and legitimacy from one system to the other. This difficulty was increased when the former religious monopoly of Catholicism (in Christian areas) was broken by the introduction and proliferation of non-Catholic denominations early this century.

At present, while only the Catholic priest in Luna may be said to command an independent power base with sufficient resources from which to challenge the authority of the municipal mayor, the overlapping nature of the secular and sacred orders prevents such a simple polarization from ever arising. This, however, does not preclude attempts by one order to encroach on the sphere of the other. I describe elsewhere (Pertierra 1976) an instance of the rivalry and tension existing between the Catholic priest and the mayor. The links between the political and social elites on the one hand, and the Catholic organizations on the other, make such tensions inevitable.

The organization of the Catholic Church at the municipal level resembles in many ways the structure of local government. Lay representatives from different barrios are recruited to form the Parish Pastoral Assembly (PPA) which is, with the priest, the body responsible for the affairs of the parish. PPA members elect officers from among themselves; it often happens, in similar situations in local government, that one faction acquires control and the representative nature of the organization is lost.

From 1975 to 1976, PPA was under the control of the Bato faction although the presence of Luna supporters, including the Catholic priest, prevented this faction from totally controlling it. The disproportionate influence of the Bato faction in the PPA results from the belief and practice that holders of political office are automatically entitled to equivalent positions in important religious and civic organizations (see appendix 2).

Historical Basis of Domination

I have mentioned that, in general, people in Luna and its associated barrios have not accepted that the poblacion should remain in Bato. These people argue that since Luna is the geographic center of the municipality, its most populous barrio and the center of most formal religious activity, it should be the poblacion. These advocates further point out that Luna, then known as Nueva Coveta, was the effective center of the area that now constitutes the municipality, at least since the beginning of the previous century.

On the other hand, people in Bato point to the proximity of their barrio to San Jose and the provincial highway, with all the advantages that this proximity implies. Until recently, Luna was frequently cut off during the rainy season because the main river running through Zamora became too dangerous to cross. But in 1968, a bridge was constructed over the main river, facilitating access to Luna and to other southern barrios.

People supporting the claims of Bato remind the members of Luna's faction that when the idea of forming the new municipality was first suggested, the elders from both factions agreed that Bato would be the site of the new poblacion. This arrangement forms part of local historical knowledge and is generally accepted by the older men of both factions. People are, however, unable to explain why Luna, with its fifteen (Ilocano) allied barrios and its long history of being the center of Spanish and later of American administration, accepted the conditions put to it by Bato, a faction that could only muster the support of eight or nine other barrios. Part of the answer might lie in the fact that when this agreement was made in 1915, much of the land in Zamora was controlled by families residing in the non-Ilocano barrios constituting the Bato faction. Since universal male suffrage was not introduced until 1916, the numerical superiority of the Luna faction would not have been significant.

In his 1905 report, M. Miller, the American colonial official who visited the non-Ilocano barrios in the municipalities adjoining Zamora, commented on how the people in these barrios, while wishing to become integrated within the political framework of the emerging nation, did not desire to come under the municipal jurisdiction of coastal Ilocano officials. He recommended that these non-Ilocano barrios be given a certain autonomy enabling them to manage local affairs in accordance with their political traditions. Such a recommendation could explain how the numerically much smaller non-Ilocano population in these interior municipalities retained their traditional political domination over the Ilocano majority. In the case of Zamora, this domination continued until the Second World War.

In the 1970 census, the poblacion (Bato) is listed as having 239 inhabitants. Many old people remember the days when hardly anyone lived in the section that is now referred to as the poblacion. The present inhabitants, who are mainly Ilocanos, settled in this section about thirty or forty years ago, when the poblacion showed signs of developing into a permanent administrative center. However, only a short distance from the poblacion is the barrio of Masingit (population:125), an old Tinggian settlement. North of the poblacion and separated from it by less than 100 meters is the barrio of Lucaban (population:326). This latter barrio traces its links to the Kankanai-Sagada culture area. While an outsider might not be able to distinguish any clear boundaries between these three communities, they nevertheless constitute separate social and political units. To such an outsider, the poblacion might well appear to consist of an agglomeration of these units.

The hub or center of this agglomeration is the plaza, bounded on the west by the large municipal hall built in 1968, and the adjoining municipal health center. North of the municipal hall is the primary school whose grounds border the barrio of Lucaban. Masingit is on the southern flank, overlooking the plaza and only a few yards away from the provincial road. The few stores in Bato are found along the provincial road facing the plaza.

Although the poblacion is the political and administrative center of Zamora, none of the municipality's economic needs are available in its stores. Zamora does not have a market and consequently, people have to travel to San Jose or elsewhere for their main purchases. Farming and household requirements are bought in San Jose and transported to Zamora in the jeepneys that regularly ply the San Jose-Zamora route.

Cement, fertilizer, fuel-oil, insecticides, building materials, and other necessities are transported to Zamora from San Jose or from the coastal centers, adding considerably to the final cost of these items. There are attempts from time to time to establish a regular market in the poblacion but so far without success. Many people express their preference for traveling the few extra kilometers to San Jose to be assured of a wider range of goods. Unless large numbers of people can be persuaded to support the local market, it is unlikely that the scale of market exchanges will attain an economically viable level. The current state of rivalry between Bato and Luna diminishes the likelihood of achieving such support.

Center versus Periphery

The poblacion of Zamora has not yet developed the features discussed by Hart (1955) in connection with what he calls the "plaza-complex." Hart lists as important elements of this complex the school, the church (usually Roman Catholic), the municipal hall, and the marketplace. In many lowland Philippine municipalities, the plaza complex represents the Spanish colonizers' partial success in centralizing and urbanizing the formerly dispersed village (*barangay*) communities. This centralization facilitated the process of conversion and control essential to the colonial enterprise. Moreover, the plaza model was one which the Spaniards were familiar with and which they took to their colonies.

A typical plaza complex consists of a square around which are found the church, the school, the municipal hall, and the houses of the *principalia* (social and political elite). The marketplace and the commercial section either border this complex or are set back a short distance from it. What is particularly striking about the complex is the often disproportionately large church dominating the plaza and the contrast between the large and solid houses of the principalia and the flimsy, thatched, bamboo huts only a few meters away, in which the great majority of the town's population live.

The plaza of San Jose conforms to this description, except that the large church, with its impressive belltower, is built on a hill overlooking the plaza to which it is connected by more than 100 steps, each step being ten meters wide. The old people in San Jose remember being told by their parents of the enormous effort that went into the building of this church, most of which was done through the system of compulsory labor.

Zamora does not have anything resembling an elegant plaza, with impressive tiled residences where the rich copy the lifestyles of wealthy Europeans. In Bato, there are several substantial houses along the main road facing the plaza, but these houses are not in marked contrast to the many equally substantial houses found in several other barrios of Zamora. The Catholic church in Bato is built on a hill overlooking the plaza, but typhoons have diminished its impressiveness.

Luna's plaza is even less impressive than Bato's. The Catholic church is at one end of the plaza and the old municipal hall, now showing signs of neglect, is found at the other end. The primary school is across the road from the plaza. Opposite the school, built next to one another, are the churches of the Methodists and the Church of Christ. There are very few substantial houses built near or around the plaza itself, and aside from two makeshift stores, there is even less of what could be called a commercial sector than in Bato. The private secondary school is near the main road leading to Luna, some 200 meters from the plaza. In the middle sixties, during the time that Luna was the poblacion, a regular market was held next to the plaza. This market only lasted for six months; it failed because of a shortage of money.

Since a developed plaza complex does not exist in Zamora, rich families do not form a residential cluster around or near the plaza, as is the case in many lowland municipalities. Instead, such families construct their houses facing the provincial road, or in a prominent place in their respective barrios.

The opposition, common enough in other municipalities, between the poblacion—with its resident elite and its social amenities—and the peripheral barrios has taken other modified forms in Zamora. One such modification is the opposition between Bato and Luna, each claiming to be the proper site for the poblacion. Another modification, although to a much less marked degree, is the opposition between those who live near a main road and those who live in less accessible areas. In all these cases, the opposition arises out of the tensions existing between markedly differentiated status groups. People who live away from the main road or who live in isolated barrios are perceived as socially inferior to those whose houses are near the plaza or on a main road. These notions of superiority and inferiority do not always stem directly from an economic base but instead, reflect values and preferences related to a particular lifestyle.

People in Zamora apologize to visitors coming from coastal towns on the ground that Zamora, being an interior municipality, lies outside the mainstream of events. It is not uncommon for otherwise well-informed people in the nearby coastal towns to express surprise when told that Zamora has been an autonomous municipality since 1919. Many of them still think of Zamora as an appendage of San Jose. One of the most senior municipal officials of Zamora who lives in an old, established town nearby—and who belongs to the social elite of this town—admits in private that he finds many of the local practices, particularly in cooking, rather crude and uncouth. This official has been associated with Zamora for over a decade, is very well-liked and considered to be approachable and congenial. This case simply shows how feelings of status are closely associated with the dichotomy between coastal and interior municipalities. Many examples of this feeling of superiority by coastal dwellers over the inhabitants of interior municipalities may be given.

The notions of superiority and inferiority are more complex than I have managed to describe above. In addition to the coastal-interior dichotomy, there are other dichotomies, such as that between Ilocano and non-Ilocano, between poblacion and peripheral barrio, between formally educated and uneducated, and finally, between rich and poor. While the dichotomies described do not arise exclusively from status differences (i.e., lifestyles), it is the differences in status, rather than the difference in class or political rank, that are stressed in them.

When these dichotomies reinforce one another, the separation between members of these different statuses assumes significant proportions. Thus, a rich Ilocano living in the poblacion of a coastal municipality is separated from a poor non-Ilocano living in a peripheral barrio of an interior municipality by such a significant status difference that many forms of social interaction become very difficult. Interaction is particularly awkward if food is involved. The only food that a member of a lower status category feels is appropriate to serve to someone of appreciably higher status consists of tinned (i.e., untouched) and preferably imported items, such as Spam, sardines, corned beef, Kraft cheese, Coca-Cola, and instant coffee. Commensality is almost never practiced by people belonging to significantly different status categories.

In this context of center and periphery, the plaza complex, besides symbolizing and being seen as the source from which urban values and innovations spread out to the peripheral barrios—as Hart argues—should more importantly be seen as manifesting and symbolizing the class, power and status divisions present in all Philippine municipalities. While these divisions are present in Zamora, their manifestation and symbolism do not take the form of a developed plaza complex. Such a complex reflected the imposition of a highly stratified colonial society. The bipartite structure of local factions in Zamora has, to some extent, prevented the development of a plaza complex, with its tendencies toward the rise of more rigid status differences. The imposition, maintenance, and transmission of the status divisions have taken other forms. Any model expressing the acceptance of new values and innovations into the municipality must consider that the center-periphery dichotomy is not as developed as it is in many older lowland communities.

Conclusion

This chapter started with a brief description of the political manifestation of Zamora's factions and argued that the pattern of transfer of political power from one faction to the other, disrupted from 1967 to 1975, has been restored as a result of the intervention of external political forces.

Factional rivalry in Zamora has manifested itself in various political forms. From 1917 to 1946, the political life of the municipality was largely dominated by the non-Ilocano barrios (including Luna), with the participation of a few rich Ilocano families. This domination was based on the ownership of land and the concomitant political advantage that such ownership entailed. A set of factors like the pattern of interior migration, demographic differentials, the introduction of universal suffrage, and the marriage practice among many non-Ilocano families brought about an increase in the number of ambitious and competent Ilocanos entering political life. Next, the disruption caused by the Second World War and the introduction of Virginia tobacco in the 1950s, with its significant effect on incomes, changed Zamora's political scenario. Although the traditionally dominant families still exercise considerable influence in local affairs, municipal politics is being increasingly dominated by men of predominantly Ilocano backgrounds. But this shift in the ethnic composition of local political leadership has not affected the main factional boundaries.

From its initial formation as a municipality from 1917 to 1919 and particularly from 1946 to 1967, political parties became identified with each of the main factions. Each party—and hence each faction—alternated in power until 1967, when an incumbent faction retained power through the manipulation of the party mechanism and the token use of interfaction links. This situation persisted until the elections of December 1975, when the holders of political power once more became clearly linked to a specific faction. In the past, disagreements within the faction in power and its inability to fulfill general expectations led to its electoral defeat. It is too early to predict whether the faction currently in power will meet the same fate but serious disputes are already threatening its stability.

Some aspects of the manifestation of this division in the religious life of Zamora have also been discussed. Among Catholics, the proper site of the parish center has been a major element contested by both sides. Because of the complexity and difficulty of manipulating the Catholic hierarchy and Church bureaucracy, the parish center has remained in Luna, where it was first established. In contrast, access to the political and legislative machinery necessary to move municipal centers has proved easier to achieve. This example illustrates the difference in the degree of articulation of the structures of authority and local political competition in relation to the Catholic Church and the national political parties. Since political parties consist essentially of personal alliances at different levels of the political structure, local political demands can eventually work their way up the structure. On the other hand, the hierarchic and bureaucratic structure of the Catholic Church does not lend itself as easily to the articulation of partisan demands at the local level.

The presence of national parties at the level of the municipality has enabled local factions to build up ties with elements of these parties at the provincial and national levels. These ties have allowed each faction to move the municipal seat of government despite the complex executive and legislative procedures involved. The Catholic Church administration has no corresponding ties with local congregations (The Parish Pastoral Assembly is a recent introduction).

The parish priest, who is usually an outsider, has acted as the main channel of communication between the ecclesiastical authorities and the requirements of his parishioners. His primary loyalties are to his religious superiors and the comparatively objective nature of his assessment has enabled the Church authorities to see the factional nature of the request to have the parish center transferred.

The nature of party support and the requirements of party politics differ significantly from the monolithic, authoritarian and hierarchical structures of the Catholic Church. It is this difference in structure that explains why the Bato faction has so far not succeeded in its efforts to transfer the parish center to its barrio.

Protestants in Zamora have also felt the divisive effects of the competition between the two factions. Their congregations have also been divided and considerably weakened as a result of it.

The dispute between Bato and Luna results from the lack of a developed plaza complex. While Bato is presently the administrative and political center, Luna can still claim to be its religious center. In a fully developed plaza complex, the political, religious, economic and social orders are spatially concentrated and markedly differentiated from the peripheral barrios.

Members of each faction in Zamora span the range of class and status categories, but the division between leaders and followers is along class and status lines. Faction leaders hold high status and belong to the proprietary (*nabaknang*) class. It is they who decide the issues on which their respective factions differ: for example, the location of the poblacion. Underlying such an issue are concrete advantages like the allocation of licenses, franchises, political patronage, and the control of national and provincial pork-barrel funds.

That the Bato and Luna factions exist, and that much of the political life in the municipality is affected by their disputes is empirically evident to any observer, including the politically sensitive inhabitants of Zamora. But the same observer will also perceive occasions when common interests unite at least some of the members of each faction. Apart from ties of kinship which at times cross factional lines, there are organizations with special interests like teachers' and farmers' associations, religious and civic bodies, which provide an opportunity for developing cooperation at the municipal and extramunicipal levels. Strong common interests like the performance of *comedia* (Pertierra 1976) often involve members of both factions.

While the factions may represent a different agglomeration of barrios, their leadership is drawn from the same status and class categories. As a consequence, each faction represents essentially equivalent political interests. The success of one faction ensures that its leaders take over from the leaders of the opposite faction, but the process leaves intact the economic and political bases of patronage and preserves both the hierarchy of status and the realities of class. In this way, much of the intense political activity associated with the competition between the main factions ultimately serves to maintain the interests of their leading members. This fundamental coincidence of dominant interests would be both symbolized and manifested in a developed plaza complex.

Zamora's integration into the national polity and economy is reflected, among other things, in the dispute about the site of the poblacion. While many of Zamora's indigenous socioeconomic structures are typical of the egalitarian features characterizing Philippine highland societies, its progressive Ilocanization—here I mean the progressive adoption of lowland political and economic structures—has generated pressures toward a reproduction of lowland Ilocano social structures. These structures are more highly stratified and are essentially pyramidal, with the privileged elites at the top. These elites dominate the political, economic and moral orders, and a developed plaza complex represents an accurate expression of their dominance.

The bipartite nature of the factional division in Zamora is found in other nearby interior municipalities. Similar disputes regarding the proper site of the poblacion have characterized much of the political activity in those municipalities. Hollnsteiner (1963) and Agpalo (1973) discuss similar examples in other areas. Essentially, such disputes occur in municipalities whose leading families are dispersed in several barrios, instead of living within an established poblacion with a developed plaza complex. The centralization and consolidation of elite interests, expressed in the plaza complex, reflect the sharp dichotomies characterizing the former centers of colonial domination, in which political, economic and religious boundaries between the center and the periphery are clearly delineated. But in areas where colonial domination was weak or disputed, the indigenous political structure that consisted of semiautonomous villages prevented the spatial consolidation of elite interests. In Zamora, this consolidation may be expected to shift elite interests and loyalties from local to regional and national issues; it may lead to the replacement of the present tensions between the coalitions of barrios by tensions between competing classes and status categories.

CHAPTER 4

Kinship and the Social Order

Kinship is a primary dimension and consideration in most social relations in Zamora. Inhabitants of the same barrio are often linked to one another by cognatic or affinal ties, and the primary mode of behavior is based on a kinship model. Terminologically, this model is extended to all Ilocano speakers. It is a common practice in Ilocos to employ kinship terms to include transitory and passing social interactions. In such cases, the terms used serve mainly to distinguish between generations, or seniority within a generation.

This chapter shall examine under the general rubric of kinship, the ways in which status, property, residence, and group membership are transmitted from one generation to the next. While societies achieve this transfer in different ways, the idiom in which much of it is carried out is often based on notions of descent, filiation, and affinity.

Although these notions are highly significant in Zamora, it would be a mistake to assume that all transfers mentioned above arise principally from them. Significant economic and political ties exist outside the domain of kinship, and concepts like class and status are necessary to explicate the way in which kinship is linked to the rest of the social structure.

Formal Characteristics

Kinship terminology in Zamora follows the general Philippine pattern. This terminology is found among Ilocano speakers (Nydegger 1963, Scheans 1963, 1966; H. Lewis 1971, Bello 1972) although its precise use may differ slightly throughout the Ilocos region. While Ilocano terms are in general use in Zamora, barrios like Macaoayan, Lucaban, Mambog, and Masingit occasionally use, in conjunction with the Ilocano terms, their own kinship terminology. In the case of the first two barrios, this is largely derived from the Kankanai culture area (Eggan 1960, Bello 1972). The last two use terms similar to the terminology employed by the Itneg or Tinggian of Abra (Fay-Cooper Cole 1915, 1922).

Descent is traced bilaterally with equal jural emphasis given to male and female links. In specific cases, the links emphasized are those that reflect the interests of the respondent in establishing the connection with some significant ancestor.

Generations are contrasted above and below ego, but alternate generations such as grandparent and grandchild employ similar terms for reference and address, i.e., *ápo* and *apó*.

In the first ascending generation, parents are terminologically differentiated from their siblings, but the terms of address for uncles and aunts is often that used for parents, namely, *tatang* (father) and *nanang* (mother). In ego's own generation, siblings are differentiated from cousins. But first cousins—sometimes second cousins—are often treated like siblings. In the first descending generation, ego distinguishes his children from those of his siblings. But the term for "child" (*anak*) is used to address all cognates of ego's child's generation.

Both address and reference terms tend to emphasize the differences in generation, rather than the direct genealogical links to ego. Thus, ego's father's first cousins (and other cousins) are referred to as "uncle" (*uliteg*) or "aunt" (*ikit*) and are addressed as "father" (*tatang*) or "mother" (*nanang*). These systems tend to use a single term for cognates or for affines of the same sex and generation, regardless of the genealogical distance from ego. However, when pressed, people can explain the direct genealogical ties (with exceptions to be discussed later) to their kinsmen. In most circumstances, it is considered unnecessary to work out the details, as long as the appropriate generational reference is made.

The system of reference distinguishes degrees of collateral kin in ascending and descending generations, but reference to kin belonging to further generations is made without indicating the degree of collaterality.

No terminological distinctions are made between matrilateral and patrilateral kin. But the system of inheriting surnames, imposed by the colonial authorities in the middle of the previous century, has a patrilineal bias.

Following a common Philippine pattern (Jocano 1968, Agpalo 1973), parts of the body are used to indicate generation. Aside from the use of terms like *tumeng* (knees) and *dapan* (soles) to indicate senior and junior generations, terms like *bagi* (body or stem) and its derivatives *kabagis* and *kabagian* are used to distinguish lineal from collateral and distant kin.

While affines are distinguished from consanguines in reference, the system of address for most affines employs an appropriate consanguinal term. No attempt is made to differentiate categories of affines (i.e., cognates of spouse and spouses of cognates), such as is reported for other Philippine groups (Eder 1975).

Extent of Kindreds

The kinship model in Zamora encompasses widening circles of kin. Each circle constitutes a category of kin whose members may be activated in appropriate circumstances. As the circle widens, including more distant kin, the ability to activate all its members decreases as the people involved see their obligations to ego progressively diminish. The first circle includes all the descendants of the four grandparents (*kaputot*). This circle includes ego's parents and their siblings and his first cousins. In practice, only some of these may actually acknowledge responsibilities toward ego, but his claim on their help and assistance is seen as proper and legitimate. There may be others, like affines, trade partners, and friends who may help ego in particular circumstances. But his claim on their assistance is neither as general nor as binding as it is among the members of this first circle.

Marriage with any member of this circle is strongly disapproved. But people claim that in the past, particularly in the non-Ilocano barrios, first-cousin marriage was practiced by the rich to consolidate family property.

The second circle includes all the descendants of ego's greatgrandparents (*kapoon*). As this circle is larger than the first, it may include members who maintain few ties with ego.

Marriage between second cousins, although disapproved, is known to occur. Marriage to a member of this circle not belonging to ego's generation is a more serious breach of the rule of exogamy (especially if one spouse is significantly older than the other) than if both belong to the same generation.

People in Zamora claim to recognize a category of kin up to the degree of fifth cousin (*kabagian*). But the large size of this circle, and the generally shallow genealogical memories of most informants, make it unlikely that most people can clearly delineate kin beyond third cousins.

These widening circles of kin constitute ego's descent category. By descent category, I mean a category of people all of whom recognize descent from an apical pair, usually two or three generations above them. Each person belongs to two or more such categories, depending on the extent to which he or she is able to trace descent from an apical pair. Several terms express this notion of being descended from a common stock, namely, *galad*, *katatao, kaputotan, kapoonan*. Occasionally, the original stock may be five or six generations beyond the oldest living member, as in the case of the yearly sharing of the mango harvest mentioned in chapter 1. But descent categories of this depth are unusual and for most purposes, ego reckons his membership to encompass at most his third cousins.

Apart from ties that ego has with his cognates and affines, he is also connected with many others through friendships, partnerships, and ritual kinship (*compadrazgo*). All these relatively permanent and stable relationships provide the individual with the opportunity to exploit whatever resources these links entail, but they also impose appropriate responsibilities.

Several terms express the various categories to which ego belongs as a consequence of kinship (*kagaboan* - descended from a common source), affinity (*agkasukob* - allies or partners), proximity (*kailian* - from the same place) or special friendship (*kagayyem* - close friends).

Household Access

People in Zamora object to first cousins marrying by saying that first cousins are like siblings in that they have been raised under the same roof—in the same household or with access to each other's household. Boys have virtually no limits placed on these visiting practices and girls are also given considerable freedom, provided they are accompanied by close kin. In a predominantly non-Ilocano barrio like Macaoayan, it is the custom for adolescent boys to sleep in the *dap-ay* while girls prefer to sleep in the house of an old widow. Even in Ilocano barrios, it is common for adolescent boys to sleep in abandoned houses; a group of girls often sleep in a house belonging to a close kin.

Access to a household means that the person is on very close terms with its members. This usually implies close kinship links and assumes a regular and altruistic exchange of goods and services among its members. People claim that it would be inappropriate and inadvisable to marry someone with whom such close links already exist.

Marriage Alliances

Marriage in Zamora is seen as an alliance between two households and brings together the respective kindreds of each spouse. The members of each household become *agkasukob* (allies of one another). To marry outside the household is an imperative and failure to do so constitutes a breach of exogamy.

Each spouse enters or is co-opted into the other's kindred. In the system of address involving different generations, the incoming spouse uses the cognatic term appropriate to the other spouse. This usage expresses certain structural properties of the kinship system. Briefly, the use of cognatic terms in addressing cognates of a spouse or the spouses of cognates (particularly for those affines who are *not* members of ego's generation) reflects the structural principle of equating spouses with siblings (i.e., sibling = spouse). This equivalence implies, among other things, that people should marry members of their own generation. It is partly as a result of this structural imperative that people object much more strongly against marrying kin of adjacent generations. The principle of equating spouses with siblings is a result of a kinship system one of whose major organizational features is the differentiation of generations.

Marriage is seen primarily as the legitimated union of the kindreds of the respective spouses. It is the usual process by which new kindreds are formed. Both spouses' personal kindreds form the basis of their children's kindred, their members being held together by a common interest in the children. The fate of the relationship between the spouses who initially brought about the union of kindreds is irrelevant. In the cases where spouses separate, remarry or simply establish other households, the relationships between the children and members of their kindred remain strong and continue despite the parents' separation. There are many examples in Zamora of spouses who have separated and established different households, but whose initial children still activate the kindred brought about by the original marriage. In the case of separation, the *sab-ong* (property contributed by the groom's parents) is held in trust for the children usually by the groom's parents, but occasionally by the bride's parents. Since the children usually remain in the wife's custody, her kinsmen help toward their maintenance until they are old enough to make use of the sab-ong. If no children result from the marriage, the sab-ong reverts back to the husband's parents.

People who refer to one another as *abalayan* (co-parent-in-law) continue to do so even if the marriage is no longer functional, as long as it has resulted in children. But if the children are produced outside marriage, their grandparents, while usually recognizing the line of filiation, do not address one another by the term *abalayan*. In this last case, the ties of the child with members of his kindred are not reinforced by affinal links.

Descent and marriage are the principal axes on which alliance groups (*sukob*) in Zamora are formed. Descent determines one's cognates, from whom one may expect help and protection. The ties generated between affines are couched and assimilated into the cognatic kinship model.

Politics and Genealogical Amnesia

While collecting information on genealogies in Zamora, it became evident that most people's knowledge of kin ties seldom extends beyond their grandparent's generation. Often they could no longer recall the names of their dead grandparents. This lack of recollection occurs even more frequently among grandparent's siblings. But when recalling collateral kin (same side, e.g., father, father's brother or sister) of the same generation, most people are able to name all their first cousins, most of their second cousins, and many of their third cousins. There is much greater interest in tracing horizontal ties (i.e., links between members of the same generation) than in remembering vertical ties. People claim that this is because horizontal links (*sangaputotan* - belonging to the same generation) provide one with potential allies (*agkasukob*) while vertical links only entitle him to claim certain rights and privileges resulting from common descent (*katataoan* - original or founding ancestor). In a community like Zamora, descent confers only a generalized set of rights and privileges in which specific claims have to be enforced. For this reason, a person's allies are a more important factor in achieving his goal than any "inherent" rights he may have due to descent.

Political support is one instance where a generalized claim has to be converted into a more specific one. A man who asks the support of a kinsman may be refused on the grounds that another, more genealogically distant but affectively (affinally) closer kinsman, has also asked for support.

Although the category of fourth and fifth cousin is said to be recognized, very few informants are able to provide explicit links with kin of these categories. When pressed, most people reply that such kin are *kabagian* (distant relatives).

Whenever it is desired to cultivate close relationships with distant relatives, people usually employ the kinship term appropriate for the desired relationship. If the desire is mutual, this telescoping of kinship ties is passed on to succeeding generations. Thus, third cousins might refer to one another as second cousins.

In Zamora, there is usually little need to remember a long line of ancestors. As a consequence of bilateral descent, no one except full siblings (children of the same father and mother) have the same set of ancestors. Spouses belong to different lines of descent and their children belong equally to the lines of descent of each spouse. If this process is repeated over several generations, the lines of descent soon increase to impractical proportions. Because there are no enduring descent groups (i.e., lineages or clans) but only temporary descent groups manifested in certain gatherings, at which people acknowledge common descent, or localized bilateral descent groups encompassing at most three generations, it is not surprising to often encounter shallow genealogical memories. It becomes too complex and difficult for ego to trace links beyond three or four generations above him. Besides the emphasis on horizontal links earlier mentioned, structural properties of the kinship model encourage genealogical amnesia.

Aside from the links that people have through common descent or ties of affinity, people in Zamora also make use of the institution of *compadrazgo*. This practice creates ties that bind the parents of a child to the child's baptismal or marriage sponsor. By consenting to act as a marriage or baptismal sponsor, one acknowledges a special relationship both to the person sponsored and to this person's parents. This relationship employs terms analogous to those used in the kinship system.

Compadrazgo can be used to publicly seal and acknowledge an already existing relationship between adults, such as that between a tenant and his landlord, or an employee and his superior. In such a case, the use of ritual kinship facilitates and supports the already existing special ties binding the parties. In Zamora, the ideology of kinship obliges one to seek the welfare and good of one's kin. Compadrazgo extends this obligation to include ritual kinsmen. This relationship does not explicitly prohibit marriage between the children of the *compadres*, since its main concern is strengthening and confirming the ties of compadrazgo rather than the obligations between sponsor and sponsored. Some informants indicated that it would be good in some cases for the children of the compadres to marry. They compared it to the former practice of cousin marriage.

Another use of compadrazgo is to build up ties between as yet uncommitted members of the community. Whether such ties are actually activated will depend on the need of the parties involved. But the links will have been established and certain opportunities will have been created by this action.

Compadrazgo is a relationship whose terminology is modeled on that of kinship; its normative and behavioral expectations are conceived and expressed in terms of the rights and obligations of close kin.

Compadrazgo ties often bind, sometimes alongside already existing kinship links, the patron/broker to his/her client. These relations range from long-term personal and moral ties with an element of altruism to less stable, pragmatic and transactional relations between equals. At present, the nature of the economy and the lack of a developed market and bureaucracy tend to emphasize the patronal and moral aspects of this relationship.

Marriage and Residence in Luna

The general comments made so far apply to the municipality of Zamora as a whole, with a population of just under 8,000 in 1975. Zamora consists of twenty-six barrios. Its smallest barrio has a population of 99 and its largest, Luna, a population of 836 distributed in 151 households.

Marriage data for 205 natives of Luna, showing the pattern of residence, is given in tables 3-5.

Table 3. Marriage and residence patterns in Luna

	Married a spouse from Luna	Married a spouse from Zamora but not from Luna	Married a spouse from outside Zamora	Total
M	66	14	20	100
F	68	15	22	105

Table 4. Patterns of residence for natives who married outside Luna

	Virilocal	Uxorilocal	Neolocal	Total
M	20	8	6	34
F	20	15	2	37

Table 5. Patterns of residence for natives who married in Luna

	Virilocal	Uxorilocal	Neolocal	Total
M	35	30	1	66
F	37	30	1	68

Table 3 shows that 14 out of 100 men and 22 out of 105 women left Luna as a result of marrying a spouse not from the barrio. On the other hand, 15 men and 20 women became residents of Luna after their marriage to a native of this barrio (table 4). This shows a balanced reciprocity between marriage in and outside of Luna.

When both spouses come from Luna, the pattern of postmarital residence is not as crucial for the spouses as it is when one of them is not from this barrio. But the choice of residence in Luna, for most cases of intrabarrio marriage, follows the pattern of virilocality (table 5); the couple resides in the compound of the husband's kin.

Initially, until the newly married couple establish their own separate household, they will usually live in the house of the parent in whose compound they reside. But while they are living in the parental house, the young couple will use their separate income and their own supply of rice. Once they have children, the need to establish their own separate household increases. The couple will build their own house near the parental home, or within the compound of houses owned by siblings or other close kin. Most of the materials and labor for the construction of the new house is contributed by kinsmen.

The stated preference for marrying within the barrio and the patterns of residence in Luna reflect the importance of maintaining close ties with each spouse's kindred. Access to economic resources and the exchange of goods and services takes place more easily between kin than it does between nonkin. People in Luna claim to want to live near their relatives to facilitate such exchanges. Exchanges between nonkin also occur, but the ideology and commitment encouraging good relations between kin are stronger than relations between nonkin. Neighborhood ties and membership of mutual aid organizations (i.e., *saranay* in times of bereavement, *comun* for marriage, *dapat* - irrigation societies) complement but rarely substitute for the bonds created by kinship and marriage.

The question of postmarital residence is one of the main matters discussed during a marriage negotiation. People in Luna generally claim that since it is primarily the husband's duty to provide for his family, he should have the choice regarding marital residence. Virilocality is the most common form of residence (tables 4 and 5). But the incidence of uxorilocality is sufficiently high for this form of residence to be considered as falling within acceptable norms. Only in the case of neolocality is this choice markedly smaller. Neolocality occurs when the couple decide or are obliged to reside outside each of their close kin's residential compounds.

One factor determining the choice of spouse is the amount of land available. People who have insufficient resources in Luna tend to marry outside of it in the hope of gaining access to external resources. People claim that this explains why younger members of the barrio increasingly favor marrying outside of it. Factors such as the rapid population growth, the increasing diversification of the economy, and the effects of high rates of barrio marriages, coupled with the prohibitions against cousin marriage, are likely to change the focus of marriage—from within to outside Luna.

The average Luna household contains six or seven members; in many cases, it includes three generations. If the oldest inhabitant, male or female, is still economically active, he/she is considered as the head of the household. But all adult members, particularly if they contribute to its maintenance, are always consulted in all major matters affecting the household.

Although married children establish their own households as soon as possible, parents often insist that at least one child, often the youngest, stays in order to care for them in their old age. This child, irrespective of sex, inherits the parental house and lot. This is the ideal arrangement, but it is not always attained. Households consisting of old parents, widows, etc., without their children or younger kin, while not very common (8 percent), occur often enough for people to realize that their security in old age is not certain.

Although the nuclear family constitutes the core of most households, the presence of other consanguines and/or affines is considered normal and proper. Often, unmarried siblings or grandparents take over the care of children whose parents are unable to do so, or who are persuaded to give this task to others. The emphasis in the kinship system on generation and seniority and the tendency to terminologically equate close kin of the same generation (i.e., cousins are called siblings) facilitate and reflect such childrearing practices.

Marriage and Residence in Macaoayan

Marriage preferences and the choice of residence in Macaoayan differ considerably from those in Luna. While people in Luna stress the advantages of marrying within the barrio (ca. 66 percent did so), people in Macaoayan prefer to marry outside the barrio (ca. 62 percent did so). Virilocality was both the preferred and the most common form of postmarital residence in Luna (ca. 56 percent) while uxorilocality was the preferred and the most common form of residence in Macaoayan (ca. 60 percent). Tables 6 and 7 show the marriage and residence patterns for 224 natives of Macaoayan. A consequence of such a pattern is that over a third of the men leave Macaoayan after marriage, to be replaced by approximately the same number of men from other barrios.

Table 6. Marriage and residence patterns in Macaoayan

	Married in Macaoayan	Married in Zamora but not in Macaoayan	Married a spouse not from Zamora	Total
M	38	12	50	100
F	50	16	58	124

Table 7. Patterns of residence involving an outside spouse

	Virilocal residence	Uxorilocal residence	Neolocal residence	Total
M	23	37	2	62
F	28	45	1	74

Macaoayan is considered to be one of the most prosperous barrios in Zamora. Paradoxically, it is the barrio's wealth that is partly responsible for the preference in choosing a spouse from outside Macaoayan. The close ties that Macaoayan people have with the barrios of the neighboring interior municipalities sharing cultural and ancestral links with the northern Kankanai-Sagada area have created a wide network of land ownership. This dispersed network gives people in Macaoayan adequate land resources in other municipalities and in Zamora. Parents thus advise their children to marry into these other barrios to maintain and reinforce interbarrio links. In such marriages, uxorilocal residence is preferred. A son is often advised to marry into his father's sister's village as he will then be able to work the land he is to inherit from his father.

Many of the senior and most influential men in Macaoayan have married into the barrio. Traditionally, these in-marrying men formed the core of the gerontocracy (rule by elders) that dominated the political and religious affairs of the barrio. Part of the advantage of in-marrying men was their ability to exploit their external ties in interbarrio disputes.

Ironically, it was also through the initial practice of uxorilocal residence that Luna eventually evolved into a barrio where both marriage within and virilocal residence became common. The mechanism of recruiting men from outside the barrio, with links in other barrios, who would eventually constitute the group of influential elders, was largely responsible for the transformation undergone in Luna during the first decades of this century. At this time, a number of Ilocano men married into the leading families of Luna, and through their influence, Luna became the center of the newly formed municipality. Luna's political importance attracted other Ilocanos, many of whom had little or no land elsewhere. As a result, the children of these marriages had only their mother's land in Luna to inherit. These children preferred to stay in Luna and marry someone from this barrio. The shift toward intrabarrio and virilocal residence accompanied the Ilocanization of Luna as it became increasingly drawn into provincial and national structures.

Macaoayan, on the other hand, managed to retain many of its non-Ilocano structures well into the present century. Several factors seem to have been responsible for the different historical experience of Macaoayan during the first decade of this century.

Unlike Luna, Macaoayan retained its religious and political institutions until the outbreak of the Second World War. During this period, no Ilocano in-marriages of any significance occurred. Religious and political control remained in the hands of the elders (*panglakayen*), many of whom came from other non-Ilocano barrios with cultural traditions similar to Macaoayan. Significantly, while Luna acted as the effective center of the new municipality, most of the political leadership came from non-Ilocano barrios like

Macaoayan, or from non-Ilocano families in Luna. But in time, those Ilocanos who had established themselves in Luna took an increasing interest in its affairs and through this, extended their influence to the rest of Zamora. Since the Second World War, the political initiative has been taken by people of predominantly Ilocano background, although these Ilocano leaders are often supported by wealthy families in the non-Ilocano barrios.

Male and Female Domains

Jayawardena (1977) rightly points out that most studies of kinship have emphasized the phenomena of procreation, generation and descent. This emphasis has, however, often neglected the basic sexual divisions that are presumed in the construction of the basic kinship categories such as daughter/sister/wife/mother or son/brother/husband/father. Jayawardena argues that, at least for Acheh society, intersexual relations are as important a feature of the social structure as are intergenerational relations. The latter usually forms the focus of kinship studies. It seems that for Acheh, the nature of intersexual relations is itself responsible for what appear to be intergenerational factors. Thus, the economic self-sufficiency of Achehnese women largely explains what appear to be vestigial matrilineal features, such as uxorilocal residence and the inheritance of certain rights and obligations through females.

Compared to Acheh, the relation between the sexes in Zamora is more egalitarian. Both men and women participate in the cultivation of tobacco and rice, and they are equally involved in market and trading activities. Politics is usually the domain of men but very few can expect to succeed in it without the active support of their wives. Religious activity involves both men and women, although the focus and quality of their behavior may stress different aspects.

The arbitrary division between the public and private domains is not significant in Zamora, except in the sense that a woman's responsibilities and interests leave her little time to become involved in activities not immediately relevant to the household. Many household activities are public in their enactment but private (i.e., household) in their orientation. Religion is the primary extradomestic interest appropriate to women, particularly those from high-status and affluent households.

In contrast, men have more time to devote to extrahousehold interests. This enables them to develop and engage in political activity. However, much of its success depends on the economic base provided by the household; and women's contribution to this economic base is an important element.

Essentially, the private-public dichotomy concerns socially defined spheres of interest and activity appropriate to each sex. In this sense, women are perceived as much more oriented toward domestic responsibilities, and their activities revolve around their own households. Men are not perceived as being so closely bound to domestic or household interests. A man's sphere legitimately includes extradomestic orientations and activities (Rosaldo 1980, Rutten 1983).

While the acceptance, maintenance, and reproduction of social structures do not depend exclusively on the principles of organization of sexual divisions, these principles underlie such primary relations as those between classes, between status groups, and both between and within generations.

Kinship, Marriage, and Residence: An Overview

At the beginning of this chapter, I defined kinship and marriage as a total complex whose basic function lies in the transmission of status, property, residence, and group membership through the idiom of descent and alliance. Kinship and marriage's fundamental aim is the structuring of social relations between generations, between sexes, and between seniors and juniors of the same generation. The final form of this structuring is not determined solely by kinship and marriage relations, but this category is a major organizing principle. Other factors like common economic and political interests, friendships, and contingent choices also shape this final structuring. As in the case of compadrazgo, the idiom of kinship is often employed even when its meaning is clearly not parentation (Southwold 1971). In the most general case of the extension of kin terms to all Iloko speakers, the terminology is obviously meant to denote parentation only in a symbolic and metaphorical manner.

In the examples of Luna and Macaoayan, the final shape of this structuring has responded to historical, economic, political and social factors. But behind these different responses, certain structural features like bilateral descent and the differentiation of generations have remained.

Kinship terminology in Zamora is concerned with distinguishing (1) the generations, (2) the sexes, and (3) seniors from juniors within a generation. This terminological concern is associated with corresponding normative expectations in the interactions between kin and affines. Seniors must be shown respect, but juniors may be treated familiarly. A mild joking relationship exists between members of alternate generations and between affines of the same generation, particularly between the *abirat* or spouses of a set of siblings or siblings of a set of spouses (appendix 1). Although uncles and aunts must be given the same respect as one's parents, they are seen as more indulgent than parents. Children are much more informal with their mother than with their father.

An important feature distinguishing a barrio such as Luna, with its preference for barrio endogamy and virilocality, from Macaoayan, with its preference for barrio exogamy and uxorilocality, is the relation between men of adjacent generations. In Luna, a man, his father and grandfather live in the same barrio, sometimes in the same household, but usually within the compound of close kin. The relation between a man and his father is one of formality but with the grandfather, one of informality. While a man and his son are on formal terms, the father must nevertheless facilitate his son's assumption of the paternal estate. As a consequence, the growing demands of a man vis-à-vis his father's privileges are a potential source of friction. In Macaoayan, the practice of uxorilocal residence often ensures that a man and his sons do not live in the same barrio. When a young man marries, he leaves his natal barrio to join his wife in her barrio. Often this means moving to his own father's natal barrio. While he can expect to be on very formal terms with his father-in-law, he usually has resident cognates who facilitate his acceptance and adjustment into the barrio. In this case, a man expects to succeed his father-in-law rather than his own father. The relations between a man and his father-in-law are even more formal than his relations with his own father, but a father-in-law is not expected to solicitously seek his own replacement by his son-in-law. This structural opposition between men of adjacent generations is openly admitted in Macaoayan but in Luna, it is felt to strike at the core of the "axiom of amity" (Fortes 1969).

The strict rule of the elders (*panglakayen*) in Macaoayan, was facilitated, at least in structural terms, by the open admission of this opposition. People in Macaoayan refer to the difficulties in maintaining this strict rule over one's own sons and point out the problems encountered in barrios like Luna, where fathers are reputed to be unable to control their ambitious sons. Both in Macaoayan and in Luna, people claim that it is much easier to dominate sons-in-law than to dominate sons.

The gradual erosion of the power of the elders in Luna went hand in hand with the increase of the pattern of virilocality in this barrio. In contrast, the retention of the practice of uxorilocality in Macaoayan was accompanied by the continued influence and authority of barrio elders.

The role and position of women is also affected by the rules of residence. A young woman who has to live with her husband's family finds this period of adjustment particularly difficult. She is on very formal terms with her husband's parents and is expected to help and obey her mother-in-law in household tasks. Only years after her own marriage and once established in her own household, with her own children, may a virilocal wife expect to possess autonomy over her own activities and those of her household's.

On the other hand, a uxorilocal wife experiences very few of these initial difficulties. She begins her married life among her own kin and is able to make the required adjustments in a familiar and often supportive environment. The tension characterizing relations between fathers and sons is absent in the case of mothers and daughters.

When marriage occurs within the barrio, the problems of residence are not as significant as when marriage involves an outside spouse. Even when a wife joins her husband in his parents' household, her own kin are nearby and she can expect their support whenever conditions become difficult.

Patterns of residence also determine the use and access to land and other resources. When marriage occurs in the barrio, as it mostly does in Luna, both spouses have continued access to their own agricultural land and they usually develop this resource together. Although a distinction is made between individual and conjugal property (*sab-ong*), the resources of both spouses are treated as a unit, particularly when they have children. But a problem is generated whenever one of the spouses dies prematurely (or separates) and the other decides to remarry.

In the case where one spouse comes from another barrio, the problem of controlling land in another place arises. In such cases, each spouse usually retains control over his/her own land, although each spouse's land is considered to be part of the entire family's estate.

I have mentioned that men in Macaoayan prefer to marry women from their father's natal barrio. This preference ensures that residence in the wife's barrio allows her husband to have access to his own father's land.

CHAPTER 5

Rituals and Social Structure

Zamora, like all societies, faces the problem of integrating its new members, of indicating significant changes that its members undergo, and of making them accept the inevitability of death. Each of these problems constitute a life-crisis that signifies a transition from one social condition to another and is expressed through an appropriate symbolism and ritual.

This chapter explains how natural facts like birth, ageing, and death are given meaning and transformed into cultural events in Zamora. Life and death are treated here as different aspects of a common reality. Their commonality is shown in the symbolism employed in birth and death rites. This common symbolism shows how the cultural appropriation of natural events like birth and death constitutes the human condition. In the northern Philippines, as in other communities, personhood is not generated by the exclusive result of ritual action alone but its main transitional phases are usually marked by an appropriate ritual. The progress from birth to death is ritually celebrated whenever a significant social phase begins or ends

(Leach 1961). Rituals are specially effective as social markers and investitures because they can simultaneously incorporate instrumental, communicative and expressive aspects. In other words, the ritually acting subject relates to the objective world, to the social world, and to aspects of his/her inner subjective world. Unlike rational discourse or other action orientations, ritual action does not attempt to separate these different situation orientations. So, ritual speech tends to be performative rather than propositional or referential, and much of ritual action is noninstrumental and expressive such as song and dance (Bloch 1974). A ritual is important in marking socially significant phases of life. But this importance depends on the social structure and on how far action orientations differentiate instrumental, normative and expressive aspects (Habermas 1979). Social structures that have tightly integrated technical, moral and aesthetic orders use ritual to indicate and generate socially significant life phases. These phases refer to changes in relationships of status and authority. Whenever the structures of knowledge and authority fail to differentiate action orientations directed to change the natural state from those meant to affirm common moral imperatives, or from actions that express an interior commitment, ritual plays a major role. It can indicate and bring about major changes in the life phase. Events like birth and death which involve significant nonempirical elements (e.g., spirits, ghosts, etc.) often employ a rich ritual mode but an event like marriage, whose principal concern is secular, employs a more specific action orientation like rational discourse to articulate normative claims based on intersubjective criteria. The conflation of different action orientations mentioned depends on how far validity claims pertaining to each aspect are argued and defended through acceptable methods. In other words, only after the normative order is conceptually and structurally separated from the technical and expressive orders is it theoretically possible to reconstitute each order on the basis of rationally motivated activity following intersubjectively accepted criteria. In such a situation, ritual would not be a valid mode of action.

Important life phases occur between birth and death in Zamora, as in other communities. Of these phases, baptism and marriage are the most important. Birth and death address themselves to the nonempirical aspects of these experiences: in contrast, baptism and marriage are primarily secular in orientation. While the distinction in Zamora between the empirical and the nonempirical or transcendent (sacred) is one of emphasis since both realities are sometimes experienced coterminously, ritual orientation however often stresses one aspect over the other. In both birth and death, transcendent aspects of reality constitute a major orientation. And ritual serves to achieve the necessary transition between the transcendent and the ordinary aspects of reality.

Baptism and marriage on the other hand, while having transcendent aspects, are mostly concerned with establishing relationships in the secular world. These latter occasions are characterized by extensive discursive episodes (talks aimed at reaching an agreement) during which normative expectations and strategic goals are conceptually separated from technical and expressive claims and judged according to clearly stated criteria. Poor families often combine a baptismal and a marriage feast since both occasions are primarily concerned with announcing the formation of a new and independent household. Baptism and marriage feasts are large public occasions that articulate wide-ranging relationships in the social structure, such as alliance groups, categories of kin, local groups, and close friends. In contrast, birth rites are mostly private affairs; they are of concern only to a small group of close kin and only some months later are wider relationships articulated. Death rites, however, are public affairs articulating significant structural changes but the dramatic and transcendent aspects of death are equally important. A well-planned baptism or wedding is hastily cancelled or postponed in the event of a death.

Rituals are a means of creating and reasserting the social order (Bloch 1974 and 1977). They do this by defining the domains of competence (i.e., role expectations, social institutions like the family) of social actors so that social relations are made to appear as external and objective elements of the natural order. By conflating the expressive, communicative and technical aspects of action, rituals prevent the discursive redemption of validity claims appropriate to each aspect; in other words, they do not allow for the fine elaboration of arguments. Thus aesthetic-practical claims referring to inner subjective states (personal feelings) are not distinguished from intersubjective (commonly accepted) normative expectations regarding the social world or from knowledge of empirical nature. Validity claims referring to privileged knowledge of the actor's own subjectivity are merged with moral-practical expectations relating to mutually acceptable normative standards and with empirical-theoretical knowledge of existing states-of-affairs.

Rituals predecide which validity claims have to be accepted, or raised in relation to whom, when, where, and why. And so, they fail to render explicit the potential reasons and interests of acting subjects (Habermas 1984). It is in this sense that rituals provide conceptually set frameworks for thinking and feeling as well as constraints and channels for actions. By using the illocutionary and performative aspects of speech, rituals attempt to achieve technical ends by projecting social relations onto the empirical world. They are effective because they regulate the transition from the subjective to the intersubjective and the objective worlds. In other words, they are able to generate dispositions and interests by "creating" social states. Truth claims are fused with normative rightness and personal authenticity.

This chapter discusses how the major *rites de passage* provide the framework for thinking, feeling and acting that ultimately reproduces objective domains of competence. Through their enactment, these rituals articulate orientations to the self, stake moral-practical claims, and perform certain technical tasks. The role of women in social reproduction, the centrality of men in alliance networks, the special claims of elders and the natural authority of the wealthy are affirmed and legitimated.

This analysis of ritual does not, however, imply a functionalist model of action. Rituals, like all other action orientations, sometimes work and at other times, they do not. Moreover, as van Gennep (1960) pointed out, healing rituals do not themselves mend broken bones although they may assist in the healing process by creating the appropriate psychological environment. Some rituals can alleviate anxieties when there are no pragmatic solutions; others can also engender them to legitimate or validate norms. Hence, death rites facilitate the control of the fears and dangers of death as well as dramatize its existential importance. Likewise, conflict-resolving rituals often operate to disguise the real source of tension in social systems marked by significant inequalities. The ideological functions of ritual are well-established (Barth 1975). In Zamora, as in other communities, rituals are used to make social claims that may or may not be reasonable. For example, during pregnancy, a woman claims certain privileges; if these privileges are not satisfied, the health of the fetus may be affected. The extent to which she presses these claims and the satisfaction she receives depends on a host of contingent factors. In a sense, for rituals to operate effectively, their cognitive, affective and technical claims must remain implicit or even unconscious. In other words, they are effective if they are not questioned. The *habitus* (Bourdieu 1977) within which they are embedded must be unchallenged and acceptably orthodox. To engage in a ritual is to participate in the construction of a world of meaning whose framework has already been given (e.g., the Pope is holy; President Reagan is good; capitalists are evil).

The fact that systems of metaphysics are not always consciously and systematically elaborated in all societies has not deterred anthropologists from analyzing public symbols and institutionalized behavior as important elements of their expression. Douglas (1966, 1973), van Furer-Haimendorf (1969), and Turner (1967, 1974), to name only a few, have analyzed non-Western metaphysical systems in terms of the rich body of symbols such cultures possess. In this chapter, I want to examine the relationship between a system of metaphysics and the social structure within which it is embedded. It is this relationship which explains why some changes but not others are seized upon and developed in a given society. It also explains why relatively undifferentiated metaphysical systems employ ritual to generate and reassert changes in the social structure.

Following the work of van Gennep (1960) on the importance of *rites de passage*, I examine the practices and beliefs associated with transitional states experienced in Zamora. These transitional states involve both natural (birth, menarche, death) and ideological (superincision, marriage) aspects that have been given social significance.

Pregnancy and Childbirth

Despite the fears and apprehensions most women have about childbirth, they regard it as their main function in life. While the beliefs associated with conception are not always clear, considerable knowledge exists regarding male and female roles in sexual reproduction. Several acts of coitus are regarded as necessary for conception. The man's role is seen as the more dynamic, while the woman provides the environment and nutrients for fetal development. The man's role is essentially one of initial implantation, of introducing the seed (bukel) into the woman who, in turn, nourishes it (agbukel) in her own body. Whenever conception does not occur, the woman is usually blamed. The beliefs mentioned constitute the public ideology (what people say in public) regarding sexual reproduction; they reflect the masculine bias of the ideology. In private, women do not always accept such male-oriented explanations for infertility.

The pain and the dangers associated with childbirth make inexperienced women very anxious. The conditions in which births occur and the generally poor health of many mothers justifies such a state of mind.

Once pregnancy is diagnosed, the woman claims certain intimidatory rights over her husband on account of her condition. She develops cravings for unusual foods, becomes moody and demands more attention than usual from her husband. He complies with most of these demands, believing that the child's health would otherwise be adversely affected.

The unborn child is believed to interact both with its internal and external environment. The mother's experiences and her desires affect the character and future of her unborn child.

Pregnancy places the woman in a liminal condition, which is manifested in her special needs throughout this period and for some months after childbirth. At any stage of her pregnancy, a woman may legitimately deny her husband sexual access. She becomes less active as her term progresses and performs the necessary rituals to ensure a safe pregnancy and an easy delivery. She rubs vinegar on her stomach to keep away evil spirits; she makes sure she has taken some salt with her whenever she leaves the house. Nighttime, dusk, and dawn are particularly dangerous times, and women take care to remain indoors. Evil spirits are strongly attracted to pregnant women and lurk in the vicinity of the house waiting for an opportunity to harm her or the child. These spirits are sometimes associated with dead ancestors but others are not believed to have ever been human.

A pregnant woman is not supposed to stand near a doorway or window, lest she experience a difficult delivery. The mimetic symbolism of not blocking openings is not consciously stated although untying knots is a common remedy against difficult births (Nydegger and Nydegger 1963). Ritual baths are always taken in the morning; but on a day she has had a massage, she is not allowed to bath. Massages generate an internal body heat incompatible with cold baths. The morning is associated with health and vigor, and late afternoon, with decline and ill-health.

The notions of hot and cold (Jocano 1973) are frequently used to explain the causes of illness and these notions are also used for difficulties arising in pregnancy. Women possessing special skills, called *dadaw-wakan* (general healers) and *parteras* (midwives), attend to the pregnant woman whenever requested. Their services are generally free, or only a token payment is made to them. The woman is massaged regularly, takes therapeutic baths and toward the end of her pregnancy, wears a tight cord or belt to prevent the fetus from retracting during delivery.

Traditional midwives (*parteras*) or experienced kinswomen attend the birth. However, kin of both sexes may be asked to help and no attempt is made to seclude the woman during her delivery. The woman is made to squat and through various manipulations, the child is eventually delivered.

The placenta is placed in a bowl that is then hung on a camachile tree (*Pithecolobium dulce*) some distance from the house or near a river. Part of the umbilical cord is wrapped and kept inside the house to ensure that the child does not wander away. To prevent siblings from fighting, their umbilical cords are tied together.

After the birth, both mother and child are kept in dark and partial seclusion. This period may range from a few days to a month, the period becoming shorter after each child. The time after childbirth is a particularly dangerous one for both the mother and the neonate. Special fish and meat broths are fed to the mother for a week or two after the birth, and she is allowed only hot or warm drinks for at least a month or two. The mother is highly vulnerable to the effects of cold and so, her room must be kept warm. She is not allowed to eat or drink any cold foods.

As mother and child grow progressively stronger, they are slowly integrated into normal household activities. After a few months, they are allowed to visit nearby households. The neonate is regularly anointed with oil on the head, armpits, palms, and soles to neutralize the effects of coldness and to repel evil spirits. The newborn is never left on its own and a blunt steel blade or instrument is placed beside him as a precaution against attack by malevolent beings.

While the care of the child is primarily the mother's task, both male and female kin are eager to share in this duty. A very young child is seldom taken out of the house. A few months later when he is taken visiting, gifts are given to him and his mother. Some coins or notes are wrapped in his shawl or blanket, and uncooked but threshed rice is given to his mother in honor of the visit. The first homes visited are said to develop a particularly close tie with the child, and the gifts are meant to ensure both the child and his host's prosperity. The homes visited are generally those of senior kin or of prosperous neighbors.

In some barrios, as soon after the birth as possible, the woman goes to the river with her child for a ritual bath, and to wash the sheets and blankets she used in giving birth. The following day, the child's male kin go to the river to fish and the success of this venture reflects the child's economic future. To ensure the child's bravery and endurance, a few days after birth, he is placed on a winnowing basket and made to cry by shaking the basket.

Sexual relations are resumed a few months after the birth, assuming that the woman has by then fully recovered. A branch of the kamachile tree is placed under the house by the husband after the birth, with the dual purpose of keeping away evil spirits and indicating when sexual relations may be resumed. Once the leaves start falling, which takes between seven and eight weeks, intercourse may be initiated.

The birth of a first child confers a new status on his parents and his grandparents. The mother has fulfilled one of her main life functions, and is henceforth treated by her kin and affines with greater respect. The father has acquired added responsibilities and his behavior is now expected to be more restrained and reliable. The families linked by the marriage share a common bond in the child, whose cognatic tie (consanguines) to each family complements their affinal links (in-laws). Since marriage is seen primarily as an institution binding two families for the purpose of having children, a childless marriage is met with dismay and pity. People see little purpose in such a marriage and do not consider the relationship between a husband and wife as sufficient justification for it.

Baptism

Baptism is the most important event marking the child's formal entry into the community. The child's and the family's status is validated by giving a feast on the day of baptism. The expense for this feast is an indication of the status of the child's kindred and of their claims regarding the child's status. The choice of baptismal sponsors is important, as this involves potential allies and patrons. The institution of *compadrazgo* allows people to initiate ties with nonkin who, in the future, are treated as if they were kin. For this reason, people seldom choose real kin for their *compadre*. Sometimes compadrazgo ties express and formalize already existing links between adults, and at others, they presage the possible development of these links.

There are several denominations that do not practice infant baptism: the Church of Christ, Iglesia ni Kristo and Mision Cristiana. Most of their members are comparatively poor and would not, in any case, be expected to give lavish feasts. But most of these denominations have a dedicatory rite (*idaton*) that is equivalent to baptism. The more affluent members sometimes celebrate these dedicatory rites; but even in their case, these feasts do not usually assume the expense and importance of the baptismal feasts given by Catholics.

All of the denominations that do not practice infant baptism are nonconformist and radical in their rejection of many aspects of folk religion (e.g., offerings to ancestors, prayers for the dead). They tend to emphasize ties within their respective religious communities at the expense of ties with nonmembers.

Catholics in Zamora distinguish between *bautizar* and *buniag*, both terms usually translated to mean baptism.[3] *Bautizar* is derived from Spanish, while *buniag* is Iloko and denotes a name-giving rite or activity. The verb *buniagan* means to give someone a name; it is derived from *buni*, a spirit associated with ricefields, and *nagan* (name). Hence, the verb may have originally implied a dedicatory rite in honor of the spirits associated with ricefields.

When an unbaptized child is seriously ill, a senior kinsman sometimes baptizes it. This informal rite, called *bautizar*, employs the standard Catholic baptismal formula which in Zamora involves two interchangeable forms: (1) "Buniaganka iti nagan ti ama ken ti anak ken ti spiritu santo, amen" (I name thee in the name of the Father, the Son and the Holy Spirit, amen) or (2) "Bautizarenka. . . ." Because of the circumstances, it is performed in the child's home and does not involve sponsors. Assuming the child recovers, no feast is given to mark the rite (i.e., *bautizar*). *Buniag*, on the other hand, is reserved for the more formal church ceremony officiated by the priest or minister in the presence of sponsors and followed by a feast.

Before the day of the buniag, preparations are carried out by neighbors and kinsmen who help cook the large quantities of rice and meat needed for the feast. In a wealthy household, delicacies like raw goat or dog meat are served with alcoholic drinks before serving the main course. Special rice cakes and other desserts are also served.

When everything is organized, a small party consisting of the sponsors, the child and his parents go to the church for the brief and simple ceremony. The party then returns home for the main celebration. There is little formality associated with the feast; guests, friends, neighbors and kin partake of the food and depart almost immediately afterwards. Important guests are always served separately.

Baptism marks the end of the transitional state of the neonate, giving it a more specific social identity. This process of identity formation starts soon after birth through a series of minor rites like ritual bathing and anointing,

---

3. See Foronda and Foronda (1972:68-81) for a discussion of these terms.

name-giving, and other rituals meant to ensure its health, bravery, and prosperity. Baptism (*buniag*) and the ensuing feast reinforce all these processes of identity bestowal and publicly link the child with members of his kindred and sponsors.

Personal Name

Many people in Zamora have had their personal name changed at some stage during their early childhood. The child's formal name is the one given to it, either when the birth was registered at the local municipal hall, or at the baptismal ceremony. This formal name is seldom used while the child is young and in its place, a more intimate name, often derived from a deceased ancestor, is given him, at least until his late childhood or early adolescence. If a child is often sick, a new name is given in the hope that the offending spirit will be appeased or confused by the change. This name-changing rite (*gupit*) requires the preparation of special rice cakes by the child's mother or other female kin. A short invocation, often of Christian origin, is said by an old kinswoman, after which neighbors and kin proceed to eat the rice cakes. As people leave, they rub their sticky hands on the child's head and call him by his new name.

Naming practices in Zamora reflect ideas regarding filiation and descent. A child's first name is sometimes formed by combining parts of the first name of his father and mother, or of his grandparents. So, a man named Benjamin and his wife Estefania call their child Befania; alternatively, a child may be named Ludel in honor of his grandfathers whose names are Luis and Delfin (Pertierra 1979).

The practice of teknonymy is particularly common in Macaoayan.

Adolescence

There are no major communal rites that mark the transition from childhood to adolescence. This transition is gradual and depends as much on the responsibilities assumed by the child. Aside from experiences like superincision or menarche, the end of childhood is indicated by sleeping patterns. Adolescents often do not sleep in their parents' house but in the house of widowed or elderly kin. Boys often sleep in abandoned or unoccupied houses. In Macaoayan, boys sleep in the *dap-ay* (meeting house).

Boys are superincised between the ages of twelve and sixteen. They undergo this operation in small groups, under the supervision of an experienced adult or an older lad. This operation is essential for boys and marks their entry into puberty. Besides cutting the foreskin, some boys pierce their prepuce membrane, inserting a thread through the hole to ensure that it remains open.

Girls do not undergo any equivalent operation. The onset of menstruation is regarded as a sign of puberty and of approaching sexual maturity. First menstruation is a matter of concern both to the girl and to her senior kinswomen. They instruct her regarding the procedures to be followed during her menstrual period. The girl's earlier freedom is severely curtailed after her first menstruation. Any display of fondness toward men, including close kin, is discouraged. From this time on, a girl may publicly display fondness only toward women.

The transition into adolescence is indicated by using the term *barito* (young men) and *balasang* (young woman) instead of the general term *ubbing* (children).

Menstruation

Menstrual fears and prohibitions are not highly elaborated in Zamora. While a girl's first menses is a cause of some initial concern, this experience is quickly relegated to the everyday natural order. Menstrual prohibitions are more developed in the case of childbearing women. After the birth of her first child, a woman takes greater interest in observing menstrual taboos. She never bathes during her period and is careful not to wet her hair. Bitter-tasting fruit and oily foods are dangerous; jackfruit may cause death. Menstruating women should not work in the fields, or pound rice. Picking certain crops like beans is forbidden and they are expected to stay away from the gardens and the main crops. Intercourse is not practiced during a woman's menstrual period. Menstruating women hesitate to enter a church lest their menstrual blood becomes particularly smelly. Stained clothes are separated from the rest of the washing. An attempt is made to ensure extra cleanliness, but the contamination of food by menstrual blood is not believed to be poisonous. Although women generally observe these restrictions, the most common attitude toward menstruation is one of acute embarrassment rather than fear.

Other Changes in Social Position

Other changes in a child's development are sometimes marked by feasting. The achievement of academic distinctions is a common occasion for a moderate feast; for this reason, graduation ceremonies have become an important occasion in Zamora. In constrast, changes in spiritual development like first communion or confirmation—or full immersion in the case of denominations that do not practice infant baptism—do not merit a feast. These latter events do not enjoy the prestige associated with distinctions in formal education.

While any event which gives prestige to a family may occasion a feast, the personal achievements of children remain essentially a private or a household's concern. None of these changes in the personal circumstances of the young adult are perceived as involving a major change in his social condition. This major change takes place on his marriage, and the importance of this latter transition is such as to require a feast rather than merely providing an excuse for one.

Marriage

Marriage is a public contract signifying an alliance between the kindreds centered on each spouse. Its main purpose is to provide the proper conditions in which to raise children. A child that results from the marriage becomes a member of each of his parents' kindred. One of the consequences of marriage is the formation of new kindreds. The child's kindred exists independently of the fate of the marriage.

The control and authority of senior kin over members of junior generations restrict the latter in choosing their spouses. Most young people, however, find sufficient ways to choose their spouses within the limits set by existing opportunities. Marrying inside or outside the barrio usually indicates such opportunities but sometimes, it also expresses a definite marriage preference.

Although seniors take an active part in the final choice of a spouse, they rarely impose their will on their dependents. There are various strategies used by young people to elicit their seniors' reluctant approval of a spouse. Elopement is one of the most effective strategies.

Courtship

When adolescent boys (*barito*) show an active and serious interest in girls (*balasang*), they are referred to as *baro* (unmarried male). This interest is expressed in formal courtship that involves serenading (*tapat*) and an exchange of letters.

Once a young man has decided on a woman for his wife (having obtained her consent in advance), he informs his parents about his choice. If the parents have no objections, they call on the woman's family to begin the necessary negotiations (*danon*). Sometimes, the man's parents ask a respected elder to initiate these negotiations. The request to the woman's parents is always made in formal and metaphorical language (*dal-lot*), requiring both poetical and political skills. On being formally informed, the woman's family show no interest and ask for time to consider the matter and to consult their daughter and kin. A date is fixed for a second visit. On this visit, the man's family expect a more definite answer, unless the marriage proposal makes for difficulties. Assuming the woman consents and her family have no objections, an affirmative answer is given at this second meeting. They are then formally engaged (*patiam*) and either party is entitled to compensation if the other reneges on the agreement. A third and final meeting is arranged to discuss matters like the expenses for the wedding feast, the date of the wedding, the transfer of property, and postmarital residence. Two-thirds of the wedding expenses are usually paid by the man's and one-third by the woman's family. The groom's parents offer the young couple money, work animals, or land (*sab-ong*).

In the case of separation, the *sab-ong* reverts to the groom's family; but if there are children, it is retained for their use. The groom's family offers a gift (*pasuso*) to the bride's mother in acknowledgment of her services in caring for her daughter.

The woman's family carefully examine the circumstances and resources of the man before giving their consent to the marriage. Although her family are also expected to contribute toward the economic resources of the young couple (women have equal rights of inheritance and can control property in their own right), the new family's main support is seen to be the responsibility of the husband.

In Macaoayan, where uxorilocal residence is common, it is also assumed that a husband should have sufficient resources to be able to provide for his wife and children. But the notion of sharing this responsibility is also present and is expressed in the Ilocano saying, "No agsusuon ni babai, agassiw ni lalaki" (Just as a woman carries a load on her head, so a man carries one on his shoulders). This implies, however, that a man should carry a heavier share of the burden.

The wedding date is planned so as not to coincide with the busiest periods of agricultural work, and it depends on the availability of cash and other resources. For this reason, the months of April, May, and June—when the tobacco crop has been sold and rice planting not yet begun—are particularly favored ones. November and December, after the rice harvest but before the tobacco season, are also a frequent choice to hold weddings. Days that are propitious are chosen and omens like a sudden death may cause people to postpone the wedding. Some days of the month are automatically propitious, and others unpropitious. Knowledgeable men and women are consulted to determine the best day for the wedding. Several methods are used for determining a suitable day. These require the use of astrological books or a system of reckoning like reciting the Apostles' Creed and counting its phrases until one reaches a phrase that coincides with the date desired. If the coinciding phrase is propitious—the seventh phrase refers to the suffering of Christ under Pontius Pilate and is therefore unpropitious, while the tenth phrase refers to Christ's ascension into heaven and is therefore propitious—the corresponding date is accepted. An unexpected accident like falling down the stairs, or a bad dream may cause people to change the wedding date. Sunday is a propitious day but Friday is unpropitious.

Church Ceremony and House Rites

The ceremony at the church, although important for status, evokes only a minimal emotional response from the participants. The solemnity of marriage, if felt, is shown during the dedicatory rites (*idaton*) performed at the couple's house or during the exhortatory speeches at the wedding feast. The church ceremony, however, is both lavish and expensive. It attempts to replicate the finery and pomp associated with urban weddings. In this situation, embarrassment and awkwardness typify much of the behavior in church, and people are clearly pleased when it is all over and everyone returns home for the main celebration.

The priest or minister is always invited to attend the wedding feast since his presence confers prestige on the occasion.

After the church ceremony, the *idaton* are held at the newly married couple's home. These rites request for the blessings and aid of ancestors and other spiritual powers associated with the household. Even when the priest or minister are present, they are not asked to officiate in these rites. These rites often evoke crying but none of the embarrassment and awkwardness present at the church is evident. A senior kinsman or woman leads the initial prayers as the couple sit on each side of an improvised altar. A statue of the Virgin Mary (or a saint) is placed on the altar and two candles burn on each side of it. The candles are watched with interest because the manner in which they burn—how long they burn and which one burns faster—foretells such things as who will dominate the marriage, how long will the spouses live, and how long will the marriage last. Raw or semicooked meat and some unsalted rice cakes are placed in front of the statue as offerings.

Prayers of Christian derivation are said on this occasion and no explicit references are made to pre-Christian spiritual beings. But when asked why they perform these rites, people reply that they want to show respect to their ancestors and other spiritual beings associated with the household. In other words, the choice of prayers and their intended functions are not always articulated, unless specifically asked.

Wedding Feast

As the wedding nears, preparations are made for a large feast at the bride's house but other venues are possible. Kinsmen and neighbors help to prepare and serve the food. Plates and other utensils are supplied by neighborhood organizations (*comun*) such as the barrio youth club. Specific invitations are seldom issued since most people know which weddings they are obliged and are expected to attend. Weddings in Zamora attract over 100 guests; some even cater for twice this number. The wedding is an important occasion for it can demonstrate the status and the generosity of the families concerned. How it can be conducted well is one of the most important matters discussed during the wedding negotiations.

Weddings usually include dancing except for denominations which do not allow it (i.e., Methodists, Church of Christ, and Iglesia ni Kristo). Special songs are dedicated to the young couple; these often contain sexual references that never fail to amuse the guests. The groom's and the bride's parents or *abalayan* (co-parents-in-law) engage in comic dancing to everyone's amusement. Such informalities indicate that the two families are now close to each other; these are in contrast with the future formality between senior affines.

At the emcee's signal, the young couple commence to dance. Relatives and friends approach them, then pin or attach money to their clothes. This procedure is repeated several times, depending on the number of guests. Specific categories of people like the groom's kin, the wife's kin, servers, and cooks may be announced and given the opportunity to show their generosity. Competition often arises between the kindreds to give the highest amount; this eventually results in comparatively large donations. Donations range from ₱500 to ₱2,000. This is equivalent to an average farmer's income for two to eight months. The amount collected is publicly announced and ceremoniously handed over to the man who, in turn, gives it to his wife. Representatives of both families give long speeches before the handing over of the collection. These speeches extol the virtues of love, honesty, and hard work. They remind the wife of her duties toward her husband and her children; they also point out the husband's responsibilities toward his family. A list of the donors is given to the young couple. This list will remind them of the help they have received; it will also inform them of all those to whom they may be expected to give help in the future.

These proceedings over, the bride and groom—accompanied by their families and friends—proceed to the house of the groom (assuming that the main feast was at the bride's) for a smaller feast (*pacating*). Sometimes the bride packs her husband's clothes; the couple will bring these clothes with them to her house. She also takes a cup of rice from the groom's granary to bring with them to her house. Access to a granary is a major privilege and the bride's taking of a cup of rice symbolizes her acceptance into her husband's household and his acceptance into hers. After the *pacating*, the couple will stay at the woman's house to spend the next few days there. They then assume their permanent residence, which initially is with one of their parents.

Sponsors

Like baptisms, weddings have sponsors. The couple's parents use the wedding to create or validate ties with important members of the community. Local officials, landlords, and other persons of high status are requested to act as sponsors for the occasion. This relationship creates very few specific ties between the parties involved and is mainly an honor given to the sponsor. In most cases, the close ties between compadre created through baptismal sponsorship are not observed in the case of the relationship created through wedding sponsorship.

These procedures constitute the most common and proper way of celebrating a marriage. There are, however, cases where these procedures are not followed. If a young man and woman wish to announce their relationship without formally celebrating it, the wedding feast is dispensed with. The couple then live together in the house of one of their parents, usually the woman's during which time, the man is expected to contribute his labor to her household. This arrangement must have the prior approval of both sets of kindred and may be prompted by special circumstances such as a shortage of funds, or the young couple's desire to continue their studies.

While the couple are married in the eyes of the community, enjoying the rights and privileges of marriage, their social transition—from *baro* and *balasang* to *casado* and *casada*, respectively—is not fully validated until the wedding feast is given. The birth and baptism of their child or a change in their economic circumstances may provide the occasion for that feast. An arrangement between the heads of their kindreds may be a sufficient condition for a young couple to live together but this arrangement must ultimately receive public endorsement for the union to be considered legitimate and proper. In general, an arrangement like this is disadvantageous to the woman and her kin; they would only accept it in unusual circumstances.

Change of Family Names

Upon marriage, a woman assumes her husband's family name but also retains the use of her father's family name. The use of her husband's name indicates her new orientation vis-à-vis him and his kindred. The retention of her father's name shows her continuing tie to her natal group. If the marriage fails, she often reverts to her previous surname, particularly when she wishes to indicate the termination of her domestic and sexual duties to her spouse. If she wishes to continue her claim to her spouse, even if their marriage has failed and her husband has left her and established another household, she continues to use her spouse's name and behaves as a faithful wife.

Men do not adopt a new surname upon marriage. This reflects a bias toward men with respect to their commitment to their wives. While women lose considerable personal freedom after marriage, men are not rushed to accept the more restrictive aspects of marriage. When a woman gets married, she is expected to immediately reorient her life to the duties and responsibilities of a wife. She becomes associated with people who exercise authority over her activities and interests. This period may extend for several years until the time when her role as wife and mother is well established both within her own and her husband's kindreds. Men, while also expected eventually to settle into their role as family providers, are given more time to grow into their new responsibilities. Their behavior immediately after marriage is often unreliable, in terms of ideal expectations, and certain privileges are extended to them, such as special rights at public dances. People are generally sympathetic to men having difficulties in adjusting to marriage. They excuse these men's shortcomings as due to their new status. People call them *baro ti kalman* (yesterday's bachelors). No equivalent expression exists to describe recently married women. They are expected to settle into marriage responsibilities immediately. They are not expected to attend dances and must show restraint and propriety on all occasions.

Death

Upon a person's death, preparations are made for the appropriate mourning ceremonies (*minatayan*). Their extent and expense depend on the status and wealth of the deceased. The body is carefully washed by close kin, and particular attention is given to combing the hair of the deceased. He/she is then dressed in his/her best clothes and displayed in the main room of the house. Relatives, friends, and neighbors gather around the coffin to pay their final respects. A basin of water is placed under the coffin; candles and other forms of brilliant illumination are placed beside it. The room is purposely not swept for the duration of the vigil.

Close kin sit near the coffin. There are always other people present in the room. As visitors and kin arrive, members of the bereaved family show their grief by loud lamentations and by reciting special chants (*dungaw*). Once the immediate display of grief is over, they prepare to feed and entertain the large number of visitors.

Prayers led by a senior kinswoman are said for the deceased, at least once a day for the duration of the vigil. Young men and women of the neighborhood play special games; they also entertain the visitors and the bereaved family with songs and poems. Many of these games are characterized by a controlled unpredictability which mimics the ultimate precariousness of life.

The vigil is maintained until all the important relatives have arrived to pay their respects and to console the survivors. A person of high status whose kinsmen live far away may not be buried for up to a week or even longer. During this time, people gather in the house of the deceased each evening to offer moral and financial support to the family. Close members of the family of the deceased are not allowed to meet or greet guests as they arrive nor to accompany departing guests to the door, for such courtesies may attract the ghost of the deceased. Guests are rubbed with oil before leaving to protect them against abdominal pains which can be caused by the ghost of the deceased. Some people take a bath on returning home, then rub themselves with *malunggay* leaves (*Moringa oleifera*). Malunggay is a tree whose leaves and flowers are a common ingredient of Ilocano food.

Women sit in the main room; men congregate outside. Coffee and other light refreshments are provided. Neighbors and relatives serve and look after the guests.

Local associations (*saranay*) help their members in a range of activities and expenses associated with mortuary rites. These neighborhood associations are often headed by women. They have their own sets of plates and other utensils which are used only for mortuary feasts.

On the day of the funeral, a large crowd accompanies the coffin to the church and later to the cemetery. Great care is taken not to bump the coffin against the door or a wall as it is taken out of the house, as a sign of respect for the deceased. The water in the basin kept under the coffin is thrown out of the front door after the coffin is removed. This action is said to remove any evil spirits that might have been attracted into the house during the vigil. This room is then swept for the first time and prepared for receiving the people for the postburial feast.

Members of the immediate family of the deceased do not go to the cemetery but delegate a more distant kinsman to accompany the corpse to its final resting place. It is said that the cemetery scene is too painful and difficult for close members of the family to bear. Distantly related women (*kabagian*) are the main mourners at the cemetery. Amid loud cries, they provide the deceased with cigarettes, tobacco, and an item of clothing having close association with him/her, like a pillow, a hat, or a shirt.

After the cemetery rites, the mourners return to the house of the deceased on a route different from the one taken on their way to the cemetery. This strategy is meant to confuse the dead person's ghost and to dissuade him/her from returning home.

Close kinfolk, who up to this day have not been allowed to bathe, wash themselves in the river after they have killed a chicken and sprinkled its blood over themselves. The chicken sacrifice is meant to appease malevolent spirits attracted by the corpse.

The major feast takes place immediately after the cemetery rites. The novena begins on the night of the burial. It consists of Christian prayers and hymns performed for nine consecutive days. These prayers are led by senior kinswomen who are not of the immediate family of the deceased. While women and children are active participants in novenas, men very seldom attend them. And even when they do, they are unlikely to take an active role. A large crowd attends the last night of the novena. After the prayers, a main meal is served and a dance is held to commemorate and honor the deceased. For the first time, senior men take an active role in the proceedings. Long speeches recall the deeds and accomplishments of the deceased, and the bereaved family is assured that their obligations have been properly fulfilled. The dance attracts many young people of the barrio and other nearby areas. The immediate members of the family, including first cousins, do not take part in the dancing; but more distant relatives, friends, and neighbors are expected to enjoy themselves.

There is a developed body of beliefs related to the spirit of the dead. People say that a person's ghost hovers near that person's house immediately after death. It attempts to reenter its body and must be convinced that this is no longer possible. The careful washing of the dead person's hair with frothy water squeezed out of burnt rice-straw is offensive to ghosts, and the singing of the death chants (*dungaw*) finally convince it of the impossibility of reanimating its body. Spirit possession (*naluganan*) is a common experience that occurs a few days after death. Messages from the dead are passed to kinsmen by the possessed agent. The medium may be a close kin of the deceased but more often, a distant kinsperson or even a neighbor acts as the agent. The third and ninth night after burial are particularly favored by the spirit to visit his/her kin. Any unusual noise or smell is quickly interpreted as a sign of its presence. The close association between the spirit of a recently deceased and its former habitat lasts approximately for forty days. Only after this time has passed are the survivors confident that the spirit no longer lurks near the house wishing to rejoin its living kin. A year after a senior person's death and yearly thereafter, the spirit is invited to share a ritual feast with its descendants and, from then on, is expected to be benevolently disposed toward them.

In some barrios, the pattern of feasting and the participation of seniors differ slightly from the one just described. There, the main feast is given while the corpse is still in the house. Relatives and friends attend this feast and consume large quantities of meat, rice, and *tapuy* (rice wine). The feast may last for several days, depending on the status and resources of the family. For example, when a prominent man in Macaoayan died several years ago, the mortuary feast lasted for four days. During the feast, one large carabao (water buffalo), eight pigs, tinned meat, and two cavans of rice were consumed, bringing the expense to ₱3,000, or the equivalent of an average yearly income. No major feast is given after the burial, but visitors are served light refreshments if a novena is held. In these latter barrios, old men and women play a more significant role in death rites. The collective role of the *panglakayen* (old men) at a death in Macaoayan contrasts with the comparative lack of participation of senior men in Luna. For ritual purposes, Macaoayan is divided into opposing *moieties* (complementary parts). The section to which the deceased does not belong is responsible for the organization of the main feast, including serving the guests and preparing the burial plot. This moiety division was in the past a major feature of barrio social structure, but it has progressively fallen into disuse except in the case of death rites where it still exercises considerable influence.

At the major feast given while the corpse is present, great care is taken to serve the guests food appropriate to their generation. Senior men and women are always served first and have the choice of special delicacies like liver and kidneys. Younger people are particularly respectful to elders at these occasions. In contrast, very young children are allowed great liberties by the elders, who share the special delicacies with their grandchildren.

In these latter barrios, there is no dancing or other amusement organized by young people on a death. The occasion is one that primarily allows old men and women to eat and drink in excess and to engage in exchanges of wit and poetry.

The activities described constitute the basic elements of death rituals in Zamora. Details vary according to the status and economic resources of the deceased. But in all cases, people exert a great effort to ensure that the death of a kinsman is properly commemorated.

Major Rites of Passage

I have described some of the more prominent beliefs and practices associated with birth, marriage, and death.

As mentioned earlier, each of these transition rites has both secular and sacred aspects. Feasting and the creation of political alliances are some of the prominent secular aspects, while ceremonial naming, symbolic washing, invocatory and dedicatory prayers represent the religious (sacred) aspects. The rites of birth and death stress the sacred aspect while marriage stresses the secular aspect.

Marriage and baptism are seen primarily as an alliance between kindreds whose members have a common interest in the children resulting from the union. The sacred aspect is secondary to the foremost purpose of strengthening the bonds between kindreds.

Birth and death, although providing splendid occasions for people to create and define social ties and status differences, also have to deal with the nonempirical aspects of these experiences. The importance of ancestors and other spirits to the health of a neonate, when added to the danger these ancestors and spirits pose during pregnancy, ensures that the religious or sacred aspect of birth rites is stressed. Similarly, the final and irreversible experience of death and the belief systems associated with it, inevitably evoke religious or sacred links. In contrast, marriage is firmly rooted in the requirements of the present life.

Despite important similarities, birth and death also have significant differences. Birth rites are mainly concerned with the termination of the state of pregnancy, with its attendant danger, and the integration of a potential member of the community. The integrative rites of a neonate precede a social relationship that has yet to develop.

The rites concerning death have to resolve the inevitable reorientation of social relationships which have had significant implications throughout the community.

A successful birth is in several senses a victory over death. The danger in pregnancy often brings a woman close to death, and her child—following its close associations with a dead ancestor—represents a reaffirmation of life. For these reasons, pregnancy is ambiguous because it signifies both a possible death and a new life. The parturient woman (woman who has recently given birth) and her child regain life after having come close to death, and this transition is symbolized in the rites of seclusion following a birth. Both mother and child are kept in a warm and darkened room for several days. They are only gradually exposed to the morning light. She washes her hair with rice-straw water, vinegar, and salt while facing east. During an eclipse, pregnant women and those who have recently given birth sit on a rice mortar and wash their hair in the manner described. The symbolism after a birth stresses life-giving elements and marks the transition from a dangerous to a safe condition. The spirits of women who die during childbirth and of unbaptized children are particularly malevolent.

While a successful birth has important effects on the relationship between the parents and their kindreds, the death of a married adult has wider implications throughout the community. Such an event brings about changes in the relations of authority within a household and often between households. Patterns of inheritance and the distribution of property following an adult's death have wide repercussions in the community. In contrast, the consequences of a birth remain tentative for some years, since the relationships presaged by it may not come to full fruition, as is the case in premature death, a common possibility in Zamora. There is nothing tentative about the consequences of an adult's death.

Marginal Situations

Pregnancy, birth, illness, and death are natural events with particular significance. For philosophers such as Heidegger (1962) and Jaspers (1963), death and other natural crises bring into question ordinary ways of comporting and of understanding ourselves and the world. Death is not simply the termination of life, but its most significant feature. It thrusts itself into our consciousness and becomes an aspect of it. This inward appropriation of death becomes a characteristic of the human condition and is exemplified in countless mythologies which attempt to explain its intrusion into human affairs.

People in Zamora generally do not reflect on the nature of their own death or on the death of others. But the experience of death and other natural crises elicit certain metaphysical and ontological themes expressed through the notions of pollution, marginality, inversion, separation, and reintegration. Rituals in general (not just death rituals) provide the appropriate cognitive, affective and behavioral responses to such crises, thereby reasserting and reproducing social order.

The notion of pollution is used to indicate the otherness of death through culturally significant oppositions such as washing-not washing, active-inactive, sociable-unsociable. Marginality is expressed in the unsuccessful attempts of the ghost to return to its body. It neither fully reenters it nor completely leaves it. Ordinary rules of greeting and entertaining are temporarily suspended by the bereaved family. The time between Christ's death on Good Friday and his resurrection on Easter Sunday is marked by the suspension of the normal rules of nature (i.e., magical powers are strong) and culture (i.e., the practice of ritual theft). Adolescents roam the barrio at night, during this period, stealing chickens and other minor items because normal rules of compensation are suspended. The notions of inversion, separation, and reintegration are expressed in behaviors such as the different routes to and from the cemetery (a direct route there and an indirect route back), the absence of immediate kin at the burial site and their proximity to the corpse throughout the vigil, ritual baths, the lifting of the prohibition of working in the fields, and the use of ordinary clothes to mark the official end of mourning.

The symbolism of water features prominently in both birth and death rites. Warm flowing water, signifying life, is contrasted with cold water which is symbolic of death. A tree like the camachile, useful only for its meager shade and tasteless fruit (mainly eaten by children) is contrasted with the malunggay, a tree whose leaves and flowers are a common ingredient of Ilocano cooking. The former features in birth, the latter in death. Sexual intercourse is resumed when the camachile branch placed under the house looses its leaves (i.e., putrefies), a period that normally takes about seven or eight weeks and during which the placenta, referred to as the second birth, is allowed to dehydrate in an old rice bowl hung from the camachile's branch.

Visiting patterns following a death are usually resumed at the end of the mourning period approximately forty days after burial, when the ghost has accepted the irreversibility of death. This interval coincides both with the resumption of sexual relations after a birth and the tentative efforts to introduce the child to neighbors and close friends. In all these cases, normal and full sociability and sexuality is resumed after a period of separation imposed by birth or death.

In contrast to the camachile's close association with birth and sexuality is the symbolism of the malunggay, whose leaves are used to make infusions for purificatory and medicinal purposes. The drought-resistant kamachile represents the triumph of vitality over putrescence, while the useful malunggay, the housewife's handiest nutritional source, ensures the continuity of life in the face of death.

The care taken to prevent a coffin from bumping against any walls as it is quickly taken out of the house recalls the mimetic rites of unblocking passages to ensure an easy delivery.

The period of dark seclusion following a birth may be contrasted with the brightly lit, large gatherings at a person's death. A mother and her newborn child, having come close to death, are gently and slowly nursed back to life in the privacy of domestic kin. A person's death is not only the occasion for a large gathering of both kin and nonkin; amid this, close kin of the deceased sit apart, refusing to greet each other because rules of pollution prevent them from touching or greeting relatives and visitors. They only resume their ordinary behavior after the burial, which they themselves do not attend.

A pregnant woman and a corpse are both ambivalent and transitory conditions. The former has an excess of life, the latter has the form but not the content of life. Pregnancy is both a physiologically and spiritually dangerous condition and for these reasons, a pregnant woman has to take precautions to ensure a safe delivery. She takes care not to stand or sit near doorways or thresholds and always keeps a supply of salt or vinegar to repel evil spirits. If she must walk outdoors after dark, she undoes her hair in the manner of adolescent girls rather than keeping it in a tight bun as is customary for a married woman. In this case, the allusion to presexuality is apparently sufficient to protect her from dangerous spirit beings intent on attacking the unborn child.

The carefully groomed corpse also attracts spirits, including its own which attempts unsuccessfully to reanimate its body. The combination of noise, light, and the death chants finally convinces the spirit not to reenter its body. The spirit stops haunting its former abode seven weeks after burial, the time alloted for the desiccation both of the camachile leaves kept under the house after a birth and the placenta hung from the camachile's branch. The contrast between sudation and dessication to express the opposition of life and death is made explicit in the practice of steaming women after parturition and the recently discarded practice in some barrios of smoking the corpse before burial. In these and other cases, the conditions of tumescence (hardening) and detumescence (softening) are seen as representing life and death.

Birth and death rites are attempts to overcome the dangers posed by pregnancy or the presence of a corpse. The former, having a surplus of life, attracts the interest of malevolent beings. Moreover, the act of parturition is dangerous and the neonate's life is easily threatened by both natural and supernatural factors. A fresh corpse also attracts spirits, including its own which must be dissuaded from attempting to reanimate its body. Death rites successfully accomplish this and the finality of death is accepted by the spirit with some initial reluctance but eventually uses its new condition to help surviving kin.

Sickly children are nursed back to life by undergoing a name-changing rite that involves rubbing their hair with glutinous (sticky) rice reminiscent of the regular anointing during infancy. The practice of rubbing mortuary guests with oil to protect them from the ire of the spirit of the recently deceased should be contrasted with the careful washing of the corpse and the special care to remove any remaining natural oil from its hair by washing it with burnt-straw water. During an eclipse, pregnant women wash their hair while sitting astride a rice mortar. This is a symbolic reassertion of female fecundity emphasized both during a discontinuity in nature and the temporary suspension of a wife's sexual obligations to her husband.

It was noted that close kin do not wash for the duration of the vigil and only do so when the corpse is taken to the cemetery. They sprinkle the blood of a sacrificed chicken over themselves before washing carefully in the river. They then return to the house to await the arrival of the guests for the postburial feast. Guests who have paid their final respects to the dead wash themselves carefully on their return home with an infusion made from malunggay leaves.

Through the complex interweaving of the symbolic elements discussed above, people in Zamora are able to express and induce important changes in the life phase reflecting a person's new status. Natural changes are given significance and transformed into cultural events within the appropriate normative and expressive structures. Empirical facts are linked to social claims and interior states of the personality. In the absence of a discourse that can reconstitute action orientations referring to the empirical world or to the inner-subjective world through the use of rationally motivated and intersubjective criteria, ritual provides a necessary mechanism to achieve this reconstitution effectively. The empirical dangers of birth and death cannot be superseded pragmatically and technically but only symbolically through the use of ritual. In the case of marriage, discursive redemption (reasons provided in argumentation) of normative claims reflects its largely secular orientation and contrasts with the more ritualized response to birth and death.

Conclusion

The acceptance of a neonate takes place within the family soon after its birth. A name is chosen, usually by the parents or grandparents, and from this time, the child possesses a personal identity. Its social acceptance by the wider community may be postponed for some months until sufficient resources have been obtained to prepare a feast. Although the immediate reason for the feast is the community's validation of the child's status and links with members of its kindred, it also signifies the entry (or reconfirmation) into parenthood and grandparenthood. Parenthood confirms a person's married status (*casado*) and grandparenthood indicates the gradual transition from respected adults (*lakay* and *baket*) to elders (*nataengan*).

Any property brought into a marriage will eventually be inherited by the children. The new household then becomes the center for future derivative households; its social, political and economic unity having started to take shape on the birth of a child. That marriage rites only place secondary emphasis on the religious or transcendent aspect indicates the weak links between this social state and the transcendent order; marriage is essentially a system of alliance. Its rites' main focus is on the alliance between kindreds and the requirements and obligations of the present life.

Death is the ultimate and the most important social transition in Zamora. For this reason, the moral and economic resources of the household are fully activated to ensure that the proper rites are fulfilled. These rites stress both secular and religious aspects. The implications of death in the social, political and economic life of the community may be considerable. The distribution of property creates new economic units, and may lead to political realignments. The corpus of beliefs about the nature of the supernatural ensures that death is closely associated with the transcendent order. The living must be consoled for the grief and the discomfort caused by the irreparable loss of a kinsperson and his/her ghost must be sent to its proper domain. The natural and transcendent spheres complement one another, but each sphere must be kept in its proper place. For this reason, great effort and expense are spent in ensuring that proper funerary rites are carried out (Hertz 1960). A sense of security is felt after customary and traditional obligations have been performed for the community and the spirit-world.

I have shown in this chapter how the transitional states of birth, marriage, and death employ a complex system of symbols to express both their transcendent and secular aspects. This complex of symbols is neither totally consistent nor exhaustive and they are employed according to practical interests (e.g., whether the child survives, whether newlyweds are compatible, whether baptism can be afforded, etc.). Moreover, the cultural heterogeneity of Zamora is at times quite marked. But within certain divergent limits, the necessities for communication and coordination create enough of a shared reality in which the symbolic elements discussed play both a performative and an expressive function. While not always consciously elaborated, symbolic systems always imply a certain ontology and metaphysics. In Zamora, the beliefs and practices related to birth, marriage, and death reflect theories of being as well as the nature of transcendent reality. Zamora culture and social structure do not always allow for the separation of cognitive, expressive and moral-practical claims. In the absence of a decentered view of the world and faced with the experience of birth, marriage, and death, ritual is able to validate ontological claims within commonly held metaphysical views. Through the use of mimetic and symbolic elements, ritual is able to combine technical efficacy with expressive and normative claims.

Within this common culture and social structure, children are treated as essentially nonsexual beings whose personalities are as yet unformed; adolescence brings with it the first clear sexual differentiation. By their control of property and other resources, parents often direct their children to desired marriage arrangements. The final negotiations and public validation of the alliance between kindreds in marriage is dominated by men.

In contrast, women play a greater role in death. Much of the mourning and praying is performed by women, while men show an interest only at the final state—when the deceased is publicly praised.

All of these transitional states are expressed within existing status and rank hierarchies. Their performance both creates and confirms the economic and political divisions in the community.

Rites of passage infuse meaning into facts of nature, turning them into events of culture. Conversely, cultural constructs like gender, generation, and status are naturalized; they are made to appear like objective elements of the natural world (e.g., men are brave; women are tender). Social relations then become external and objective elements of an impersonal reality. Through ritual, nature is socialized and society, naturalized. While women play a prominent part in the conversion of natural facts like birth, menstruation, and death into their cultural constructs, men mimic this conversion from nature to culture in superincision and through their control of the ideology of procreation. Birth and death are the most fundamental natural facts and appropriately, these are closely though not exclusively associated with women. Marriage is an example of a cultural construct that attempts to mediate between birth and death; it comes before birth and denies the finality of death. Men play their most important role through their control of the ideology of procreation. The complement of *genetrix* and *mater religiosa* (moral guardian) is *homo politicus*.

Church wedding of a *nabaknang* family

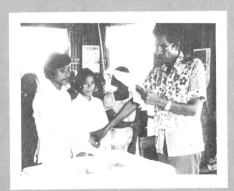

Senior kinsman advising newlyweds following church ceremony (*top*); mayor officiating marriage of a *napanglaw* couple (*bottom left*); house rites following church wedding of a *kalkalaingan* couple (*bottom right*); A *nabaknang* family paying their last respects to the dead (*top right*); Reyna Elena and her consorts in the Flores de Mayo (*right*).

Top: house of a *nabaknang* family in Macaoayan; *above left*: *napanglaw* house in the same barrio; *above right*: *dap-ay*, or men's house, in Macaoayan;

Top: Catholic Church in Luna; *above left*: former municipal hall in Luna; *above right*: present municipal hall in Bato.

Top: a family sorting and staking tobacco leaves; *above left*: a rice granary built in the traditional style with modern materials; *above right*: two tobacco curing flues.

CHAPTER 6

Indigenous Beliefs, Moral Values, and Behavioral Models

The agricultural economy of Zamora centers on the growing of rice and Virginia tobacco. Rice is the basic subsistence crop; it is associated with traditional notions of wealth and status, while Virginia tobacco provides farmers with a cash income.

Rice-growing requires control of the water supply so the crop will mature efficiently. Several irrigation associations, whose members build and repair canals, ensure an adequate water supply. At present, a large canal maintained by the government supplies parts of the south, west, and north of Zamora with some water for ricefields. There are also much smaller canals that are maintained by members of the associations owning watering rights in them.

Agricultural Rites

Irrigation canals (*pay-as*) are opened in June when a sufficient rainfall has raised the water level in the local dam. The larger irrigation associations (*dapat*), whose members come from different barrios but whose lands adjoin one another, perform a ceremony in June called *paayos* to mark the opening of the irrigation canals. In this ceremony, an invocation is addressed to *Kabunian* asking him for a good harvest so that people may fulfill their social obligations. These obligations include giving feasts, extending hospitality to visitors, or being generous to kinsmen in need. A pig is killed using a bamboo knife; its blood is allowed to run into the canal to ensure a good flow of water. Its meat is distributed to those members of the association using the canal and who contributed to the cost of its construction. But a portion of the meat is kept by the ritual practitioner, usually an old man. In September, a small pig or chicken is sacrificed (*apuy*) in the ricefield by individual farmers. This rite is done to ensure the growth of the crop. It usually does not require the services of a ritual specialist, but farmers unfamiliar with the form and structure of the appropriate prayers enlist the help of old men. These prayers may be said in Iloko or Kankanai, and their contents vary from one practitioner to another. In general, an appeal is made to the ancestors and other spiritual beings to extend their help and protection for the coming crop. Most people agree that to implore Kabunian's help is essential for the paayos rite but not in the case of the *apuy*. Kabunian is seen as concerned essentially with collective needs, while ancestors and other spirit beings look after the interests of individuals.

In Macaoayan and in the other non-Ilocano barrios until recently, *bignas*, a collective rite, was performed during the dry months—from April to May—before planting rice. Senior men carry it out for the benefit of the entire barrio. For the duration of the bignas, usually two or three days, no one is allowed to leave or enter the barrio. Work and sexual intercourse are prohibited, and people are exhorted to put aside their disputes during this period. This rite is no longer performed today, but the paayos and the apuy may be seen to have similar functions. The change from the public and collective bignas rite in favor of the paayos and apuy rites marked the decline of the indigenous tradition. Collective rites are presently monopolized by Christian denominations, although domestic and private rituals still retain strong elements of the indigenous tradition.

There are no significant first-harvest rites in Zamora, but a portion of cooked rice from the previous harvest is offered to the spirits by the household head to ensure the safety and health of all its members.

The response of Christians to rites like the paayos and apuy is one of mild toleration, recognizing Christianity's limited hold over the domestic and private spheres. Christians with scruples about performing an indigenous rite themselves get others—their kinsmen or neighbors—to perform it for them.

There is no religious rite associated with the cultivation of Virginia tobacco. People appreciate its importance but they do not consider the growing of it to be as socially meaningful and satisfying as rice.

There have so far been no consistent efforts by Christianity to include within its liturgy the main agricultural activities. In general, the Christian attitude has been to oppose and ridicule the remaining indigenous practices rather than to provide corresponding rites. The areas of life most affected by Christian ritual are those concerned with the main social transitions (i.e., baptism, marriage, death) and calendrical rites like Christmas and Easter.[4] But rituals associated with subsistence activities and illness still depend primarily on the indigenous tradition.

In a sense, all the main Christian rites are also linked to the agricultural year, since their performance depends on the availability of surplus created by the local economy. Feasting during Christmas, the New Year and the fiesta is possible only because these events occur soon after the rice harvest. Weddings are often held in December, for the same reason, or in May, after the sale of tobacco. The lean months of August, September, and October are not associated with religious activities requiring major expense. Easter and All Souls' Day sometimes involve a major expense and are celebrated when resouces are available.

Domestic Rites and Practitioners

Apart from Christian rites that usually take place in a church, there exists a corresponding set of indigenous rites that take place in the home. A church rite is often preceded or followed by an indigenous rite at home. For example, many people are married in church in a ceremony officiated by the priest or minister. This ceremony carries considerable prestige and is essential for anyone claiming high status. After the church wedding, another rite is conducted at home; it is performed by a senior kinsman of either spouse. In the case of death, church rites are considerably less important than the corresponding home rites. Church rites are usually performed by a priest or a minister, while home rites are conducted by experienced seniors.

Unexpected and recurrent illness is often blamed on ancestral or environmental spirits. There are several rites performed by senior kinsmen (*mambunong*) or local curers (*dadaw-wakan*) to appease offended spirits. In the case of children, a name-changing rite (*gupit*) is usually performed. For adults, the ritual ranges from a simple offering (*atang* or *singa*) by a curer to a more complex rite (*baños*, *koskosip*) involving several offerings and procedures calculated to placate a host of offended spirits. The *baños* is performed by a

---

4. Fr. Leonardo Mercado (1970:42-89) suggests changes in the Catholic attitude toward "domestic" rites, particularly rites in relation to death.

senior kinsman of the patient but the *koskosip* may require the services of a ritual specialist.

Baños or Banyos

On the day of the baños, the senior kinsman goes to the cemetery, either at noon or just before dark (when the Angelus is rung). At the cemetery, he prays for the release of the souls from purgatory. Then, using a large knife (bolo), he digs out a clod of earth which he takes home. On his way to the cemetery, he is not allowed to talk to anyone, or to reveal his destination. But on his way home, he may gesticulate to indicate where he is going. At home, he boils water and puts in it nine leaves of *calamansi* (*Citrus mitis blanco*), several bamboo leaves, rice wine, and the earth. The mixture is boiled for several minutes and allowed to cool in a basin. It is then rubbed on the patient, particularly in parts that have caused him pain or discomfort. While the patient is being rubbed, a short invocation is recited asking for the restoration of his health. The invocation is addressed to the ancestors and any spirits that may have caused the patient harm. A short Catholic prayer, like the Hail Mary or, in the case of Protestants, a biblical passage, is said. Then the mixture is thrown away. Great care is taken to wash the bolo, the container, and the basin with hot water lest the contamination be transferred to others. This rite is performed as often as is necessary to restore the patient's health. The baños illustrates the eclectic nature of Zamora ritual.

Koskosip

Unlike the baños, which is specifically a curing rite, the koskosip is performed whenever it is felt (following a dream or an omen) that ancestral or environmental spirits should be propitiated. The emphasis of the baños is magical (i.e., the specially prepared mixture has strong healing powers), while the koskosip stresses the propitiatory and communicative element of ritual. The former is principally an instrumental action, while the latter is an expression of an ethical and moral relationship between members of a household and their spirit-guests. The koskosip is a commensal rite expressing the links between the living and the dead.

On the day of its performance, a white chicken, two eggs, nine pieces of native tobacco, betel nut, and glutinous rice are prepared. Only the tender parts of the chicken—wings, breast, legs, thighs—are used. These are cooked in boiling water for a few minutes without adding spices or salt. The eggs and rice are also partly cooked and the prepared fare, including some rice wine, a glass of water, and the tobacco, is placed on a mat. The sponsor of the rite goes outside the house to summon the spirit-guests. Deceased ancestors may be called by name or by referring to an appropriate kinship term (e.g. grandfather). A general invitation is also issued to all the former and present spirit-inhabitants of the immediate neighborhood and any of their spirit-friends. The spirits are asked to help other spirits wishing to attend who might otherwise have difficulty, for example, lame-spirits, blind-spirits. These invitations are issued several times and are called out facing all the cardinal points: north, south, east, and west. After some time, the host returns inside and recooks the food, adding spices and salt. A short prayer is said—nine Hail Marys or the rosary—and the food is served to assembled kinsmen and friends. All the offerings are used, including the wine and tobacco, but the water-offering is kept as a cure for skin ailments. To wash the plates and other utensils immediately after use is considered disrespectful to the spirits, and for this reason, they are stacked in a corner and washed the next day.

The main purpose in performing a koskosip is to reaffirm the moral ties between the present inhabitants of a house-site and its former occupants (including ancestors), but an added motive is the acquisition of the water-offering with healing powers.

Like the baños, the koskosip has Christian elements but its main purpose is to reaffirm obligations to spirits closely associated with a household. Some of these spirits may be ancestors, but others are not genealogically related to the sponsor of the rite. Private rites, like the baños and the koskosip, are focused on a household, and use senior kinsmen or local curers as practitioners. Kinship and residential ties are activated in these rites, and a parallel set of obligations linking the living and the dead are simultaneously confirmed.

Religious Syncretism and National Structures

The Spanish and later, the American colonial system stressed the power difference between the colonizers and the colonized. However, the colonized were themselves differentiated into groups with varying access to a range of political and economic resources. Iberian Catholicism and later, American Protestantism were imposed, with varying success, on this complex socio-political structure, bringing a complex Church bureaucracy, the idea of conformity to the implacable will of an all-powerful and ethical deity, and the constant striving to attain religious merit.

As Zamora gradually became integrated into the nation's economic and political structures, the indigenous religion progressively weakened. At the present time, apart from some agricultural rites (paayos, apuy) performed inconspicuously, the only remaining viable corpus of indigenous rites occurs at the domestic level. The gradual disappearance of indigenous religion does not result in its replacement by a form of "orthodox" Christianity. Instead, the result is a religious syncretism containing elements of both traditions. This syncretism may be seen in the way with which Protestant denominations with egalitarian values have easily attracted converts in non-Ilocano barrios or in the contractual ties between saints and their Catholic devotees (i.e., saints proffer help in exchange for novenas or offerings).

While Christianity has taken over public rites, significant areas still exist where the indigenous tradition exerts a major influence. Agricultural rites and those associated with illness still retain strong non-Christian elements. The urban orientation of Catholicism and other Christian denominations has resulted in hegemonic control over the definitions of prestige in the religious sphere. Urban religious practices are therefore accepted as the ideals for people aspiring to high status. For these reasons, the private and daily concerns of subsistence households have not received the same attention from the urban-oriented Christian tradition. Moreover, the existence of structural relations within the household (i.e., the authority of seniors, obligations to members of the kindred, the division and regulation of labor) prevents the bureaucratic and specialized tendencies of the Christian traditions from penetrating domains presently under the control of the household. The growing of crops and the curing of illness still constitute the domain of competence of household members. As the household economy becomes increasingly less self-sufficient and more dependent on national forces, one can expect the religioideological component of these external forces to replace the indigenous religious tradition.

Virginia tobacco and other cash crops are examples of household economic concerns resulting from the progressive integration of Zamora into a market economy. Unlike rice, Virginia tobacco and other cash crops do not require the performance of religious rites. The inclusion of these crops in religious ritual is unlikely to take place within the indigenous tradition, but more likely to come under Christianity. The successful cultivation of a crop like Virginia tobacco leads to a progressive reinterpretation of local ties and obligations such as has occurred in Macaoayan and Luna. This reinterpretation falls more easily within an ideological scheme provided by Christianity.

Methodism provides a good example of an interpretation of religious allegiance in association with the growing of Virginia tobacco. Methodists in Luna frequently argue that their Church's objections to the cultivation of Virginia tobacco work against the Church's interest.[5] Virginia tobacco is the only readily available source of cash for farmers. Local Methodists point out that to support the Church and its ministers, one needs money. Partly for these reasons, Methodists grow Virginia tobacco, convinced that by doing so they are better able to discharge their religious duties, despite official

5. This denomination generally objects to smoking, drinking alcohol, and dancing, but the degree of implementation varies consideraly from one congregation to another.

disapproval of its cultivation on the part of their senior (urban) Church leaders.

There are other reasons why growing Virginia tobacco lessens the people's dependence on indigenous religion. With money, people are able to consult and pay for the services of the doctor or the priest, instead of having to rely on the indigenous practitioner. People with means often resort to both traditions.

Moral Values and the Spirit World

Aspects of the moral world in Zamora have been discussed in preceding chapters. Morality ultimately involves the internalization of certain principles that govern the proper relationship between human beings and the world. These principles are not characterized by their causal efficacy or practical utility but by their deontic or obligatory nature. This view does not deny that moral principles have pragmatic consequences. But the justification of these principles is not solely evaluated pragmatically. Moral norms are simply proper ways of acting (*umno*) befitting the human condition. These views regarding the nature of morality are often expressed in conversation by Zamorans.

Human nature is seen as inextricably bound up in this world. Man's relations with the supernatural are pursued primarily to benefit his present life rather than in reference to a future or past existence. The natural and supernatural worlds contain harmful and beneficial forces affecting this life. Religion provides people with the knowledge of propitious forces— knowledge which they are able to apply to this life. Distinct from this knowledge is the technical knowledge involved in house-building, fishing, planting, etc., and the properties of the organic world.

Relations with the spirit-world are modeled on relations experienced in the empirical world. Spirits have their favorite haunts and individual personalities. Their dwelling-place—bamboo clusters, large trees, virgin forest, cemeteries, certain springs or parts of the river—should be avoided and proper respect should be shown when trespass occurs. Some spirits are inherently evil, others benevolent, but most simply react to the behaviors of humans toward them. This spirit-ideology is neither consistent nor elaborated. A general term (*anito*) is used for spirits, but other terms describe specific manifestations, for example, *al-alia* for ghosts, *karkarma* for ancestral spirits. A person's soul (*espiritu* or *kararua*) occasionally has a physical manifestation, but it is unable to exist for long periods outside the body. A dead person's soul eventually becomes an *anito* and joins the rest of the spirit-world.

Spirits form close attachments to their material habitats, cultivate friendships with animals and occasionally enter into regular relationships with humans. Ancestral spirits are most likely to be benevolent and are often asked for assistance. Spirits associated with familiar and cultivated areas—for example, a copse, ricefields, cleared land and areas of secondary growth—are usually benevolent, while those associated with unfamiliar and wild areas—for example, virgin forest—are malevolent. The spirits of people who suffered a violent death are also malevolent. These last are the most dangerous since they hover near human settlements, ready to inflict harm on the unwary.

Apart from spirits, there are other beings with natural and supernatural powers. Some of them are malevolent, others benevolent, but most are neutral unless offended.

The *bulalakaw* is a fiery monster whose approach causes insanity and sometimes death. Mischievous beings (*engkantada*) play tricks on humans, for example, luring them into the forest by mysterious lights seen on treetops or hills. The *engkantada* are harmless unless deliberately offended by desecrating their caves or killing their favorite animals.

The bulalakaw and engkantada, although taking material form, are essentially supernatural creatures similar to the anito. Their powers stem from their ability to cause fright or inflict illness through supernatural means. In contrast, beings like the *mangkukulam* (witch), *mangagamod* (sorcerer), and *kumao* (kidnaper) use natural means, and are, in other respects, ordinary mortals. People often distinguish a mangkukulam from a mangagamod. The former are mostly women whose malevolence is indiscriminate and uncontrolled, while the latter are men who use their knowledge of magic in a rational manner to achieve comprehensible goals, like inflicting illness on an enemy or opponent. While both witches and sorcerers are feared, their powers are limited by their victim's capacity to take direct retaliation. In many cases, they are regarded as community members whose nature and inclinations cause them to pursue clandestine activities, but who are nevertheless partly constrained by certain norms and sanctions. They are treated with the caution and deference extended to others like the rich and powerful or those with a record of violence.

Unlike resident witches and sorcerers, the kumao are strangers who visit the barrio for the express purpose of kidnaping people to offer as human sacrifices. These sacrifices are said to take place during the construction of bridges, dams, and other main engineering projects. Kumao are the agents who supply the victims needed to propitiate the spirits whose favors ensure the success and completion of such projects. They prowl around the barrios at night, looking for victims, usually children or old people. Being strangers, they are not subject to normal constraints, which include the obligation to compensate the victim's family. The threat of direct retaliation by the victim's kin and their demands for compensation restrain the malevolence of resident witches and sorcerers, but no similar controls apply to the kumao. This agent acts for a distant and powerful patron (e.g., the project engineer, the local politico or other influential persons) against whom ordinary barrio people have little hope of obtaining adequate compensation. These beliefs may have their source in an indigenous tradition involving human sacrifice for certain public rites which was widespread in the highlands before colonial rule was imposed.

Relations with the supernatural world do not differ significantly from relations with the natural world. Both worlds contain dangerous beings and forces. They must be approached with caution and measures must be taken to reduce the possible dangers. Such things as steel, salt, ginger, and garlic are common talismans (*sublay*) against malevolent supernatural forces. Corresponding measures are taken to guard against natural dangers; for example, not venturing outside at night, watching out for snakes, not provoking the anger of witches or sorcerers, not angering men with influence or those noted for their violence. These measures require prudence, discretion and sensitivity. *Nakem* is the Iloko word for expressing the attitudes necessary to operate successfully in a world inhabited by dangerous natural and supernatural forces.[6]

Reciprocity and propriety are the main attitudes expected both in people's relations with their fellows and in their relations with the supernatural. The ideal relation is between kinsmen. Kinship behavior stresses respect for seniors in exchange for their aid and protection. This ideal is extended to include relations between superordinate and subordinate social categories (i.e., between *nabaknang* and *napanglaw*).

Ancestors are expected to look after the interest and welfare of their descendants in exchange for the latter's ritual offerings. These ties weaken as the links with one's ancestors widen. In a cognatic system, the number of ancestors increases rapidly after the first few generations. Consequently, only certain lines of descent are remembered; the others merge into the general anito category, whose members no longer recognized special obligations toward the living.

The relations between living descendants and dead ancestors is generalized to encompass other members of the supernatural world. The dead in general—whether kinsmen or simply former inhabitants of a house-site—are invited to partake of any offerings to the spirits, as in the koskosip rite. When people fear or suspect that they have offended an anito or engkantada by encroaching on its habitat or by killing one of its pets (i.e., birds, rats, and other feral creatures), they make a propitiatory offering indicative of goodwill and willingness to compensate for the offense. Reciprocity and mutual

6. *Nakem* means propriety and sound judgment; *agnakem* means act sensibly; *manakem* means considerate or conscientious; *agpakinakem* means reflect or consider carefully or judiciously.

consideration are the moral attitudes expected to hold between humans and supernatural beings.

Human or supernatural retaliation is the consequence of having committed an offense against the social or the supernatural order. The only way to prevent this retaliation is to admit fault and to offer compensation. Such an offer acknowledges membership of a common moral universe and mitigates the fury of the offended. This common moral universe includes members drawn from the natural, social and supernatural orders.

Animals in close association with man (e.g., farm animals, creatures living in the ricefields and surrounding woods) are seen as belonging to this common moral universe (Pertierra 1979). Man's ecological environment and his position in it express his membership in this common moral universe. Some of the difficulties of introducing technology—new rice varieties, pesticides, irrigation—which affects the natural environment arise out of the obligations of this common membership. Objections to new technology are expressed in aesthetic or religious terms; for example, people commonly complain that new rice varieties are tasteless and lack nutritive value, and that their ancestors prefer certain traditional varieties. But underlying these objections are often unstated moral norms binding people to their physical environment. These norms become explicit in the prohibitions against the indiscriminate killing (e.g., using pesticides and other poisons) of animals, including man's natural competitors (e.g., ricebirds, rats, snakes) and in the notion of usufruct covering certain resources (i.e., grazing rights; access to frogs, small fish, and other animals living in the wet ricefields and irrigation canals; access to firewood and bamboo; gleaning rights). People share their physical environment not only with animals but also with members of the supernatural world. The haunts and favorite places of these beings must be respected in the same way that people respect the homes and property of covillagers. An unwarranted trespass results in retaliation unless the offender offers compensation.

Some aspects of the natural and supernatural orders do not come under the moral domain. Wild, uncultivated, or unfamiliar places represent the spatial boundaries of the moral universe. Humans, animals, and other beings inhabiting these places are thought to be more dangerous and are greatly feared. Supernatural beings associated with these groups are thought to be more malevolent than local and familiar ones.

Apart from these spatial boundaries, there are cognitive factors affecting the application of moral norms (i.e., certain times of day or year, like midnight, noontime, Good Friday, etc.). Cognitive ambiguities, transitional or marginal states, and structural dilemmas threaten the order implied in membership of the moral universe (e.g., menstruation, illness). Animals with feral and domestic characteristics like rats, cats, house lizards and bats, menstruating women, and natural events like eclipses, are instances of cognitive ambiguities threatening the moral order. Times such as dawn, dusk, midnight, and such occasions as Good Friday and All Souls' Day are characterized by a suspension of moral rules.

Death poses the ultimate threat to all order, and for this reason, it is fraught with anomalies and ambiguities. The spirits of the recently deceased are particularly dangerous. This danger is compounded in the death of parturating women and unbaptized children. Their spirits are especially malevolent and often injure people closest to them. The stereotype of witches often consists of ambitious and successful unmarried women. The structural dilemmas that the given examples illustrate are expressed in the inversion of the moral order. That is, what is appropriate becomes inappropriate, e.g., in baños rite you cannot answer someone who asks you where you are going. The time between a person's death and the end of the novena prayers—usually nine days after burial—is the time when malevolent forces and witches are particularly active.

Behavioral Ideals

Reciprocity (*subalit*) and propriety (*umno*) are behavioral ideals often breached in the daily interactions of people in Zamora. In most cases, this breach results from a different interpretation of the norms, rather than their outright rejection. However, situations arise in which the norms themselves come into question. The progressive monetization of the economy and shifting political loyalties create conditions where it is difficult to determine how far should reciprocity and propriety apply. For example, in the relations between landlords and tenants, members of different generations; in the obligations to kinsmen and neighbors, what should be the extent of observing reciprocity and propriety? These conditions give the moral order a quality of openness which, in association with the problem of determining boundaries, is responsible for the state of moral flux typically encountered in Zamora and ultimately resolved according to pragmatic principles. In other words, the moral order is not totally fixed but rather consists of general expectations which have to be interpreted in specific instances.

Nonreciprocity and the total lack of propriety epitomize evil. This condition is found in the world, for example, in encounters with hostile strangers and some supernaturals. Evil is an existential quality of the world and not a result of people's presence in it. Human nature is inherently good. All men naturally seek reciprocal and proper behavior, even if contingent factors sometimes cause them to negate these values in practice.

The view of human nature frequently expressed in Zamora makes no mention of a fall from God's grace, a central tenet of Christianity. Fault on man's part results from an offense against the multitude of spirit agencies with whom he deals. Some of these faults involve a deliberate breach of the moral code, like when descendants consistently fail to meet their ritual obligations to ancestors. This breach may result in supernatural punishment for the offenders.

Spirit beings may also punish men even when no fault has occurred, or at least be known to have occurred. Thus, a person who unknowingly trespasses into a spirit's domain may incur its wrath. Like humans, spirits sometimes act on impulse, out of envy, or to display malice, even against those whom they are expected to protect. An offering is usually sufficient to persuade an erring spirit to meet its obligations.

Human frailty, recalcitrant spirits, and preexisting evil are the factors responsible for the misfortunes and difficulties of this world. The first results from people's competing interests, limited resources, and incomplete knowledge, rather than from any intrinsic or inherent defect in their nature. The second may be remedied by regular offerings reminding the spirits of their obligations. The third is an existential component of this world that one must learn to accept.

The role of Kabunian, the high God in the indigenous system, is not significant in the daily and practical encounters between humans and the supernatural. Like the Christian God, Kabunian is an elevated, distant, and abstract entity whose concerns normally do not impinge on people in their daily lives. Indigenous ritual specialists claim that he is the ultimate source of well-being, and the origin of all knowledge. It was Kabunian who taught men all they know, by sending Lumawig (a culture-hero) to this earth to teach the arts of cultivation and government. Having intervened once, Kabunian is largely content to allow man to shape his own destiny on this earth. Knowledge of the roles of Kabunian and Lumawig is limited, and aside from a few remaining rites (i.e., paayos, apuy), their help is rarely invoked. Unlike the spirit beings who intrude more often into people's lives, Kabunian is seen as a truly ethical being and as the source of all moral imperatives. It is difficult to disassociate the idea of Kabunian from the Christian notion of God, since borrowings from the latter tradition have clearly intruded into the former. The presence of a supreme deity in the pre-Christian religious system of northern Luzon has been disputed by numerous writers (i.e., Scott 1974b, Barton 1946, Moss 1920, de Raedt 1964, Reynolds and Grant 1973). The early penetration of Christian influence makes it difficult in the case of Zamora to argue for the independent existence of a concept of a supreme being. What is apparent is the relatively insignificant role a being like Kabunian plays in the daily activities of most people. Whatever might have been his role in the indigenous system, it is clear that ancestral and other spirits were the main supernatural concerns of ordinary folk. Religious specialists in pre-Christian days may well have had developed notions of an ethical supreme being (as both Christian and indigenous specialists at present have), but these notions are unlikely to have constituted the system of publicly or generally shared beliefs and practices.

Just as the notion of the fall is absent from most people's religious conceptions—except for some members of separatist Protestant denominations—ideas regarding the afterlife seldom form a major interest. After death, a person's soul attempts to maintain its links with this world, especially if it has descendants who honor its memory, but eventually, the soul joins the anito category. Souls of the dead lead lives similar to the ones they led on earth (e.g., the rich are looked after by dependents, the poor till the soil) but ultimately, the soul disintegrates or some part of it may be reborn. In this spirit ideology, questions of punishment and reward after death are unimportant. Divine justice manifests itself in this life, in terms of health, fortune, and children. The punishment of wrong-doers is seldom carried out by Kabunian since this is left to the appropriate offended spirit. However, in a case of obvious and gross injustice such as pestilence, drought or floods, Kabunian's mercy and help may be implored.

Local Christianity

The influence of Christianity in Zamora dates back to the mid-eighteenth century, when Augustinian missionaries established the mission of San Jose. From there, Augustinian priests visited what is now Zamora, and by 1832 had established the mission of Nueva Coveta. After their initial success with the coastal populations, the Augustinians experienced much more difficulty proselytizing in the mountain areas. By 1900, after 150 years of missionary effort, many of the mountain people still retained their indigenous religion. The influx of coastal (Christian) Ilocanos into Zamora and intermarriage throughout the nineteenth century led to the progressive Christianization of most communities, although others (Macaoayan, Mambog, Lucaban, Masingit) retained their indigenous system well into the twentieth century.

Protestant missionaries began visiting Zamora early this century, and by the 1930s, several congregations had been formed in Luna, with members coming from other barrios. The Catholic authorities responded to these conversions by establishing the parish of the Santo Niño de Praga in Luna in 1932. Since then, there has always been a Catholic priest residing in the parish.

It is within this multifaceted and syncretic religious tradition that present folk beliefs and practices have developed. These traditions (i.e., autochthonous, Protestant, Catholic) share a common field of practice and dogma which people utilize according to their preferences, needs, and resources.

Catholicism

The success of Catholicism has been most marked in areas where it has reinforced already existing expectations and attitudes. For example, such

central Catholic institutions as baptism and marriage meet the local requirements for the validation of status and the affirmation of significant
political ties. The doctrinal aspects of these sacraments are often unknown
and ignored. Thus, while the Church limits the number of sponsors and
specifies their duties, people are primarily interested in using these occasions to extend alliances as widely and effectively as possible. They arrange
to have a large number of sponsors (exceeding the limits stipulated by
Church authorities) and show more concern for a sponsor's material resources than for his or her spiritual capacities. The pomp and expense of
Catholic baptisms and weddings are largely status-validating exercises. The
importance of feasting on these occasions has been mentioned. While these
Catholic practices are widespread, their doctrinal and transcendental aspects (heaven or the afterlife) are of negligible interest to most people.

Often, while the practice is derived from the Catholic tradition, its
rationale is supplied by the indigenous base. Thus, despite the importance
of baptism, a child's acceptance into its kindred and village community
takes place before it is baptized. Rituals of acceptance employ symbols
often drawn from non-Christian sources, are conducted by senior kin or
indigenous ritual specialists, and invoke the protection of ancestors and
other spirits. For much the same reasons, a church wedding is followed by
dedicatory rites performed at the wedded couple's home under the supervision of senior kin. These rites stress the obligations of ancestors and ask for
their blessings. While divorce is not allowed by the Catholic Church (or the
State), little disapproval is expressed in cases where married couples have
separated and established new households. If a marriage does not result in
children, people feel that the couple are not suited for one another and
should therefore terminate the relationship, possibly to embark on another.

Death is an area where formal Catholic doctrine has had least effect.
While novenas and other Catholic rites are performed for the dead, their
intention is to banish the soul into its proper domain, rather than to ensure
its salvation. The priest rarely participates in the domestic rites for the dead,
his main concern being limited to the brief church ceremony before burial.
In most cases, the priest does not accompany the body to the cemetery.

The rich corpus of folk beliefs and practices associated with death is
drawn largely from the indigenous system. These beliefs and practices are
primarily concerned with banishing the soul into the appropriate realm and
ensuring its goodwill. Local eschatology seldom mentions Christian concepts of punishment and reward, and instead, views the afterlife in terms of
the present life.

The mortuary feast marks the highpoint of the celebrations for the
deceased. Speeches are made extolling his or her virtues and the large
number of people who attend add a corresponding honor to his or her
memory.

In this context, Christian notions of the afterlife are mostly inappropriate. One of the most significant structural relations in Zamora is that between kinsmen, in particular between members of different generations. A death mobilizes and expresses these feelings through the performance of the appropriate rites.

Death illustrates the differing attitudes to man's position in the world found in the Christian and indigenous traditions. The former largely denies the importance of this life in anticipation of the next. The latter focuses its interests on this life and tries to employ transcendental forces to diminish life's misfortunes and increase its benefits.

Those aspects of Catholicism that stress the links and benefits of this world (e.g., the acceptance of a child into the community, the public creation of marital contracts) fit easily into the indigenous attitude while soteriological aspects are mostly ignored.

Calendrical rites performed during Easter or Christmas also draw much of their support from indigenous attitudes and expectations.

Among the most significant of these rites are Good Friday and All Souls' Day. These involve respect for the dead and stress their obligations to the living. The fiesta and the Christmas-New Year celebrations are essentially rites of renewal. They occur when surplus is available, allowing its conversion into prestige through lavish feasting. In a time of surplus, the Flores de Mayo (Mayflower) festival converts potential obligations into actual support. The October rosary devotion taps the solidarity existing in local neighborhoods.[7] Its domestic orientation and concern for protecting household members reinforce existing expectations. The moral and altruistic ties binding members of a neighborhood (indicated in activities of mutual-help associations) are given ritual expression in the October rosary devotion.

The main calendric rites express significant cultural expectations; for example, the relations between the living and the dead (modeled on the exchange relationship between inferiors and superiors); or they manifest structural forces that ultimately lead to an increase in solidarity, at times through the open expression of conflict. Thus, the October rosary devotion concretizes and reflects neighborhood ties, while the Flores de Mayo creates the conditions for competition resulting in a clearer expression of obligations and alliances. The Christmas-New Year period and the fiesta are opportunities for restating and legitimating the relations between and within social strata.

For these reasons, the calendric rites mentioned elicit popular support,

---

7. The devotion involves the recitation of the rosary in every household of a neighborhood throughout October, culminating in a major feast held on the last night at the house of the local dignitary.

while other equally significant liturgical events (i.e., Epiphany, Ascension, Assumption, Immaculate Conception, Easter Sunday, All Saints' Day, Corpus Christi) are overlooked.

Protestantism

The main thrust of Protestant conversion in Zamora took place soon after American colonization. This conversion occurred at a time of significant economic and political changes. Interior municipalities had until then exercised considerable political autonomy. The rapid Ilocanization of these municipalities, as a consequence of American intentions to create national structures, posed a threat to their non-Ilocano inhabitants. Conversion to Protestantism was a response to this threat.

Organizational features of Protestantism—for example, the prominence of laymen, the lack of a developed ecclesiastical bureaucracy and the stress on congregational autonomy—facilitated its acceptance in communities with similar equalitarian political structures. This ideological response to the political and economic encroachment of the Ilocano majority ultimately proved inadequate. The gradual introduction of universal suffrage, the importance of political patronage, and the rise of an urban and national consciousness, introduced new parameters as a result of which Protestant conversion lost much of its initial appeal.

Protestant congregations (i.e., Methodists, Mision Cristiana, Church of Christ) have adapted their theology to meet local requirements. Obligations to ancestral spirits are indicated in mortuary rites similar to those practiced by Catholics. Rites commemorating the deceased, dedicatory feasts for young children (idaton), and elaborate weddings are standard practices among affluent Protestants. Many of them play an active role during the Flores de Mayo and the fiesta. The Christmas-New Year period is used to celebrate their religious commitment, but also to reaffirm links with their Catholic kinsmen.

In contrast to established Protestant denominations are the separatist groups: for example, Christ Jesus' Holy Church, Iglesia ni Kristo, Jehovah's Witnesses. These groups stress their exclusive rights to salvation and repudiate traditional links with other members of the community. They are mostly drawn from the class of tenants and agricultural laborers.

The Christ Jesus' Holy Church (CJHC) is a neo-Catholic denomination whose liturgy and doctrine combine nationalist elements with Roman Catholic practices (i.e., mass and the sacraments). Its primarily rural orientation enables it to fuse elements of indigenous belief and practice with Christian notions. While its formal structure resembles Roman Catholicism (i.e., priests, bishops, sacraments, grace), its social origins, participant membership, and nationalist aspirations bring it closer to the Iglesia ni Kristo (INK).

The INK is one of the most successful indigenous religious movements. Its success is due to the charismatic appeal of its founder and a shrewd understanding of organizational structures. The INK has survived the chronic schismatic tendencies present in most Philippine religious movements through its insistence on rigid discipline, doctrinal orthodoxy, nationalist aspirations, and an active membership. Unlike the CJHC, the INK has a strong urban orientation, and a doctrine which firmly rejects many of the traditional beliefs and practices. It discourages lavish feasting and prohibits the traditional obligations toward deceased kin. The validation and extension of ties and status achieved through feasting is replaced, among INK, by a deliberate cultivation of a political consciousness and the security of belonging to a solidary and powerful organization. Obligations to the dead are replaced by a strong conviction of being God's elect, and surplus is redirected to proclaiming his glory through the construction of elaborate and distinctive churches.

Christian Hagiarchy

The most distinctive feature of indigenous religion is the contractual character of the tie between humans and the spirit world. These relations stress the need for reciprocity on both parties, rather than the insistence on a fixed standard of behavior or a total trust in ultimate beneficence. The natural and supernatural worlds are distinct but interact mutually. Relationships in the natural world also apply to the supernatural world and the former realm is more desirable and ultimately more real than the latter. Numerous myths are found throughout northern Luzon (de Raedt 1964, Scott 1974b, Vanoverbergh 1955) describing how spirit-beings came to earth, married a human and raised a large family. These myths illustrate the desirability of life on this earth, often in preference to other lives. In Zamora, preference for this life is shown in the attempt the dead makes to return. While such a return is impossible, souls of the recently deceased have to be induced to accept their new state and to extend their aid to living kin.

In contrast to these beliefs, Christianity insists on the ethical rather than the contractual nature of the relationship between man and God. Man's condition is so debased in God's sight that any concept of negotiation or contract between the two is inconceivable. The doctrine of the fall and the undeserved nature of salvation are central tenets of Christianity. This religion also stresses the insignificance of this life in comparison to the next. Hardships in this life are more than compensated by the rewards of the next. God's magnanimity, if not shown in the present, is assured for the future.

These central tenets are not part of most people's religious expectations. In the past, Kabunian may have had attributes similar to the Christian God, but relations with Kabunian differed significantly from the tenets above since human nature was not thought to be debased, nor were Kabunian's rewards reserved for the afterlife. I have argued that Christian notions of God, salvation and sin have been adapted to fit preexisting religious expectations. The preexisting religious expectations conform more closely to people's experience of a world in which an abstract notion of universal justice is undeveloped, where security is best achieved by using surplus in the present rather than storing it for future use, and where notions of outward display and shame are more common than notions of interiority and guilt.

God's inaccessibility is compensated for by the possibility of establishing relations with the Virgin Mary and the saints. Catholics are much more likely to initiate relations with saints than they do directly with God. Saints are seen as God's agents with whom people may establish contractual relations. The most efficacious link to God is through the Virgin Mary. Her favor is sought so that she may intercede with God. All the religious associations/organizations in Zamora have the Virgin Mary or a saint for their patron and object of devotion.

Boissevain (1974) discusses the transition from the emphasis on saint-worship to Catholic monotheism in Malta, in terms of the associated changes in the system of patronage. Hagiolatry was associated with a system of direct patronage while Catholic monotheism reflected the growing importance of bureaucratic and national structures in which social and political brokers replaced the previously direct links between client and patron.

The importance of saints in Zamora has been mentioned. Their worship has its origin in the indigenous spirit ideology, reinforced by existing sociopolitical structures. Patronage is dispensed directly by those who control economic and political resources and is often justified in terms of kinship. But the role of political brokers and social intermediaries (backers and contacts in the local terminology) is also highly developed, and the increasing importance of national structures may, in the future, significantly affect both the pattern of patronage and access to resources. It is this change that, according to Boissevain, led to the replacement of hagiolatry by a christocentric monotheism in Malta during the last few decades. In Zamora, such a shift is effectively found among the Iglesia ni Kristo, but its minority status and the nature of its membership does not permit one to assume a more general shift against hagiolatry in the wider community. The importance and popularity in Philippine Catholicism of saints and the Virgin Mary is readily evident. This may well be due to the persistence of locally based structures and patronage systems—structures similar to those discussed by Boissevain in relation to Malta—but equally important is the persistence of an indigenous spirit-ideology.

The relationship with saints is based on an exchange of services. The novena, a devotion whose effectiveness depends on its being carried out for a prescribed period of nine days, is an example of this exchange. The saint obtains regular worship for which he or she dispenses a favor, similar to the relationship with ancestral and environmental spirits. In contrast to this exchange relationship is one emphasizing spiritual merit as the basis of salvation. This latter relationship is the one emphasized in orthodox Christianity.

While Protestants do not resort to saints as often as Catholics, the use of spiritual intercessors is found among them. Protestants implore the spirits of the recently deceased, for whom they perform novenas, to intercede on their behalf. They perceive Christ as more accessible than do Catholics; the former address their prayers to Christ while the latter address them to Mary. Protestants in Zamora consider Christ to be distinct and separate from God and often compare Christ and God to Kabunian (Creator God) and Lumawig (Kabunian's main agent and a culture-hero).

The shift from contract to merit is usually accompanied by a development of the notion of interiorization (conscience) and an objective ethic. This shift has not occurred in Zamora and explains why people prefer to make full use of the available and eclectic religious field. Even educated and conventionally devout Catholics and Protestants resort to the non-Christian tradition when the need arises without a feeling of having transgressed against objective ethical rules. For these reasons, a developed notion of sin is largely absent. People have difficulty in enumerating sinful actions, except where these result in social disruption or personal grievance (e.g., disrespectful behavior, violent or aggressive actions, failure to fulfill social obligations). To offend against an abstract set of rules is seen as far less serious than offending a particular person or a spirit.

The concept of fault (*basol*) is highly developed and sin is subsumed in this category. Fault requires compensation, but procedures for determining it depend as much on the relations between the parties as they do on the nature of the offense.[8] It is the negotiable and situational component of fault—who does what to whom—that distinguishes it from sin (and demerit), a breach against a universal and objective set of rules.

Sexuality is an area where breaches of Christian norms frequently occur. These breaches are rarely seen as morally reprehensible, except when they lead to disputes. Adultery, premarital and extramarital sex, homosexuality, masturbation, and other practices strictly forbidden by Christianity are usually tolerated so long as they do not cause disharmony in the community. These practices are mostly seen as breaching relations between people but have no import for relations with the supernatural order.

---

8. Barton (1969, 1973) and Schlegel (1970) make a similar point when describing the adjudication of disputes and the allocation of fault among the Ifugao, Kalinga, and the Tiruray.

Men are given more sexual freedom than women, and male celibacy is seen as unnatural, for which reason male homosexuals, though generally tolerated, are urged to marry and have children. The regulation of sexual behavior so central to Christianity is absent from the indigenous tradition. Even violation of the strict prohibition on incest seldom brings immediate and automatic supernatural sanctions. This breach is shameful rather than sinful.

In his study of moral values in a number of Asian societies, von Furer-Haimendorf (1969) points out the range and variety of moral and religious conceptions. Apart from general features, such as the existence of a stable moral order and the presence of certain sanctions, very few moral universals connect the societies examined. Notions of sin, merit, salvation and retribution differ significantly from one society to another, depending on their exposure to Hinduism, Buddhism, and other world-religions. Societies not deeply infused with Hindu or Buddhist notions are characterized by their orientation to this world and the comparative absence of the idea of sin in preference to stressing equitable social relations. These latter observations also apply to Zamora. Despite several centuries of Christian influence, the moral and religious life of its people retains significant non-Christian elements. These elements may be seen in the importance given to ancestral and other spirit-beings, the emphasis on contract rather than merit, the notion of fault instead of sin, and the stress on pragmatic and situational factors, rather than on an inviolable set of moral rules.

CHAPTER 7

Material Interests and Religious Ideology

A s part of a wider ideological system, religion is embedded in material and social structures. This chapter examines the relationship between religious behavior and membership of class and status categories.

Since Zamora is predominantly Roman Catholic (75 to 85 percent), I will examine in some detail how the political, social and economic elites extend their control into the sphere of Catholic practice and morality. The control of Catholic activity is an important aspect of the process of legitimation of these elites. In contrast, poor tenants and agricultural laborers sometimes turn to radical non-Catholic denominations, thereby rejecting traditional religious obligations and challenging the elite's control of Christian orthodoxy.

In Zamora, there does not exist a significant degree of regular, mass participation in Catholic worship, despite the fact that the municipality is predominantly Catholic. This lack of mass Catholic participation is a consequence of local economic and political structures that ensure that the average barrio Catholic is effectively prevented from taking an active part in his religion. There are other avenues that allow a more active role for the ordinary barrio believer. An example is the complex and variegated folk religious tradition composed of Catholic and pre-Catholic elements.

At one end of this folk tradition are indigenous elements such as ricefield, household and ancestral spirits, and a morality that emphasizes a contractual rather than an ethical aspect in man's relation to the transcendent order. At this end of the spectrum, Christian notions of sin, hell and alienation from God are irrelevant and incomprehensible. The other end of this same tradition encompasses rites like Holy Week, All Souls' Day, the fiesta, and Christmas, all of which are Catholic in origin.

In this chapter, I show that the average peasant's commitment to the indigenous elements of folk religion explains why he participates in Catholic ritual. When traditional religious rituals become unsatisfactory to him, in fact, he and many of his kind turn to radical non-Catholic denominations rather than to Catholicism.

The elite's monopoly of Catholic activity and of the religious associations involved in such activity has prevented the majority of Catholics in Zamora from defining and constructing a Catholic moral order. This exclusion of the ordinary believer is both a consequence and extension of the economic, social and political privileges enjoyed by the elite. The history of Catholic proselytization, with its emphasis on urban centers (*poblacion*), its active cooperation with the *principalia* (urban elites), its reliance on a largely foreign priesthood and on an alien theology may be expected to generate fundamental difficulties in convincing and retaining the allegiance of the average Ilocano peasant. The symbols of the Church and their expression, as well as the Church's political and economic links with the colonial powers and their native supporters, create significant barriers. These barriers—high status, expensive rituals, foreign languages, etc.—prevent most peasants from taking an active part in Catholic activities.

Theoretical Orientation

Lenski, referring to Durkheim and Weber, wrote in 1963: "We do not know much more today about the influence of religious institutions on secular institutions in modern society than was known half a century ago" (1963:6).

I. M. Lewis, ten years later, repeated Lenski's assessment: "Except in such specialized areas of interest as witchcraft, initiation rites or pollution behavior, the subject (i.e., sociology of religion) remains as a whole very much where it was left by Durkheim and Weber" (I. M. Lewis 1971:11).

Studies in the Marxist analysis of religion, from a sociological or anthropological perspective, are not much more developed.[9]

Anyone who doubts the lack of substantial progress in the sociology of
religion need only refer to a standard monograph like the *Anthropological
Approaches to the Study of Religion* (ed. M. Banton, 1966) or to the works of
contemporary sociologists like Berger (1973) or Luckman (1967) to become
convinced that apart from certain important gains in empirical detail, the
theoretical formulations in this field have not substantially improved since
they were first suggested by Marx, Durkheim, and Weber.

The data on religion in this chapter uses a systematized conceptual
framework drawn from the insights and suggestions of these classical
writers. This chapter examines the ways in which secular institutions,
beliefs, and practices are related to a transcendent moral order. In other
words, it shows how religion's cognitive and normative aspects reflect,
express and analyze the secular world and its everyday interests. Also shown
is how much of regular religious behavior is embedded within social
structures representing the sectional interests of participants. Thus, intrabarrio and extrabarrio interests are expressed in membership and degree of
participation in particular denominations.

The theoretical syncretization of elements drawn from Marx, Durkheim
and Weber offers a satisfactory account for the ways in which material
interests interact with existing conceptual and normative structures (i.e.,
ideologies). The question of the ultimate validity of religious belief and
practice does not fall within the accepted competence of sociology or
anthropology. My interest is limited to providing a partial explanation for
the content and the expression of religion in Zamora.

Roman Catholicism

Catholics constitute between 75 to 85 percent of the people in Zamora.[10]
The rest are Protestants, in the generic sense of this term, or belong to
religious denominations with a neo-Catholic orientation: Iglesia Filipina
Independiente or its schismatic branch, Christ Jesus' Holy Church. There are
still a few old people who have resisted conversion to Christianity, but their
influence in the community is not significant.

Most Catholics—assumed to be Roman unless otherwise stated—think
that being Roman Catholic does not mean they have to discard the practices
and beliefs taught to them by other churches, including the indigenous

9. A good analysis of Spanish Catholicism from a Marxist perspective is found in Navarrò's
Las Hermandades Andaluzas (1974).

10. The 1970 census estimate, based on 5 percent random sample.

tradition. For example, a Catholic couple were married by the Protestant minister because they were unable to obtain a priest. In most other ritual matters, they follow Catholic practice and would not think of themselves as other than Catholic. The majority of Christians—Catholics and Protestants —in Zamora regularly resort to the indigenous tradition in matters such as the treatment of diseases (*gupit* and *baños* rites), the propitiation of ancestors (*koskosip, atang, singa*), or the entreatment of the various indigenous spirits. It is within this eclectic understanding and practice of Roman Catholicism and Protestantism that the terms *Catholic, Protestant,* etc., are used.

Other investigators (Lynch and Makil 1971) have noted the positive correlation between educational attainment and frequency of church attendance in municipalities throughout the Philippines. Zamora is no exception. The usual Catholic congregation (this applies to a much lesser extent among non-Catholics) consists largely of the well-educated and affluent members of the municipality. Besides regular church attendance, this elite plays an active and almost exclusive role in running the religious associations that define and maintain what is locally regarded as an appropriate Catholic lifestyle.

The barrios of Luna and Bato are the main centers of Catholic worship. Two masses are celebrated in Luna, and one in Bato, every Sunday. The main church is in Luna, but Bato also has a large church befitting its status as the *poblacion.*

The regular Sunday congregation at Luna and Bato averages seventy-five adults at each mass, with slightly more women than men. Regular church attendance averages less than 6 percent of Catholics aged over fourteen, which is less than the estimated national average. The national average is 10 percent (Piron 1965). Most Catholics in Zamora do not attend mass regularly, nor do they participate in other weekly devotions like novenas. Their main contact with Catholic rites happen during life-crises (baptism, marriage, death) or during the main calendric festivals (Good Friday, All Souls' Day, fiesta, Christmas).

Catholics in Luna and Bato, or in nearby barrios, have easy access to church services, but most of them do not make use of their proximity to a church. In contrast, many of the most active Catholics come from relatively distant barrios. The most important factor in predicting regular participation in church activities is a person's status or rank. Catholics enjoying high status or holding political office see their participation in church matters as a necessary validation of their position.

While there is a connection between political success and church participation in Zamora, this link is not a causal one. Local politicians do not cultivate the image of being a good Catholic to win votes. Winning a local election is a consequence of more specific and tangible factors, like political patronage and economic resources. But political success confers prestige and part of the obligations of success is an involvement in church affairs. There are also more practical reasons for becoming involved in Catholic activities. Membership of church associations provides links with influential allies and possible patrons, besides acting as a platform for monitoring the feelings and mood of the community's leading members.

Parish Organizations

The organization mainly involved in running the affairs of the parish, in association with the priest, is the Parish Pastoral Assembly (PPA). The PPA organizes several activities like the fiesta, Christmas-New Year celebrations, and other important calendric events. This body is also responsible for arranging religious instruction for children attending government schools and any other matters touching on the Catholic life of the municipality. General funds are raised in activities like Flores de Mayo (Mayflower) competition, or by imposing fixed levies on all Catholic households in the municipality. The money raised is used for the repair and maintenance of the main church in Luna or the priest's residence. Occasionally, individuals make donations to the church, but in such cases the priest, rather than the PPA, controls this source of revenue. The weekly collections and any payments made for the services of the priest constitute part of his personal income, for which he is accountable only to his religious superior: the Archbishop in Vigan.

The PPA is mainly concerned with financial and administrative matters; the more specifically devotional concerns are left to the various religious associations. These associations are under the spiritual patronage of a saint (i.e., St. Joseph, St. Anthony, Virgin Mary) and are often under the authority of the priest.

Members of the PPA are voted into office yearly and are meant to represent a cross-section of the Catholic community. In practice, some barrios are much better represented than others and only those members of the community enjoying high status—either through wealth, education, or political office—are elected to this organization. As can be seen from appendix 2, members either occupy political office, are comparatively affluent, or have had tertiary education. The mayor is the most powerful local politician, and appropriately, he is the president of the PPA. The list of PPA members indicates, among other things, the political faction currently in power.

There are other Catholic bodies whose concerns are more specifically devotional. Unlike the PPA, these bodies are primarily exemplary in their interests and functions.

While the PPA has a certain autonomy over the activities under its jurisdiction, its final authority and effectiveness depend on the priest's approval and cooperation. The priest acts as the link between the PPA and the Church hierarchy. While the Catholic Church in the Philippines, as in other parts of the world, is making increasing use of laypersons, the final authority still rests with the clergy. The local priest embodies this final religious authority at the parish level. However, it would be wrong to assume that the PPA is totally under his control. Its membership, consisting of the municipality's leading citizens, assures it an independent power base, even if this base rests on secular rather than sacred sanctions. Many activities, like the proper celebration of the main calendric rites, depend on the PPA's active cooperation and their fulfillment is seen as an essential part of the community's Catholic life.

Bodies with Exemplary Functions

These can be divided into those that stress a public Catholic lifestyle and those that emphasize states of private piety.

Knights of Columbus

The Knights of Columbus (KC) is an example of an organization that stresses a public lifestyle. It is the most influential Catholic body after the PPA and a considerable overlap in membership occurs between these two organizations. In the lists provided, 40 percent are members of both bodies (appendix 2).

The KC is a semiautonomous exemplary organization without a clearly specified range of devotional commitments. It is not under the spiritual authority of the priest; KC members have to account only to their superiors within the larger body of their organization. Technically, the chapter of The Knights of Columbus based in Zamora is not a fully autonomous body but is affiliated to a larger chapter in San Jose. In practice, however, this local KC exercises full autonomy over its affairs.

Membership of the KC is limited to men, and prospective members have to satisfy certain criteria. These criteria are sufficiently general to allow any Catholic to join, provided he is recommended by an influential sponsor. Although many of the KC's rituals are performed in secret, the main orientation of this organization is public. Reciprocal feasting among members is an important feature of its activities. Its secret ritual is seen as a mark of exclusiveness, rather than an attempt at concealment. A main function of the KC is to provide a forum, free from public scrutiny, for discussing and reaching decisions affecting the community.

The activities of the KC include, among other things, the sponsorship of various fund-raising competitions or arranging the visits to the municipality of well-known religious images. The money raised through these activities is controlled by the leadership of the organization, and often used to support existing factional claims. For example, in 1975 and 1976, the KC organized the Flores de Mayo competition in Bato and used the proceeds to upgrade the church in this barrio, as part of the strategy of the Bato faction to transfer the parish center. At the present time, the leadership of the KC is controlled by the Bato faction, and its members use this organization to challenge Luna's claim as the Catholic center of Zamora. The Bato faction also exercises partial dominance of the PPA, but its control is often challenged by Luna's supporters, including the priest. The KC does not fall under the priest's jurisdiction, and for this reason, the Bato faction is more effective in using it to press their claims against Luna. While the priest was not consulted about the use of the funds raised by the KC during the Flores de Mayo at Bato, he obtained control of the funds raised in Luna (with the support of Luna members of the PPA) and used part of it to install an electric water-pump in his residence. Since the funds raised to determine the Queen and her consort for the Flores de Mayo depend on local and personal support, each geographically based faction would not tolerate its use by its opponents. For this reason, the KC could use the funds raised to improve the church at Bato, while Luna insisted—through its representatives in the PPA and supported by the priest—to use the funds generated by its supporters for the benefit of Luna.

All the other Catholic associations in Zamora are, at least technically, under the authority and guidance of the priest. His position and authority symbolize the moral unity of the Catholic community.

Even the KC attempts to project a feeling of solidarity and unity both among its members and the rest of the Catholic community. In its meetings, feasting and drinking figure as prominently as prayer, a behavior typifying the pre-Catholic religious tradition. This feasting generates a feeling of camaraderie and egalitarianism among its members, some of whom come from opposing factions. In most cases, ties of alliance and patronage bind its members; resources and opportunities are made available, through the formal channels controlled by some and through the informal networks of members and their kin, to one another.

Catholic Women's League

The Catholic Women's League (CWL) is an organization of influential, college-educated women. In some respects, it acts as a female equivalent of the KC, although its activities are not as closely related to the factional division of Zamora. The CWL comes under the authority of the priest, and in most cases, he ensures that its activities do not emphasize the political cleavages of the municipality. He achieves this by ensuring that its membership does not unduly favor one faction.

Although the mayor's wife was, from 1975 to 1976, president of the CWL, its factional leanings were comparatively unemphasized. Apart from the control exercised by the priest, who attempts to depoliticize its activities, the CWL's female membership makes it less likely to pursue an explicitly political line. Political links between women are relatively undeveloped, and political action by women in Zamora usually requires that these links be mediated by men. It is the political links that men have with one another that generate a subsidiary set of links involving women, which on certain occasions cause women to pursue an explicitly political line.

Both the KC and CWL are concerned with expressing an acceptable, public Catholic lifestyle. The semisecret nature of the KC's ritual does not prevent membership and the prestige attached to it from being public knowledge. Both of these organizations sponsor programs, conferences, visits by popular religious images or prominent religious leaders, and other activities stressing public behavior rather than private piety. This public orientation requires that its leading members hold appropriately high status. While the stress on public behavior by these organizations does not preclude an interest—on the part of some of their members—in private piety, this interest is neither presumed nor required.

Corporate Organizations

Religious bodies like the KC and the CWL are well organized groups which are part of larger structures extending beyond the municipal level. These links connect the local chapter to provincial and national bodies. The term *religious organization* will be used to describe these groups and to distinguish them from other much more loosely structured associations (sodalities). Members of religious organizations act collectively in a wide range of devotional and nondevotional matters.

Corporate and collective religious organizations with specific politicoeconomic functions, like the *hermandades* or religious brotherhoods found in other parts of the hispanic Catholic world (Navarro 1974), are not found in Zamora. The KC, while having politicoeconomic interests, does not, unlike the hermandades, have special links with a particular saint. The KC's devotional interests are dispersed rather than centered on a particular image. Unlike the hermandades, membership of the KC is not inherited, and the feeling of unity of the KC that enables it to pursue politicoeconomic goals results from common class and status interests, rather than from sharing special links with a particular supernatural patron.

Noncorporate Associations: Sodalities

Apart from the organizations mentioned, there are others whose main interests lie in developing inner states of private piety. These have fewer members than the religious organizations discussed, are more loosely structured, and focus their devotional activity around a specific supernatural patron (e.g., Our Mother of Perpetual Help, Santo Niño de Praga, St. Joseph). The term *sodality* conveys their loose and unstructured nature. Most of their members are women. Aside from performing devotions in common, their members do not act collectively in nondevotional matters. The relation of members to their spiritual patron is individualistic rather than collective. Any gains which an adherent may derive from the patron is seen as a private transaction between the patron and his/her devotee. For these reasons, even though sodalities have special links with a particular supernatural patron, are usually single-sexed and often hereditary in membership, they do not have a strong feeling of corporate unity resulting in collective action. Unlike the hermandades or the KC, sodalities do not pursue politicoeconomic interests.

The Society of Our Mother of Perpetual Help (SMPH) and the Apostolados y Apostoladas de la Oracion (Apostolates of Prayer) are sodalities. Their members perform weekly devotions in church and their activities come under the authority of the priest.

Aside from the sodalities mentioned, whose activities are based in Luna, there are two other sodalities: The Society of St. Anthony and The Society of St. Joseph; their members come from the barrios of Mambog and Bato, respectively.

They all have a relatively small membership, often no more than eight or ten people. With the exception of two effeminate men who are active in the Apostolados y Apostoladas de la Oracion (AAO), all other members of sodalities are women.

The Legion of Mary is an association whose members are all women. Its structure and activities are intermediate between a corporate organization like the KC and the much looser sodalities like the AAO. Like the KC, the Legion of Mary (LM) is a local chapter of a national body with a bureaucratic structure. It is activist rather than contemplative in its orientation, and its proselytizing interests inevitably project the image of the good Catholic. But like the sodalities, the LM is also significantly concerned with specifically devout behavior. Unlike the KC and the CWL, the LM requires its members to practice weekly devotions in addition to taking a public interest in Church activities.

Aside from the PPA, whose members include men and women, other religious associations in Zamora do not include members of both sexes (except the AAO).

The primary concern of organizations like the KC and the CWL is to project and maintain a public Catholic lifestyle. Their members enjoy high status and are active in a wide range of public issues. These organizations do not assume an emphasis on private and inner devotional states as long as their members fulfill their public obligations.

In contrast, associations like the AAO and the SMPH are less concerned with public displays. Instead, they stress a personal and private devotion to a particular supernatural patron. These associations often attract wealthy and elderly women (widows or spinsters). Their structure is looser and less hierarchical than in groups like the KC and the CWL. Members of sodalities gather as a group only to perform the ritual in honor of their spiritual patron. These gatherings are small; they involve no more than six to eight people. Sodality members make no attempts to establish links with other similar sodalities in the municipality. Their interests are totally devotional, and apart from the occasional participation of a priest, the absence of men in their group is conspicuous.

Men do not participate in sodalities due to several factors. Propriety and personal preference usually discourage the formation of associations involving both men and women. Kinship ties or the pursuit of one's livelihood (i.e., certain agricultural activities, marketing or trading) are the main conditions which allow a regular and easy social relationship involving both sexes. For these reasons, women would normally resist the inclusion of men in what could otherwise remain a female association. This opposition to male membership would not arise in the case of effeminate men since they are given female status in a range of situations (i.e., female gossip groups, easy access into the more private parts of the house, the display of physical affection). Noneffeminate men who show an interest in joining female groups cause suspicion among the women and their menfolk.

Other factors discourage the formation of male sodalities. Men in Zamora, especially those holding high status, are primarily interested in establishing political alliances. Sodalities do not constitute an effective base for building such alliances because the interests and orientations of sodalities are primarily local and devotional. Furthermore, these are generally under the authority of the priest, a situation that high status men find unsuitable and uncongenial.

Sodalities like the AAO and the SMPH are primarily concerned with developing a special relationship with their respective spiritual patrons (e.g., St. Anthony, Virgin Mary, Sacred Heart). This relationship requires the development and expression of a specifically pietistic attitude on the part of the devotee. This ethical state may be achieved through the repeated and mechanical performance of certain rites and devotions. For example, members of the SMPH have to take part in a series of prayers (novenas) each week for a period of nine weeks for this rite to have merit. It is the attainment of religious merit that predisposes the spiritual patron to grant the favors asked. In this kind of relationship, there is little scope for negotiable maneuvering beyond performing or not performing the ritual concerned. An essentially supplicatory and ethical attitude is seen as more befitting the nature of women than the nature of men. The self-image of most men causes them to avoid, if possible, purely supplicatory relationships, even with supernatural entities, in favor of contractual alliances. This distinction between ethical and contractual ties with the supernatural was discussed earlier.

In 1975-76 (a similar trend is present in other years), there were 54 Zamorans—33 men and 21 women—who held office or participated regularly in the activities sponsored by their respective body. There were, of course, more active Catholics in Zamora than the 54 whose names were on the lists mentioned, but these people, who constitute less than 2 percent of adult Catholics, are primarily responsible for defining, controlling, and maintaining a public and a private Catholic morality and lifestyle. The majority of the 225 people who attend mass and other Catholic activities regularly is constituted by the 54 people mentioned and their close kin. The rest are elite members of the political faction currently out of power.

Non-Catholic Denominations

Several Protestant, neo-Catholic and biblically based separatist denominations in Zamora compete with Roman Catholicism for membership.

The Methodist and the Mision Cristiana (Christian Missions) were established in the municipality soon after the American invasion at the turn of the century. They achieved success by proselytizing in the predominantly non-Ilocano barrios. At present, the numbers of these Protestant denominations are stable and their congregations are small. Small congregations of Seventh Day Adventists and Jehovah's Witnesses are also established in Zamora. All of these denominations have ties with their overseas counterparts. While their level of local autonomy and their degree of indigenization varies from one to the other, most of these denominations have difficulty in making their foreign ideology adapt to local needs. One such important need concerns the problem of national and cultural incorporation of the believer into the religious community.

The politics of conversion and religious practice involves a complex interweaving of cultural patterns, economic interests, and private needs. The initial success of Protestant conversion in the predominantly non-Ilocano barrios early this century reflected the political expression of significant cultural and economic changes undergone during the preceding decades. The influx of coastal Ilocanos into the municipality and the introduction of a cash economy toward the end of the nineteenth century had important consequences for cultural identity and the pattern of land ownership. Conversion to Protestantism was a political response to some of these changes. But this response did little to alter the fundamental course of cultural and economic trends in the municipality during the succeeding decades. At present, the impetus for conversion to Protestantism is largely over, although the appeal of marginal groups like the Jehovah's Witnesses is somewhat stronger. The swing of conversion from orthodox Protestantism to more radically oriented foreign denominations has been noted as a general trend in the Philippines (Ellwood 1968). This trend is not significant in Zamora. The degree of conversion to the Jehovah's Witnesses and the various Pentecostal groups, although higher than the conversion to the more orthodox Protestant sects, does not compare with the increasing activities of nationalistic sects like the Iglesia ni Kristo and the Christ Jesus' Holy Church.

It was mentioned in the preceding section that the large majority of Catholics do not participate regularly in church activities, except during life-crises and the main calendric festivals. Only members of the elite participate regularly in devotional and nondevotional activities associated with Catholicism.

Elite participation in such activities may generate feelings of solidarity among its members, but more importantly, this participation is seen by the general community to be an essential aspect of its members' status. An important aspect of high status is a corresponding interest and involvement in a range of public activities and issues. Religion, politics, and education are the most common areas where high status is expressed and validated.

The common interests of members of this elite arise from their equivalent status positions in the community. The class base from which these status positions are derived is seldom consciously expressed, but whenever the economic base of status is challenged, members of the elite are quick to realize their common class interests.

Challenges to their economic dominance—like the attempt by some tenants to insist on the legal proportions of harvest shares or public pressure to bring down high fares illegally imposed by privately owned passenger vehicles plying the San Jose-Zamora route—were quickly met by the threatened elites' collective action. Challenges to their social, political, or religious domination cannot be illustrated so directly. Such a challenge requires the presence of viable alternatives. Only in the religious sphere are these readily available.

Mision Cristiana and Church of Christ. Protestant missionaries first visited Zamora early this century. In 1905, members of Mision Cristiana were proselytizing in Luna and nearby barrios. The Mision Cristiana initially included members of several denominations such as the Methodists and the Presbyterians. In 1925, the Methodists formally broke away from the more fundamental group then known as the Filipino Missionary Church. Since that time, the Methodists and the Filipino Missionary Church—locally known as the Mision Cristiana—have pursued their separate paths.

The Mision Cristiana was formally established in Luna in 1913 by an American missionary referred to in the local records as Mr. Hanna and his Filipino assistant, Mr. Francisco Gatbonton. Close links were maintained with the Methodists until 1925 when the Mision Cristiana formally repudiated the Methodists.

In 1951, the minister of the Mision Cristiana encouraged an influential widow and her supporters to break away from this denomination. The dispute concerned the use of musical instruments in Church services and the partaking of animal blood. The schismatics—who eventually joined the Church of Christ—were opposed to these practices and accused the Mision Cristiana of having romanized its doctrine and its practice.

In 1966, this dissident group established itself under the name of the Iglesia ni Cristo (Church of Christ) after having persuaded a minister of this denomination to lead their congregation. The English name of this sect will be used from hereon so as to distinguish it from another of the same name (the Manalo-led INK).

The Church of Christ was introduced to the Philippines by American missionaries in 1928 and many of its ministers have had dealings with the Mision Cristiana. This denomination has its own chapel in Luna and has access to funds from the Philippine Bible College, an American-funded missionary organization. The small Luna congregation is responsible for the maintenance of church property, but the pastor's salary is paid from outside. Members of the Church of Christ are linked through kinship ties with many members of the Mision Cristiana; to a lesser extent, with the Methodists.

Although the doctrinal differences between the Church of Christ and the Mision Cristiana are still strongly felt by their respective adherents, there have been attempts by visiting ministers and some influential community leaders to merge these separate congregations. Factional and personal differences have so far caused these attempts to fail, and as long as access to separate national bases exists (i.e., funds from abroad), a merger will not likely take place.

The importance of issues—like the use of musical instruments in Church services and the prohibition of animal blood—must be seen in the context of feasting and the role of blood in indigenous rituals. Feasting and animal blood figure prominently in traditional rites; attempts to exclude them from Church ritual indicate the degree of rejection of these traditions. Members of the Church of Christ, Jehovah's Witnesses, Iglesia ni Kristo and the Seventh Day Adventists all stress ritual simplicity and prohibit partaking of animal blood. They criticize Catholics and other denominations for not being sufficiently radical in rejecting indigenous ("heathen") practices.

Both the Mision Cristiana and the Church of Christ have ties with congregations outside Zamora. The inland municipalities adjoining Zamora consist primarily of non-Ilocano barrios and many of these barrios have large congregations of Mision Cristiana and Church of Christ.

Each of their congregations in Luna has between thirty and thirty-five active members (twenty female, fifteen male) and the same number of nominal adherents. Many of the most active members are women. The activities of these denominations mainly take place in their respective chapels in Luna, where most of the active members come from. Members of these denominations in other barrios seldom participate in services held in Luna.

In 1976, the Mision Cristiana did not have a permanent minister and depended on visiting preachers and the local Church elders (*panglakayen*). These elders are responsible for the affairs of the Church and for interpreting its doctrine. These are men, mostly in their sixties or seventies, and are active heads of extended households. They are assisted by several old women (*panginaen*), mostly widows, who are also household heads.

The control over the administrative and doctrinal affairs of the Church by members of the senior generation is reminiscent of the indigenous pre-Christian religious structure. While the *panglakayen* and the *panginaen* of the Mision Cristiana effectively control local affairs, this Church is affiliated with and depends on a national body whose direction and interests are beyond the control of the local elders. Visiting ministers are often young men who have undergone theological training in the seminary at Vigan, the provincial capital. These factors impose limits on the control by Church elders.

Members of the Mision Cristiana and the Church of Christ come from many of the core of non-Ilocano families of Luna. Despite Luna's long history of contact with urban centers on the Ilocos coast, it managed to retain many of its non-Ilocano political and religious structures until the beginning of this century. The increasing political exposure of Luna to the wider national community gradually eroded most of its indigenous structures. By the 1950s the Ilocanization of Luna was virtually complete. Indigenous structures still functioning in other non-Ilocano barrios like Macaoayan and Masingit no longer exist in Luna. The traditional religious structure came under serious threat toward the end of the nineteenth century, when the problem of the pacification of the municipality was solved, and coastal Ilocanos began to settle in the area. It is within this context of Catholic Ilocano migration that many indigenous families accepted Protestantism. As Luna participated increasingly in provincial and national politics, the number of Catholics in the barrio increased, and some leading indigenous families shifted allegiance from Protestantism to Catholicism.

Methodists. The Methodists have an active congregation in Luna. In 1975-76, there were forty-five adult members in Luna (nineteen male, twenty-six female) and twenty in Bato. There are at least as many nominal members in other barrios.

The Methodists in Luna belong to the more affluent and better educated section of the barrio's population. The neat and prosperous-looking chapel in Luna, supported entirely through local funds, contrasts markedly with the much poorer-looking chapels used by the Mision Cristiana and the Church of Christ. The larger Methodist congregation only partially explains this difference. While many members of the Mision Cristiana and the Church of Christ are descended from the indigenous families of Luna, the Methodists are descended from marriages of Luna women to coastal Ilocano men. Following traditional practice, many of these in-marrying men settled uxorilocally and eventually came to play an active role in barrio and municipal politics.

Unlike their counterparts in the Mision Cristiana and the Church of Christ, Methodists of the senior generation have considerably less influence in administering and interpreting local Methodist orthodoxy. The role of the Methodist minister is more authoritative and the participation of the younger generation is actively encouraged. Methodist doctrinal and administrative structures are much more developed than in the two previous denominations. Methodist congregations throughout the province are more definitely linked to one another. This greater administrative and doctrinal unity enables them to develop wider intercongregational activities. These increased contacts between congregations break down much of the local content of theological disputes that one may find in the Mision Cristiana and the Church of Christ. Perhaps for these reasons, in-marrying coastal Ilocano men, coming from a Catholic background, found Methodism more suitable than the Mision Cristiana, the latter being controlled by resident elders.

Aside from holding regular weekly services, the Methodists have several organizations complementing their devotional activities.

The United Methodists Women's Organization is mainly concerned with raising funds for the maintenance of the church and other necessary expenses. All Methodist women are eligible to be members of this organization, but only ten out of twenty-six women belong to it.

The Methodist Men's Organization and the Youth Organization are currently defunct. Men's lack of support explains the plight of the former, but the latter was discontinued because its activities were disapproved of by the minister. Young members used this organization to engage in social activities (outings, dancing, etc.)—activities that the minister personally disapproved of.

Scripture classes are held every Sunday and young children are encouraged to attend. These classes are supervised by the minister with the assistance of several respected men and women.

There are Methodists in other barrios adjoining Luna but, like their counterparts in the Mision Cristiana and the Church of Christ, very few attend regular services in Luna. The present minister is an active man who attempts to involve as many members as possible, those residing in Luna as well as those living in other barrios. There is a small but separate Methodist congregation in Bato, at present without a resident minister. Despite attempts by the minister to have the Bato congregation rejoin the one in Luna, the former insists on retaining its separate status. Ironically, it was partially through this minister's support that the Bato congregation achieved separate status in 1961. He was then the minister in San Jose town and supported Bato's claims for separate status.

All the Protestant denominations mentioned so far share important features. Their relatively small numbers and their local base make possible the development of strong personal bonds between the minister and members of his congregation. The kinship network linking many of the members of these denominations has been mentioned, and is an important dimension separating the community of believers from nonbelievers.

Religious participation by the average Protestant is much higher than for Catholics. But the correlation of this participation with the different status categories is lower for the Protestant since for him religious attendance is not a function of status. For Catholics, going to mass regularly is a sign of high status, e.g., mayor and his family, school principal, etc.

The administrative and doctrinal autonomy of Protestant denominations is significantly higher than that for Catholics. The Mision Cristiana and the Church of Christ have the greatest autonomy, but even the Methodists have more control over doctrine and administration than do Catholics. Questions on a range of moral issues, like the sale and use of alcohol and tobacco (the latter is particularly relevant in the Ilocos provinces), the propriety of public dancing, contraception and divorce, are often decided by each of these Protestant congregations. At certain times they go against the official views of their respective national councils.

The indigenous religious structure was based primarily on the differentiation of generations—seniors or elders control the performance of major rituals. The continued significance of the principle of seniority among the Mision Cristiana reflects this indigenous base. In contrast, the urban bias of Catholicism is indicated in the significance of factors such as class and status in determining religious participation.

The Methodists occupy an intermediate place between these two positions. Their comparatively small congregations (forty-five members) allow the average member to participate more fully in many Church activities than is the case with Catholics. But the values given to formal education and the political interests of some Methodists allow some of them to monopolize certain activities and roles.

In the case of Catholics, their large number (ca. 4,000 adults) makes it less likely that the ordinary member is able to experience a feeling of solidarity through the interaction in common worship. Those Catholics who partici- pate regularly in religious activities and who control the various Catholic associations belong to the socioeconomic elite. The status of members of the elite is public acknowledgment that they share certain interests and life experiences. Religious participation does not in itself generate a feeling of solidarity but merely constitutes part of that community of interests and experiences that entitles the elites to their status.

The fact that this elite is often divided into hostile factions does not preclude their members from sharing basic interests in relation to their less privileged neighbors. These common interests are not always consciously articulated, except on the rare occasions when they are threatened.

The response to charismatic and nationalistic denominations like the Iglesia ni Kristo and the Christ Jesus' Holy Church may be given as examples of the reaction by religiously disenfranchised classes to the elite's control of the religious and moral orders.

Charismatic and Nationalist Denominations

The Iglesia ni Kristo. The Iglesia ni Kristo (INK) is a biblically based Church founded by a Filipino, Felix Manalo, in 1914. This Church has grown dramatically, has congregations all over the Philippines and in some coun- tries overseas. While the INK shares some of its eschatological and soterio- logical claims with other separatist groups like the Seventh Day Adventists and the Jehovah's Witnesses, its explicit nationalist roots and its conscious elaboration of Manalo's prophetic role give it an important place in the religious history of the Philippines.

In 1975-76, there were 110 adult members (65 female, 45 male) of the INK in Zamora. Many of these members reside in the barrio of Taliao, where its services are conducted, but other members come from Luna and other barrios. Taliao is one of the poorer barrios and most of its inhabitants are tenants of people in Macaoayan, the adjacent barrio.

The INK has been active in Zamora only in the last decade. Most of its members first discovered this Church during visits to Manila and other urban centers. In 1974, the members began to construct a church of considerable proportions in Taliao.

The pattern of conversion to the INK is similar to that for other recently introduced denominations. A member of a household is converted and his/her dependents usually follow suit. In some cases, nondependent cognates and affines also join. Although most INK members come from the Ilocano barrio of Taliao, others come from non-Ilocano barrios like Mambog and Lucaban. But irrespective of the barrio of origin, most INK members are either poor tenants or agricultural laborers.

The INK is an aggressive, well-organized and nationalist religious movement whose main support comes from the large numbers of poor and exploited rural and urban workers. Its tight organization gives it considerable political influence, seen particularly in elections held before martial law. Most INK members in Zamora come from the class of landless laborers or tenant families with inadequate holdings. The comparatively small number of INK and its relatively recent arrival has so far prevented it from generating a political base at the municipal or barrio level.

The hostility of the Iglesia ni Kristo to the Catholic Church in particular and to all the other denominations in general may be expected to create tensions at household and barrio levels. But six out of seven households in Luna with INK members also have members belonging to other denominations. The relatively recent arrival of the INK in Luna partially explains the high proportion of mixed affiliation households. The need to maintain good relations with kinsmen, both within and outside the household, mitigates the fervor with which members of the INK espouse their cause.

In Taliao, where the INK has been more active, the majority of INK households (nine out of twelve) have single religious affiliation. Significantly, Taliao households are dependent on land owned by people in Macaoayan who are not their kinsmen, while tenants in Luna often work on the land owned by wealthy kin. The more rapid rate of conversion to the INK in a barrio like Taliao is related to the fact that ties with Macaoayan landowners are not reinforced by the obligations of kinship. The ties and obligations of kinship impose restrictions on the separatist tendencies of INK membership. In Luna, the obligations of tenants to their wealthy kin (landowners) involve a range of noneconomic exchanges and relationships that inhibit religious separatism. Tenants in Taliao are not obliged to their landlords in the same way, making it possible for denominational separatism to develop. The urban situation, which strongly favors the separation and atomization (fragmentation) of relationships, is more conducive to religious separatism, and for this reason, conversion to the INK is easier in these circumstances. INK members in Zamora often point out the difficulties of continued membership to this Church while living in the municipality, and contrast this situation with the relative ease of membership in a city.

Christ Jesus' Holy Church. The Christ Jesus' Holy Church is based in the barrio of Dirdirig, a short distance across the river from Luna. Until 1965, the members of this denomination worshipped in Luna as members of the

Philippine Independent Church (Iglesia Filipina Independiente), but during this year, internal disputes had led to the schism that ended in the formation of the Christ Jesus' Holy Church (CJHC). For some years before this dispute arose, most members who worshipped in Luna came from Dirdirig, the local minister's barrio. The doctrinal and organizational changes that eventually led to the schism and the consequent formation of the CJHC were brought about through the influence of Pedro Aglipay, a close associate and distant kinsman of Bishop Gregorio Aglipay, the founder of the Philippine Independent Church. In 1955, Pedro Aglipay formally broke away from the Philippine Independent Church to establish his own religious organization. Several Philippine Independent Church congregations with whom he had had close personal contact (Luna being one) joined his schismatic movement. The local minister had been trained by Pedro Aglipay and through his efforts, the Luna congregation became increasingly alienated from the mainstream of the theological tradition of the Philippine Independent Church. The supporters of the traditional wing of the Philippine Independent Church had, since after the Second World War, become less numerous. In 1965, the local minister decided to formally secede from this Church to attract his supporters to the CJHC. Since most members of the Luna congregation came from Dirdirig and were the minister's kinsmen, they supported his decision to transfer their religious activities from Luna. The Dirdirig members dismantled the church in Luna and reconstructed it in their barrio. The land in Luna, on which the church had stood, reverted by a court decision to the original Luna donor, who had been one of the strongest supporters of the Philippine Independent Church. The few remaining members of this latter Church no longer conduct regular services in Luna.

The CJHC draws most of its members from Dirdirig, a barrio whose inhabitants, like Taliao, are mostly poor tenant farmers. Many of the 150 (80 female, 70 male) regular members of this denomination are linked to one another by ties of kinship or marriage, aside from sharing the obligations of common barrio residents.

The CJHC shares its nationalist origins with the INK. Both these denominations were founded by Filipinos after they had undergone visionary experiences marking them as God's chosen prophet. But while Felix Manalo (Sta. Romana 1955) came from a fundamentalist Protestant background, Pedro Aglipay (details from a personal interview in Dirdirig, February 1976) had been raised in the neo-Catholic tradition of the Philippine Independent Church. Aglipay accepted the role of the Church as a source of revelation, as well as its capacity to mediate salvation through institutionalized grace. The CJHC minister in Dirdirig has recently been elevated by Pedro Aglipay to the position of Bishop and he exercises the prerogatives of this office, which include ordination and the interpretation of Church doctrine. In contrast, the local INK minister has no autonomous doctrinal or ecclesiastical privileges. For the INK, the Catholic notion of collegiality (i.e., joint responsibilty of bishops) is replaced by a rigid and well-defined hierarchy, ensuring that the interpretation of official doctrine remains under the control of Manalo or his deputy.

The CJHC has so far not been as successful as the INK in proselytizing among the urban or rural poor. It has only six rural congregations in the Iloko-speaking portion of northern Luzon, compared with the much greater number of INK congregations.

While both the INK and the CJHC depend on the charismatic appeal of their respective founders for the success of their proselytization, the INK has managed to generate an effective bureaucracy, allowing it to transcend the personal appeal of its founder. To this extent, it has solved the problem of routinization (Weber 1970:297).[11] Whether Pedro Aglipay will achieve this for his movement is still to be seen. The question of succession poses further problems to the processes of routinization and bureaucratization following the death of the founder. Both the INK and the CJHC have opted for a genealogical link: Manalo and Aglipay have appointed their sons to succeed them. This strategy seems to have worked in the case of the INK, following the death of Manalo and the apparently successful accession of his son Eraño to the position of Supreme Bishop. Since Pedro Aglipay is still living, the problem of succession has not yet been faced by his movement. Moreover, the CJHC is neo-Catholic in orientation. As such it is possible that the principle of apostolic succession and collegial responsibility may interfere with Aglipay's personal choice. In the case of the INK, this transfer of charisma (i.e., apostolic succession) has been decided (de facto) on genealogical grounds, without at the same time developing (de jure) an ecclesiastical theory of succession.

A basic difference between the CJHC and the INK is the rural orientation of the former and the urban success of the latter. Pedro Aglipay's main support comes from Iloko-speaking rural congregations with which he has close personal ties. Felix Manalo's success is most marked in the towns around Manila, and in Manila itself. Manalo's success did not rely exclusively on close ties with his supporters. While the CJHC continues the Catholic tradition of giving centrality to the principle of apostolic succession and institutional grace, the INK combines a strong sense of Manalo's prophetic role with the Protestant emphasis on direct access to divine faith. The more traditional religious practices of the CJHC—its hagiological theology and the importance of ancestors in its soteriology—are consistent with its rural orientation, while the INK's most marked success has been in

---

11. Routinization is the transfer of charisma to succeeding generations of adherents who have not personally known the founder.

comparatively urbanized areas, where traditional obligations and relationships face their strongest challenge.

Other Denominations

The presence and activity of Pentecostalists in the barrios of Macaoayan and Lucaban must be mentioned. These barrios mainly have non-Ilocano inhabitants who, in general, are more prosperous than their Ilocano neighbors.

Pentecostalism was introduced into these barrios, initially by American missionaries, during the first decades of this century. Since then Filipinos, mostly from outside the municipality, have replaced the American missionaries. Because of the prosperity of its members, the Pentecostalist congregations based in Macaoayan does not depend on outside support. This congregation (100 female, 50 male) is very loosely linked to other Pentecostalist congregations and no attempts are made to form national structures resembling those of the Methodists. In this regard, the Pentecostalists are similar to the Mision Cristiana.

The case of the Pentecostalists (as to a lesser extent the Methodists, Mision Cristiana, Church of Christ) is an instance where the acceptance of a minority, non-Catholic religious status does not necessarily imply social or economic marginality. The converse is also true (i.e., social and economic marginality does not imply religious minority status), since most of Zamora's poor tenants choose to remain Catholics, albeit only nominal. However, this is not to deny that some denominations like the INK and the CJHC have features that may be of inherent interest to disenfranchised classes. Examples of these features are nationalism, a theory of suffering, scope for participation, and politicoeconomic links. The interests of disenfranchised classes may be met in a number of ways: one is the conversion to an appropriate denomination, and another is to join secular political movements advocating radical change. So far, the former response has been the more common.

The barrios of Dayanki and Taliao each have small (15 female, 10 male) but active congregations of Jehovah's Witnesses. Their members are mostly poor tenants. Despite their poverty, their religious commitment has caused them to reject State institutions and services such as government schools, hospitals, and social welfare benefits. For these reasons, Jehovah's Witnesses have a reputation for stubbornly resisting governmental intrusions and for replacing a dependence on outside institutions with a strong feeling of internal solidarity. On Christmas Day 1976, several houses in Dayanki belonging to members of the Jehovah's Witnesses were accidentally burnt to the ground. Household furniture and the rice supply were lost in the fire. The families affected chose not to apply for the benefits offered in such circumstances by the Department of Social Welfare. These families made no attempt to solicit, nor were they offered aid from non-Witnesses in Dayanki.

Although the Witnesses are a separatist religious denomination, they are not (unlike the INK and the CJHC) strongly nationalist.

An Overview

To summarize what has been discussed so far regarding the various Christian denominations: in addition to the pervasive and dominant presence of Roman Catholicism, a number of non-Catholic, mostly fundamentalist, denominations with active congregations are also found in Zamora. Much of this religious activity, including Catholicism, is centered in Luna. But barrios like Bato, Macaoayan, Dayanki, Dirdirig, and Taliao have their share of regular religious activity. Luna is the seat of the Catholic parish and the center for the Methodists, Mision Cristiana and the Church of Christ.

Bato has attempted to replace Luna as the center of Catholic worship but so far it has had only limited success. The small Methodist congregation in Bato is not as active as the one in Luna. Although there are nominal members of the Church of Christ and the Mision Cristiana in Bato, and for that matter in other barrios, the only regular religious activity associated with these denominations takes place in Luna. There is a Seventh Day Adventist chapel in Bato, but regular services have not been held in it for some years.

For most people, regular participation in religious activities occurs within the social relations bounded by the limits of the barrio. In other words, the expression of regular religious behavior is embedded within the social structure of barrio relationships, rather than constituting an autonomous set outside barrio ties. These barrio ties revolve principally around kinship and residential obligations. With the exception of Catholics and members of the INK, whose congregations consist of members of different barrios, most other religious congregations recruit their members from a principal barrio. Thus, the CJHC draws its members from Dirdirig, the Jehovah's Witnesses from Taliao and Dayanki, the Pentecostalists from Macaoayan and Lucaban, and the Methodists, Mision Cristiana, and the Church of Christ from Luna.

While the barrio forms the focus of interest and activity of most people, members of the elite are characterized by their interest and involvement in extrabarrio affairs. For the elite, intrabarrio ties are supplemented by extrabarrio obligations and commitments. A manifestation of this different orientation of elites is expressed in their membership of Catholic organizations and their participation in the regular religious activities like the main calendric festivals.

While the remarks regarding extrabarrio interests of the elite apply in particular to their involvement and control over much of Catholic religious affairs, they also apply to a lesser extent to the members of the INK. The latter are mostly drawn from the poorer classes and their participation in a congregation composed of people from different barrios is an indication of the extent to which their members have been able to transcend ordinary barrio interests.

Apart from the ability of the INK to form a tightly organized congregation drawn from several barrios, this denomination has also been successful in discouraging its members from taking part in many traditional religious practices: for example, obligations to dead kinsmen. While denominational differences exist over a wide range of matters covering the nature of proper religious behavior in Zamora, a set of shared concerns and practices also exists. Life-crisis rites, the treatment of disease, and the obligations to dead kinsmen are areas of common concern to most Catholics and Protestants, despite the differing orthodox views held by each denomination.

A person's ritual obligations to ancestors are important for most people. These obligations often involve expensive feasting before burial and thereafter in the annual rites commemorating the memory of the deceased. Illness and other misfortunes are attributed to the ill will of neglected ancestors and propitiatory rituals must be performed to alleviate these misfortunes. The INK does not accept these traditional obligations, and its rejection of them reflects its radical orientation vis-à-vis social, political and religious aspects of the traditional view of the world. This radical religious position is to some extent shared by other separatist denominations like the Jehovah's Witnesses and the Seventh Day Adventists. But unlike the INK, these other separatist groups do not combine this radical stand with a strong nationalist emphasis, a shrewd political sense and an effective well-disciplined Church bureaucracy. The first two conditions may have characterized the early stages of the Philippine Independent Church and indigenous religious movements (i.e., CJHC), but the last condition seems to be the most difficult one for indigenous movements to achieve. Even the INK cannot be said to have completely solved the problem of organizational continuity and bureaucratization. Ellwood reports four schismatic groups originating from the INK (1969:382).

By comparison with the INK, the CJHC is not as radical in its rejection of the traditional order. Its members subscribe to many neo-Catholic practices, and in most respects, this denomination represents the total indigenization of the structure of authority of the Catholic Church, with the inclusion of nationalist elements in its doctrine and ritual. Its congregation is recruited mainly on the basis of kinship and residence, and there is little attempt made to transcend or deny these traditional links for others emphasizing a more direct tie to God.

Household Religious Affiliation

The following data for Luna indicate the degree of denominational heterogeneity at the level of the household. Out of 151 Luna households, 23 (15.2 percent) contain multiple religious affiliations. The remainder, at least nominally, contain only one religious denomination. In 15 out of the 23 households mentioned, the members of different affiliations belong to the same generation, being either spouses or siblings. In 13 out of this same 23 households, the members of different affiliations belong to different generations. In the last case, there appears to be no pattern predicting the affiliation of the junior generation given the affiliation of the senior generation. In 5 out of the 23 households where members of the junior generation can exercise a choice, this appears to be idiosyncratic. Some children follow the affiliation of the father, others of the mother. In 8 out of these 23 households, members of the junior generation do not follow the religious affiliations of any member of the senior generation.

Although there may be difficulties in households with mixed religious affiliations, the tensions that could develop are mitigated by the requirement to maintain good relations with kinsmen and the necessity for economic cooperation within and outside the household. As the data for Luna indicate, mixed religious households are a minority (15.2 percent) and all the other barrios in the municipality have an even higher rate of homogenous households.

The tensions that could arise in multiple affiliation households could be particularly strong whenever the denominations involved stress separation from and opposition to nonmembers. I have discussed the effects of membership in the INK and the consequent problem of dealing with non-INK members. In the case of Luna, following the pattern of tenant-landowner relationships, INK members are forced to meet their obligations to non-INK kinsmen. But in Taliao, INK members, not being dependent on kinsmen for land, are more able to pursue their separatist inclinations. While INK households in Luna often include non-INK members, they seldom do so in Taliao.

Conclusion

In this chapter, I discussed the composition and interests of the religious denominations in Zamora. In particular, I described the role of the municipality's elite in controlling much of Catholic religious activity. This control is an instance of elite resistance to any infringement of their power and authority over the poorer and dependent classes. The election of elite members to the main religious bodies ensures their continued domination, and constitutes an aspect of power in the moral domain. Since Catholicism is the dominant religious ideology, their control is an important aspect of the process of legitimation, and forms part of the institutional and ideological hegemony exercised by these elite. The close association in the indigenous political system between the holders of secular and ritual authority has persisted, though in a modified form, into the present. The *nabaknang* (wealthy) class in Zamora still wields secular and religious authority, although the sources of wealth and the links to religion have become more complex.

The elite's monopolization of the religious and moral domain is challenged by some members of the poorer and dispossessed classes when these join separatist sects that stress the radical and exclusive nature of salvation. All of these radical sects (i.e., Iglesia ni Kristo, Christ Jesus' Holy Church, Jehovah's Witnesses) essentially preach the salvation of the poor and wretched of this earth and assure them the rewards of the life to come (Luke 6:20, 13:22). Their rejection of the dominant religious ideology masks a more fundamental rejection of the social order. The repudiation of traditional ritual obligations, for example, to deceased kinsmen, and the emphasis on separatism and on the construction of a new social order should be seen in terms of their experience of exploitation and marginality.

Marx's (1975:38-39) comments describing religion as an inverted world-consciousness is directly applicable to these separatist sects, but a different explanation must be given for the role of religion among the elite. In other words, the role of religion as an ideology varies for different classes. Thus one should see religious domination as reflecting the state of social relations in which one class has control over the means of ideological production.

The dual nature of the local economy in Zamora imposed certain constraints on the relevance and effects of Christian ideology. The domestic orientation of this economy is reflected in the importance given to ritual obligations of household members. The folk religious tradition is strongest in matters affecting the interest of the household. Planting and harvesting, repeated illness, and other life-crisis rituals have a pre-Christian orientation and emphasis. As Zamora becomes progressively more integrated into the wider economy and polity, this folk tradition and orientation may be expected to change.

The largely urban orientation of Catholicism and even of the Iglesia ni Kristo, with their emphasis on urban household patterns and, in particular, their views regarding intergenerational obligations, is a factor that must be considered in explaining the acceptance or rejection of their doctrines among the peasantry.

Durkheim (1965:257) emphasized the importance of religious symbolism in expressing significant social relations and social boundaries. The initial patterns of conversion to Protestantism in non-Ilocano barrios may be given as an instance of religious symbolism being used to express significant social relations and social boundaries. Non-Ilocanos in Zamora at the beginning of this century wished to retain their cultural distinctiveness in the midst of the growing Ilocano majority. Since the indigenous religion was no longer viable in the new political climate, conversion to Protestantism played an equivalent function.

The initial success of the Mision Cristiana and the Methodists in Luna and later, of the Pentecostalists in Macaoayan and Lucaban, are instances of significant cultural and political boundaries being expressed in religious terms. The fact that religious rather than secular symbols are used for expressing these significant relationships is an indication of the consciousness that people in Zamora have of their material circumstances. In the case of denominations like the INK, and to a lesser extent the CJHC, religious goals are, at the same time, consciously linked to economic and political objectives. In these latter examples, material and social conditions are seen as being linked to transcendental goals.

Following Durkheim (1965:475), the rituals practiced by organizations like the Knights of Columbus and the Catholic Women's League may be seen as reinforcing already existing collective sentiments and ideas. These sentiments and ideas should not be interpreted as arising exclusively from the performance of such rituals but rather from the material and ideal interests that determine people's conduct (Weber 1970:280).

The factional nature of Catholic organizations has been mentioned. In this case, the use of religious structures and symbolism to express political cleavages within an elite that essentially acknowledges a common moral order is an instance (Durkheim 1965:257) where religion provides the symbolism for expressing unconscious but intimate relations members of a community have with one another.

The views of a separatist group like the INK regarding the obligations to dead kinsmen have been discussed. Since INK members are mostly poor tenants, the advantages of holding an ethic that does not require expensive feasting may be expected to have beneficial material consequences. Such an ethic is present within a tradition that holds deceased ancestors responsible for the material well-being of their living descendants. As a consequence, poor families may feel aggrieved against their ancestors if their poverty is not the result of their initial neglect of ancestral obligations. In such cases, conversion to the INK, whose ideology absolves the believer from ancestral obligations, is morally and experientially justified. The popularity of the INK among the urban poor should be seen in the context of changing kinship norms under economic and material conditions that increasingly favor the atomization or fragmentation of kinship ties.

The material consequences of an ethic, such as the INK's denial of traditional religious obligations, constituted Weber's predominant concern in his study of religion. Weber (1970:280, 1971:1) emphasized the practical and this worldly orientation of the religious attitude. For him, religion was ultimately a quest for meaning at the cosmic level which the believer attempts to put into practice. Whether these ultimate meanings will always be expressed in religious or transcendental terms—that is, as lying outside the capacities and ordinary affairs of men, as Durkheim (1965) affirmed and Marx (1975) denied—is not finally resolved by Weber. While he points to certain tendencies, at least in Western civilization, such as secularization, disenchantment and rationalization which may conceivably end in a totally demystified world, Weber does not inform us if, under these conditions, religion will disappear.

This last question is particularly relevant in the changing political and economic circumstances facing Zamora. The acceptance or rejection of secular ideologies espousing radical reform, like those advocated by clandestine political groups operating in nearby areas, will partially depend on the extent to which religious ideologies continue to satisfactorily answer significant moral dilemmas. As long as people's ideal-moral interests enable them to accept and to explain their material conditions, it is unlikely that secular ideologies will succeed.

While these ideal-moral interests are being redefined (such as the denial of certain obligations by the INK), social, economic, and political success in Zamora, as exemplified by the local elite, remains tightly articulated in an ideology and epistemology with significant transcendent or religious elements. One should not, however, overestimate the transcendent elements in Zamoran ideology. Enough examples are present to indicate that secular elements continue to constitute a major component of the indigenous religion which make it possible for people to appreciate radical and materialist political programs.

Conclusion

In the preceding chapters, I have linked aspects of religion to political and economic interests. The penetration of Christianity and the survival of non-Christian beliefs and practices in Zamora can be seen to be related to political and economic exigencies (Gluckman 1968, 1971). These exigencies may be classified into three main stages of equilibria (1) the Spanish colonization, (2) transition from Spanish to American rule, and (3) the Japanese occupation and political independence. These ultimately resulted in an eclectic religious view combining elements of Iberian Catholicism, American Protestantism and Indo-Malayan animism.

Ideological and Religious Formation

The period of Spanish colonization marked the first stage of this process of ideological formation. It was characterized by the dominant influence of the foreign religious orders, the suppression of a native Catholic clergy, and the rising demands of the mestizo-led urban bourgeoisie, finally culminating in the nationalist and revolutionary movements of the late nineteenth century (Roth 1977). In northern Luzon, the period from 1575 to 1898 saw repeated and largely unsuccessful attempts by the friar orders and the Spanish authorities to christianize and subjugate the "wild" pagans of the highland interior (Scott 1974a). The end of the colonial regime and the expulsion of the Spanish missionaries coincided with the rapid rise of the Iglesia Filipina Independiente, a nationalist Church controlled by an indigenous clergy and supported by elite-urban interests. This brief interlude (1898-1902) saw the transition from Spanish to American rule and introduced the second stage of ideological formation.

The Spanish Period

Several paradoxes regarding Spanish colonization of the Philippines exist. One of these concerns the methods and ease of conquest. On the one hand, we are informed that "the conquest was, for the most part, peacefully accomplished. . . . Armed resistance broke out mainly among coastal peoples with histories of external aggression and raiding, and among Tagalog communities. . . . . But in every case resistance was futile. This is attributable to the extreme political fragmentation of native society, which allowed the Spanish to progressively meet and defeat small clans or communities" (Anderson 1976:12).

In contrast to this apparent facility of conquest is the view that "periodic uprisings have characterized Philippine history. Major rebellions have occurred at least once every generation since the inception of Spanish rule" (Sturtevant 1958:105). These insurrections were mostly local affairs successfully suppressed by the Spaniards with the aid of native allies. Between these upheavals the "individual attack on Spanish priests and officials, messianic religious movements, and widespread banditry interrupted the tranquility of the countryside" (Sturtevant 1958:105).

These views imply that Spanish rule, while not entirely benign, was nevertheless tolerated in large areas of the Philippine lowlands except for regular but uncoordinated uprisings mainly, though not exclusively, by elements of the disenfranchised rural masses.

This view of colonial history is inconsistent. On the one hand, it points out the facility of and tolerance toward Spanish domination. On the other, it simultaneously records repeated cases of violent and unsuccessful rebellions. These views have not been, in my opinion, adequately reconciled. Explanations either stress the breakdown of local norms and the consequent need for revitalization movements (e.g., Sturtevant) or the desperate and largely irrational responses to colonial exploitation (e.g., Anderson).

The former explanation often neglects the continuity and vitality of local traditions while the latter rely mostly on external, often unsympathetic assessments of possible strategies and alternatives.

Philippine historians (e.g., Anderson 1976, Phelan 1964) who cite the political fragmentation of native society as the reason why resistance to Spanish conquest was futile ignored the fact that this same fragmentation made conditions of chronic rebellion possible.

As noted earlier, the northern highlands and the Muslim south were not conquered as quickly by the Spaniards. One could argue that the Muslim south was not as politically fragmented (Majul 1973) as other parts of the Philippines; for this reason it was able to halt the Spanish advance. But northern Luzon was more fragmented than the easily conquered lowlands. Nevertheless, the north's resistance was fierce and successful; the Spaniards barely managed to establish a foothold in the region three centuries after their conquest of the lowlands and only after a series of punitive expeditions had failed (Scott 1974a). In this case, the political fragmentation and strategic advantages of highland societies enabled them to resist Spanish penetration. The *conquistadores* had difficulty with the terrain and logistical support. But what characterizes these highland groups is not so much the size of the polity as the absence of politically significant internal divisions.

The frequent use of a religious idiom for radical political discourse both reflects and is constrained by the fundamental divisions in the social structure. The northern highlands, in contrast to the Christian lowlands, was traditionally characterized both by the secular orientation of political discourse and by the absence of politically fundamental divisions in the social structure. Millenarian or Christian-based sentiments have only comparatively recently spread to the highlands (Smart 1970, Eggan and Scott 1965) in association with a drastic restructuring of traditional society along Christian lowland models. The political resistance in the highlands was also accompanied by an equal reluctance toward religious conversion which lasted throughout the Spanish colonial period. Missionaries were unsuccessful in religious conversion even though they were regularly settled among non-Christian peoples for long periods (Scott 1974a). When these highland groups converted to Christianity at the beginning of the American colonial period, many communities rejected Catholicism in favor of Protestantism (Jocano 1971, Pertierra 1981). A parallel rejection is recorded for Christian lowland radical movements (McCoy 1982). In all these instances religious belief and practice resulted from changes in the political structure that effectively prevented the use of a secular political idiom but allowed the use of a religious one.

The same may be said of the Muslim communities in the southern Philippines. Resistance to Spanish colonization was articulated in religious terms both by the secular authorities such as the sultan and religious leaders such as the ulama. But when the secular power of the sultanates declined toward the end of the Spanish era, the ulama provided much of the focus for political resistance. This latter period was characterized by the increasing number of *juramentados* (Majul 1973:301) or Islamic zealots prepared to die for the cause, not unlike their Christian millenarian counterparts.

It seems that religion has always impinged on most aspects of Filipino life. Or, put differently, religion served as the idiom and provided the concepts for articulating significant relationships and interests. The earliest Spanish reports portray native society as one in which the "sacred and profane were often indistinguishable" (Phelan 1964:72). While the reliability of such reports may be questioned, the conceptual distinction we make between religion and politics was not a marked feature of the native's perception of social reality. The conditions for the separate conceptualization of these spheres did not arise until the late nineteenth and early twentieth century. Even in the present time, the progressive intercalation of the local economy and the rise of a secular State have failed to make this separation between the religious and political domains as marked as it is in the West.

Religion and politics during this period were closely linked. Mass religious conversions followed the initial conversion of chiefs and men of influence. The early Catholic missionaries exploited this and succeeded. But the same links also enabled astute native religious practitioners, many of whom were women or transvestites, to mobilize resistance against the Spaniards (Anderson 1976:69). While religion and politics may not have been conceptually distinct, in many Philippine communities this separation coincided substantively with the legitimate concerns of each sex. The imposition of Catholicism and institutions like the *patronato real* (i.e., State support of Church expenses) not only formalized the existing symbiosis between the religious and political domains but also merged these domains into one under the responsibility of men. In such cases, conversion implied among other things a restriction of the proper sphere of competence of women (Owen 1978).

The special role of the clergy, particularly the members of the main religious orders, is acknowledged by most scholars as having been a major factor in the long-term success of Spanish colonization of the Philippines. It was mainly through their efforts, both martial and ideological, that an otherwise decaying and disintegrating colonial power managed to impose its rule on its most distant colony for nearly four centuries. In contrast, the role played by indigenous religious practitioners in opposing early Spanish rule and their involvement in local rebellions has, until recently, received little attention. It is clear that the traditional interests (political leadership) of native religious practitioners were against conversion but their response particularly after the, at least, nominal conversion to Catholicism only emerges several generations after the conquest (Anderson 1976).

Pax Americana

The close and direct links between religion and politics were considerably weakened at the onset of the American period. Instead, the Americans embarked on a massive and largely successful education and indoctrination program, expanded the state bureaucracy and formed a highly effective national constabulary. While Spanish political sovereignty ultimately rested on the moral legitimacy granted to it by Catholicism, American imperialism shifted its basis of legitimation from the religious to the secular order, substituting the concepts of democracy and literacy for hierocracy and predicancy, having previously ensured monopoly of military force. The weak, premodern colonial Spanish state maintained its control over the islands largely through religious means, effective enough until an emergent Filipino entrepreneurial class eroded both the material base (i.e., the economy) and its ideological superstructure (i.e., the rise of a Filipino clergy and intelligentsia). By the last decades of the nineteenth century the *principalia* class, in conjunction with the growing interests of Anglo-American capitalism, had not only consolidated its control over the local economy but increasingly challenged Spanish monopoly of the local ecclesiastical structure. The gains achieved by the principalia did not extend to other classes. In various areas like central Visayas and northern Luzon, economic conditions worsened significantly, forcing mass migration from these regions to others which were being developed with the newly gained resources of the principalia. In these conditions, we may expect significantly different class responses to the political and social changes brought about by the replacement of one colonial mode by another: from religious legitimation to direct political control. While the 1896 Revolution temporarily coalesced the interests of members of different classes in native society, the American conquest repolarized society resulting once more in distinct patterns of response to the new colonial master. The new economic and political order encouraged by the Americans created opportunities for members of the principalia without significantly reducing the grievances felt by large sections of the peasantry. This would have required a radical alteration of native society and its relation to the new metropolitan power. Neither the Americans nor members of the principalia had the inclination or the ideology for such a program. Despite the democratic rhetoric accompanying Anglo-American imperialism, the savagery of the Philippine-American War coupled with nineteenth-century capitalism's search for new markets and raw materials excluded any serious attempts to redress inequalities in native society. As expected, sections of the peasantry resorted to familiar attempts to relieve their grievances, initially employing a religious idiom that spawned religiopolitical movements but later including elements of secular revolutionary programs.

Pax Americana was quickly extended to areas in the northern highlands and the Muslim south previously uncontrolled by the Spanish authorities. Protestant missionaries embarked on a mission of conversion. As early as 1900 (Schmitz 1971:130), they began visiting Zamora and the surrounding municipalities. Their success among the coastal and lowland populations was unremarkable, as most people either retained their loyalty to Rome or joined the newly formed nationalist Church. Protestant conversion, however, was much more frequent in the previously non-Christian interior areas, like the non-Ilocano barrios of Zamora. In these areas, Protestantism became a viable alternative to Catholicism and was used by the indigenous highland populations to defend themselves from encroaching coastal Ilocano domination. This conversion was accompanied by the rapid integration, under American auspices, of these interior municipalities into the national polity. As Zamora came increasingly under provincial and national structures, the first consistent moves to create the municipality were initiated by people in the politically dominant barrios of Luna and Macaoayan.

The American colonial period saw a rapid expansion of national structures such as universal primary education, an expanding bureaucracy, an effective national constabulary, and vocal demands for political independence. Political parties were established under American guidance and a generation of national politicians competed for increasing control over the nation's political future. The orderly and gradual assumption by native political leaders of the mantle of government, planned by the American colonial authorities, was interrupted by the sudden and unexpected Japanese invasion of 1941.

The period of Japanese occupation (1941-1944) brought to the forefront the underlying conflicts and tensions in Philippine society which were present during the American regime, but successfully contained through a judicious use of military force and the introduction of liberal reforms (Wolff 1960, Steinberg 1967).

In chapter 1, I discussed some of the consequences of the Japanese occupation. Contrary to what is often assumed (e.g., Steinberg 1967), the Japanese presence, at least in Zamora, led as much to an escalation of internecine conflict between factions (caused by the dilemma of obligatory allegiance, i.e., America or Japan) as it did to a feeling of Filipino solidarity against the invading Japanese. This period set the parameters for the third and last stage of ideological formation.

Post World War II

The end of the war and the granting of Philippine independence in 1946 saw the emergence of a strong Ilocano identity in Zamora, even in barrios like Macaoayan, Masingit, Mambog, and Lucaban. The new political order favored those with ties to powerful ethnic groups such as Ilocanos, Tagalogs, Visayans, rather than members of cultural minorities like the Igorot, Kankanai, and Itneg. The earlier attraction of Protestantism which offered a viable religious symbolism (autonomy, raising of status of non-Ilocanos) for members of these cultural minorities lost its major advantage (i.e., official status and American support) in the new political climate. The emergence of an Ilocano identity in Zamora coincided with the conversion to Catholicism of the leading political families residing in the predominantly Protestant barrios of Macaoayan, Lucaban, Masingit, and Mambog.

With the possible exceptions of the Iglesia ni Kristo (INK) and the Christ Jesus' Holy Church (CJHC), it seems unlikely that the position of Catholicism as the dominant religion is seriously threatened. The Iglesia draws its support from the dispossessed classes and from those seeking a break with a religious tradition emphasizing kinship and a developed hagiolatry (saint worship). The rise of a rural proletariat, following the growth of a money economy, and the substitution of a strident nationalism in the place of local kin-based loyalties are factors contributing to the appeal of the INK. In contrast, the CJHC relies on the continuation of traditional kin-loyalties and contractual ties with supernatural patrons, but differs from Catholicism by including nationalist elements in its doctrine and liturgy. The persistence of a subsistence economy amid nationalist aspirations may be expected to favor the CJHC.

To a certain extent, Catholicism can contain many of these conflicting trends and tensions in Zamora. Although much of the public practice and expression of Catholicism is dominated by members of the elite, a large majority of ordinary barrio people are able to utilize parts of Catholic liturgy and doctrine for their religious needs. Occasions like baptisms, weddings and funerals employ Catholic ritual to serve both secular and transcendent ends. Catholic practices—the fiesta, Good Friday, October Rosary, All Souls' Day, and Christmas-New Year—meet the requirements of a subsistence economy in which kinship and neighborhood ties are a primary consideration in most social relations; where the concept of fault rather than the loss of merit is stressed; and where the moral order and relations with the supernatural emphasize an orientation to the present life instead of the next. For all these reasons, the religious experience of people in Zamora constitutes an amalgam of practices and beliefs derived from Western and indigenous sources.

Local Economy and Polity

I have questioned the cultural homogeneity of the Ilocos region assumed by writers such as Keesing (1962), Fox and Flory (1974), and H. Lewis (1971).

I have also pointed out the unreliability of much of the data gathered in government surveys. I have argued that the hypothesis regarding the lowland origins of highland populations (e.g., Keesing 1962) is not supported by Zamora ethnohistory; quite the contrary, highland groups appear to have settled Zamora during the late eighteenth and early nineteenth centuries.

The political allegiance of the peasantry in the Philippines is "terra incognita," into which political scientists and historians enter at their own risk. For instance, generalizations about peasant attitudes to the Japanese occupation, at least in Zamora, were not as straightforward as some (i.e., Steinberg 1967) would have us believe. Historians like Ileto (1975) and Guerrero (1977) are presently rewriting history as seen from below and are exploring, like McCoy (1977), the economic conditions of the peasantry in the past.

My study has shown the dangers of accepting national and elite categories in the analysis of local society. External notions of economic development and technological innovation are seldom examined in terms of existing local structures. As a consequence, they often fail to explain the nature and direction of social change. In Zamora, this change occurs within a polity with strong urban biases and entrenched elite interests. For example, the development and innovation associated with rice and Virginia tobacco may be expected to take different courses as a result of their distinct roles in Zamora society.

The increasing penetration of market-relations and state institutions in Zamora are associated with changes in the system of stratification, e.g., *nabaknang* status being used in new contexts. These changes have consequences for the nature of political activity.

As in other parts of the Philippines (e.g., Agpalo 1972, Hollnsteiner 1963, Lande 1964), political parties in Zamora act mainly as vehicles for articulating disputes between factions headed by members of the local elite. Much of this political activity takes place within a stable political order whose essential features are seldom seriously challenged.

External political factors like President Marcos's decision to change parties has had important consequences for local political alliances. In Zamora, the imposition of martial law has led, at least in its immediate effects, to a reemergence of previous political alliances, illustrating the fundamentally stable and conservative nature of most political activity.

Local political divisions are also manifested outside the party structure as in religious denominations, civic organizations and cultural orientations.

Much political activity in Zamora is associated with and reflects the absence of a developed plaza-complex. The rise of a market economy may be expected to contribute to the rigidification of the system of stratification and to the hostility between classes. These conditions favor the creation of a developed plaza-complex, with its attendant consequences.

Cultural and Structural Constraints

Kinship and marriage offer people both structural and organizational principles on which to allocate and transmit status, property, residence, and group membership. While the formal properties of Ilocano kinship are common throughout much of northern Luzon, significant differences related to historical, economic, and cultural factors exist. The differences in marriage and residence patterns in Luna and Macaoayan have been discussed in relation to these factors, e.g., the availability of land affects choices regarding postmarital residence. A given residential pattern (e.g., virilocality) generates pressures in the social structure, e.g., the relation between men and women of adjacent generations, which may ultimately lead to the instability of certain roles, e.g., the importance and authority of elders.

A major feature of kinship and marriage in Zamora concerns the maximization of political and economic opportunities. As these opportunities change, the focus of kinship and marriage likewise changes, e.g., the shift in preference against cousin-marriage on the part of the rich is related to such things as the erosion of former political boundaries in favor of national bureaucracies and mass parties as well as the progressive monetization of the local economy with its emphasis on secondary rather than primary (i.e., face-to-face) relations.

Significant ideas concerning the nature of the secular and religious orders reflect structural features of Zamoran society. The conscious model of this society comprises three basic dimensions: (1) sexual differentiation, (2) the opposition of generations and seniority within a generation; and (3) status and rank. The secular and religious orders articulate social relations arising out of these basic dimensions.

Although sexual differentiation permeates many aspects of social life, some areas are significantly more affected than others. Thus, while electoral politics is the exclusive domain of men, women exercise considerable autonomy and control over the local economy. Collective rites are generally controlled by men, but women often actively participate in them. Women are able to hold high status through tertiary education.

Each sex is allocated a distinct but equal role in the ideology and practice associated with reproduction and childrearing. While the man initially implants the seed, the woman nourishes its growth—this metaphor is consistent with the division of labor in agriculture. Interest in young children is both a man and a woman's concern.

The onset of puberty initiates the public separation of the sexes. Henceforth, boys and girls maintain a degree of aloofness which is seldom publicly discarded.

Dangers associated with pregnancy make this condition an ambivalent one, particularly for women. A pregnant wife's intimidatory rights over her husband reflect this ambivalence. She often refuses him sexual access during her term; she is excused from working in the fields. Menstrual taboos are more strictly followed after the birth of the first child—when a wife's procreative power has been verified but before she exercises her authority in the household. These taboos become less important after each succeeding child, as a wife becomes progressively more secure in her role and begins to wield considerable domestic authority.

The necessity to differentiate generations and to differentiate seniors within a generation constitutes the second feature of Zamora social structure. Showing appropriate respect to seniors is an important aspect of social relations and is manifested in the modes of address and reference. The ritual importance of seniors is repeatedly stressed, from simple curing rites like *gupit*, *koskosip*, and *baños* (*banyos*) to exhortatory speeches delivered at weddings and other social occasions. As members of the senior generation progressively detach themselves from economic activities, they turn their attention to ritual matters. On occasions like baptisms, weddings, and funerals, senior men and women play important roles and are deferred to by juniors.

Status and rank are important matters in Zamora and these are expressed in the secular and religious spheres. There is a complex pattern of consumption and display that shows a person's status or rank. Marriage arrangements, elaborate feasting, the use and participation of ritual specialists such as the priest or minister reflect differences in status and rank in the community. Men and women of high status (*nabaknang*) take great interest in public religious activities; they often pay for the performance of collective rites and play leading roles in them.

The Politics of Belief

The local elite's control of political institutions is reinforced by their control of most public religious activities. Hence the elite's monopoly of political power and the religious disenfranchisement of the masses, experienced through their nominal adherence to Catholicism, must be seen as coming from identical sources within the social structure. At present, the ordinary villager's possibilities for religious expression lie in (1) the rich folk-Catholic tradition with its emphasis on spirits and ancestors, (2) neo-Catholic denominations like the CJHC which provide ample scope for participation combined with a nationalist ideology, (3) conformist Protestant denominations like the Methodists, Church of Christ, Mision Cristiana, Pentecostalists, and (4) separatist and radical groups like the INK, Jehovah's Witnesses, whose doctrines often combine a rejection of established secular and religious positions. In the case of the INK, its strong opposition to the established religious orthodoxy (i.e., Catholicism) is matched by its attempts to influence political and economic institutions. For instance, it organizes its members into voting blocks and opens up employment opportunities for them. The INK has arrived in Zamora only recently and its small numbers have so far not made it possible for them to obtain any benefits resulting from these secular orientations.

The pattern of religious conversion, particularly the early success of Protestantism in some barrios soon after the American invasion, must be interpreted in the light of changing demographic and political pressures. The Ilocanization of Zamora had progressed rapidly toward the end of the nineteenth century. The new political order encouraged by the Americans soon threatened to overwhelm the existing privileges of the non-Ilocano minority. This minority converted to Protestantism because it wanted to preserve its position. Non-Ilocanos, through surviving traditional socioeconomic structures, managed to exercise considerable influence until the Second World War. Later, when a cash economy was introduced and other national institutions were created, local structures of power were affected considerably and this change largely favored the Ilocano majority. In this situation, Protestantism holds few advantages and as a result, most politically ambitious men have become Catholic.

The increasing monetization of the local economy has, however, also led to a proletarianization of rural workers and to the increasing appeal of a denomination like the INK.

Economic resources and political aspirations are important factors affecting the degree of participation in Zamoran Catholicism. For this reason, the elites usually control most formal Catholic activities. Elite women and men take an active interest in Catholic affairs. But members of each sex, consonant with their political role, emphasize some aspects over others. Thus, men join organizations with protopolitical functions like the Knights of Columbus and combine religiosity with external display (i.e., feasting). Women prefer apolitical associations which emphasize the development of inner states of private piety.

Collective rites like the *bignas* and the *paayos* were formerly associated with agricultural events corresponding at the present time to the Easter ritual cycle and an activity like the Flores de Mayo. The indigenous and Christian traditions may be used to supplement one another or they may result in a form of ritual eclecticism, e.g., banōs, koskosip, gupit.

Structural features of Zamora society—sexual differentiation, generation and seniority, status and rank—are expressed within the indigenous religious tradition in a manner very similar to the way they presently do in Christianity. Domestic rites were usually performed by women (*dadaw-wakan*) and collective rites by men (*mambunong*); senior men (*panlakayen*) and senior women (*panginaen*) enjoyed special ritual privileges; wealthy members of the community (*nabaknang*) were expected to contribute generously toward

collective rites and to redistribute surplus through lavish feasting to gain
Kabunian's blessings.

Zamoran morality is essentially concerned with establishing good and
viable relations with the members of one's community. It is relations between people (i.e., the secular order) rather than relations with the supernatural order that characterize moral concerns. Man's relations with the
spirit-world are modeled on relations with his fellowmen and stress values
like reciprocity and propriety. Difficulties attributed to the supernatural
order usually arise from displeasing or offending ancestral or environmental
spirits, to whom compensation and propitiation is offered just as one would
do to an offended kinsman or neighbor. Offenses against abstract moral
principles such as those represented by Kabunian rarely become the main
religious concern, which also explains, *mutatis mutandis*, the prevalent interpretations of Christianity.

The native theory of reciprocity and propriety (i.e., behavior appropriate
to one's life-situation) constitutes an effective rationale for many aspects of
social inequality. It emphasizes contractual rather than ethical or meritori-
ous relations and is extended to encompass the supernatural order. In such
a schema, the notions of sin and salvation do not occupy a central role.

Soteriological concerns are not a major feature of Zamoran religion,
except for members of denominations like the Iglesia ni Kristo and Jehovah's Witnesses. Significantly, these latter sects also challenge prevailing
models of social relations, particularly in situations of economic uncertainty
and increasing exploitation.

The dispute about the site of the *poblacion* has affected various aspects of
religious commitment and practice in Zamora. The absence so far of a
clustered residential elite has prevented the development of an ideology
that stresses the differences between the poblacion and its peripheral
barrios. However, the shift in the economy from subsistence to commodity
production may eventually consolidate elite interests and so, develop an
ideology that conforms to a center-periphery model. When Hart (1955) used
this model to explain the diffusion of cultural values, he overlooked the
historicopolitical conditions that led to this model's legitimation. What Hart
suggested as an explanatory model is in reality an ideological consequence
of a particular historical social structure.

Ritual and Social Structure

Rituals to ensure good relations with deceased kin, like All Souls' Day
and Good Friday, are among the most significant religious events in Zamora.
But only those with adequate resources can perform them; the poor can not.
These poor sometimes solve their predicament by joining a denomination
like the INK, which repudiates the links between the living and the dead.

While Christ's death is seen as religiously significant by the majority of local Catholics, his resurrection receives scant attention. Redemption, rebirth, and regeneration do not constitute dominant themes in local eschatology. Death is given existential significance, but it is not perceived in the context of salvation. Hence death is seldom seen as being transcendentally significant.

In contrast to All Souls' Day and Easter, the other major calendric rites in Zamora stress the renewal of social relations with living members of the community: neighbors, friends, patrons. They generally occur during periods of agricultural surplus and are propitious occasions for celebrating marriage or baptism or for expanding one's networks and alliances.

Through rituals social claims are expressed and fulfilled. They provide conceptual grids for behavioral and normative expectations. To participate in and initiate rituals imply the construction of a pregiven world of meaning where rights and obligations have an external and objective reality. Social relationships are given the appearance of belonging to a naturally existing reality by merging constative, normative and expressive claims. Natural domains of competence are created and reproduced. Birth, marriage, death, and other rituals reproduce Zamoran culture and through it, generate the social structure that allocates to gender, generation, and status categories their appropriate privileges and obligations. Rituals create the present out of the past for the future (Bloch 1977).

Sacred and Secular Models

Behavior during the major religious rituals satisfies what Durkheim considered as "a system of ideas with which individuals represent to themselves the society of which they are members, and the obscure but intimate relations which they have with it" (1965:257). Durkheim considered this a quintessential feature of religion. But, for him, another important element of religion is its sacred or transcendental emphasis, a feature absent in many collective gatherings such as feasts and dances. While such occasions uphold and reaffirm the collective sentiments and ideas that give Zamoran society its unity and personality (Durkheim 1965:475), they do not do so primarily in transcendental terms. In this sense, Durkheim overestimated the importance of the sacred and the transcendental in expressing collective sentiments and ideas. He failed to realize that a secular situation can adequately fulfill the functions he attributed to religion.

An important feature of Zamoran religion is its emphasis on relations in the natural world. As Marx (1975:46-48) repeatedly stressed, religious ideology arises out of social practice—in the relations of exploitation and contradiction between sections and classes of society. It is these social forces that are responsible for the creation, the form, and the content of religion. Religious ideology in Zamora is firmly rooted in social practice and experience. Within this ideology, relations between people—e.g., status and the position of seniors—rather than their relations with nature (i.e., the animal world, forests, rice, etc.) or with God, constitute the major concern of morality.[12]

Both Durkheim (1965:257) and Weber (1970:280-81, 1971:1) stressed the cognitive functions of religion. For them, religion provides people with a rationale for their most intimate and essential relationships and bestows meaning on otherwise impenetrable aspects of experience. It is on the basis of this ideal model (i.e., religion and morality) that people respond to and sometimes alter their material conditions. Engels (1975:239-42) admits as much in his letter to Joseph Bloch but, as Weber pointed out, the conse-quences of a religious ethic are often unexpected and unintended. In earlier chapters, I have explored some of the consequences of holding a particular ethic, e.g., Methodists, Iglesia ni Kristo.

Native models of Zamoran society include secular and transcendental aspects. But in the case of religion, secular aspects predominate and provide a model for relations with the supernatural. For this reason, an event like a feast is as important as collective religious rites are in express-ing significant relationships. Examples of collective religious rites are Good Friday and All Souls' Day. In this sense, I agree with Durkheim that societies must regularly celebrate their collective sentiments to express their moral unity and thereby bestow meaning on significant aspects of experience. But I disagree with his implications that they necessarily do so largely in transcendental terms. The importance of the transcendent and the sacred play a major role in certain religions like Christianity, Buddhism, Hinduism, and Islam, but not in others (von Furer-Haimendorf 1969, Wilson 1971). Both the indigenous religion and current Christian practices in Zamora are an example of the latter. Part of the explanation for a lack of emphasis on the transcendent sphere lies in the theory of society manifested in the relations between the sexes, the generations and status categories. These relations refer to a conscious set of norms and values legitimating various aspects of social inequality, e.g., male-female, senior-junior, rich-poor. The native model of society has implications for the system of production, allocating and legitimating class positions. But since class relations are not a major element of the conscious model, the consequences of class are not fre-quently examined. Structural contradictions, like the discrepancy between women's economic and political roles, are unresolved and generate tension and conflict in intersexual relations. For instance, the notions of female

12. See M. Wilson (1971:137) for a similar assessment of some African religions.

subordination and romantic love coexist with the belief that women control household finances because they have greater self-control and are more reliable in such matters than men.

While Zamora does not entirely meet Marx's requirements of a society in which "practical relations of everyday life offer to man none but perfectly intelligible and reasonable relations with regard to his fellow men and to nature" (1906:118), the prevailing ideology stresses both the practical relations of everyday life and intelligible relations with one's fellowmen. The partial satisfaction of Marx's requirements may not lead to a reduction of a need for religion, but it may well contribute to an acceptance of the ideology advocated by radical political groups in which the transcendent or sacred element is unimportant. Hence what may appear to be an extraneous source of change and disruption should instead be seen to lie within certain internal features of Zamoran social structure. This partly explains why peasant society can respond simultaneously to secular and transcendental ideologies.

Rationality and the Rationalization of Social Life

One of the major concerns of fieldwork was to examine the basis for religious conversion and practice in Zamora, a municipality which had had a long experience of Catholic proselytization. In an earlier publication (Pertierra 1981), I pointed out that the original inhabitants of Zamora initially rejected Catholicism but eventually accepted Protestantism because of the strategic and political advantages resulting therefrom. This interior minority group adopted such a strategy to retain its cultural and political boundaries against the growing encroachment of the coastal Ilocano majority. While I had stressed the strategic aspects of the behavior, I neglected to emphasize that this response represented an equal concern to maintain maximum conditions for religious discourse. In other words, the behavior mentioned exemplified both strategic and communicative rationality. The strategic aspect was concerned with maintaining cultural and political boundaries; this was intended to preserve the privileges and resources they enjoyed as the original inhabitants of the valley from the growing domination of the coastal Ilocanos. The communicative aspect of the behavior was meant to preserve the relatively open nature of religious discourse; accepting a form of Protestantism guaranteed the religious autonomy of each congregation, whereas conversion to Catholicism would have represented the loss of autonomy over the conditions of religious discourse to the control of Western-educated, urban Ilocanos. For those who accepted Catholicism, certain areas of their lives are more permeated by Catholic belief and practice than others. Hence, for Catholics, public life is characterized by Catholic rites while private-domestic life is marked by the performance of traditional, pre-Catholic rituals. The former rituals coincide with conditions of restricted communication while the latter duplicate the relative autonomy of the peasant household in domestic matters. In contrast, conversion to Protestantism often results in a break with the traditional religious past, since Protestantism, unlike Catholicism, satisfies the earlier conditions of autonomous discourse. These different responses to Christian conversion represent an attempt to maintain a domain of autonomous discourse, in one case by taking advantage of a break in the structure of power (i.e., from the public to the domestic domain in the case of Catholic conversion) and in the other by exploiting a feature of ideology (i.e., religious autonomy of each congregation in the case of Protestantism). Both represent attempts to preserve maximum conditions for communicative rationality.

Similar comments may be made regarding the arbitration and adjudication of disputes. People in Zamora often decide to settle disputes through customary procedures rather than undergo the more expensive, unpredictable, and often alienating experience of formal courts. However, the progressive commoditization of land and the recently completed cadastral survey increasingly force people to settle land disputes through the courts. This procedure is not necessarily seen as preferable to traditional methods but people are aware of the state's growing ability to enforce its decisions in such matters. However, in other areas people resort to traditional adjudication. In contrast to formal court proceedings—which are generally held in English and which involve complex and for most people, incomprehensible rules of evidence and testimony—village disputes are settled through respected local mediators after exhaustive and unrestricted discussions by all interested parties. Instead of a court bringing down a judgment, customary adjudication aims to reach an understanding (Barton 1919, Schlegel 1970). The court only considers evidence and testimony directly pertinent to the case and restricts discussion accordingly. Village mediators, while concerned with procedural and evidentiary practices, must take equal notice of the recognized needs and intentions of the parties; hence, discussion covers normative and strategic aspects (Pertierra 1978).

Moreover, in theory Western jurisprudence may be predictable and distributive, but in practice, it is often unpredictable and nondistributive. This difference between formal and substantive rationality arises whenever a system of jurisprudence is embedded in a highly inegalitarian political structure. Customary adjudication is also constrained by procedure and form but it is closely attuned to the particular needs and intentions of all parties, including the general community. Hence it is more likely to achieve a practical understanding than a court judgment.

For these reasons, whatever may be said concerning the systems-rationality of formal court proceedings as compared with traditional methods of settling disputes, we can say that the latter are more rational for individual actors. They are more predictable and explicitly related to acceptable notions of distributive justice. In this case, the formal rationality of court proceedings conflicts with its substantive practice. Moreover, formal rationality is achieved only after disembodying and restricting the conditions of discourse. In Habermas's terms, customary adjudication is based on mutually recognized and discursively redeemable validity claims that bring into play notions of propositional truth, normative rightness, and subjective truthfulness. In contrast to this emphasis on communicative rationality, court proceedings stress strategic rationality and restrict or formalize both normative claims and subjective truthfulness. Because of this, traditional methods persist in areas where the State is unable or unwilling to exercise its sovereignty.

What has been said for formal legal discourse applies equally to formal political discourse in Zamora. Nationally imposed village political structures are often ineffective and characterized by the rhetoric of their incumbents. Men and women manage most village affairs through informal channels. Their experience and affiliations enable them to perceive local needs and normative constraints. Some of them may hold formal political rank, or enjoy high status as religious leaders and schoolteachers, or possess considerable economic resources. Despite the considerable importance of these factors, village influence ultimately relates to a person's ability to elicit and sustain a generally recognized understanding of a particular issue or problem rather than on the ability to coerce or mobilize a solution (Pertierra 1976). While the element of coercion in one form or another is ever present and often resorted to, most people make a clear distinction between a "forced" understanding or solution and a subjectively acceptable one. The latter necessarily relies on the discursive redemption of normative, propositional and subjective claims and is carried out during long and unrestricted discussions.

In contrast, formal political discourse is conducted under restricted conditions of communication marked by rhetoric and laudatory commendations. Since the basis of compliance is not founded on rational and subjective assent but on coercive force, formal political discourse need not elaborate its normative claims. Both the form and the content of political discourse reflect the structure and nature of power within which the discourse is situated (Bourdieu 1979). External political ties occur in a power structure marked by great disparities and by predominantly strategic interests. In such a context, the value of an utterance does not lie in its content but on the power of the utterer. Rhetoric or other restricted codes predominate (Bernstein 1973) and discourse tends to be ritualized (Bloch 1974). A dominant idiom such as English limits the ability of peasants to assert and justify their discursive claims. Internal political relations are less marked by power differentials and are more characterized by normative interests. In this latter context, utterances depend more on their content for their value and there is a corresponding tendency to employ discursive models using the rich vernaculars.

Self-interest is an aspect of village behavior but moral-practical concerns require that some actions at least are aimed toward reaching an understanding. This concern for understanding becomes less marked in dealings with powerful outsiders. Relations between villagers and outsiders are exaggeratedly deferential and circumscribed. When Zamora people deal with outsiders, strategic considerations often come ahead of mutual understanding; the relationship is oriented toward success rather than toward mutual understanding. In such cases, peasants may initiate links attuned to the most recent political practices and may advocate radical change. The political life of Zamora consists of external alignments along instrumental and strategic lines combined with internal relationships based on mutually recognized normative claims.

The tension between these contradictory tendencies—the gains from externally based alliances versus the moral claims of internal ties—is never completely resolved. This tension or contradiction often leads to the erosion of internal political support or to the repudiation of external ties. The regular and predictable rise and fall of political careers in Zamora reflect the conflicting claims exerted by, as well as the lack of articulation between, the demands of village life and the realities of external politics.

The rapid acceptance of tobacco and other cash crops among Ilocanos proves that peasant farmers are not conservative. After the war, these farmers grew Virginia tobacco with enthusiasm. This is proof that given adequate conditions, peasants will seize the opportunity to increase their cash incomes (Torres 1982, Pertierra 1979). While the farmers quickly adapted the required techniques for tobacco production, its capitalization and sale were just as rapidly monopolized by urban capitalists who used the occasion to increase and expand their bases of power. This resulted in the progressive demoralization of most farmers, many of whom attempted to compensate for their losses by taking illicit advantages of government programs like the Green Revolution and land reform. The latter response is often seized upon by outside observers as evidence of peasant recalcitrance and poor planning, while contributory factors such as unpredictable prices, spiralling interest rates, misclassification of tobacco leaves and other discriminatory practices are conveniently ignored.

While new crops like tobacco and cotton are easily accepted by peasant farmers, new varieties of rice are not as enthusiastically received. Farmers in Zamora are quick to point out the difference between venturing into crops grown for cash, on the one hand, and risking the year's harvest by trying out new rice varieties, on the other.

Apart from changes in the methods of planting, weeding, harvesting, threshing and storage—some of which involve significant reorganization of labor—the new rice varieties require capital investments in fertilizer and pesticides which then tie the farmer more firmly into urban-controlled financial and technical institutions. Moreover, formerly corporate resources such as the various edible species found in the rice paddies (e.g., frogs and fish) and in the river (e.g., shrimps) are affected either by the pesticides in the fields or by the uncontrolled use of river-water for irrigation. The largely private gain in rice production is offset by the loss in corporate resources.

Finally, some traditional rice varieties (glutinous) are necessary for major religious and festive occasions such as ancestral feasts, weddings, and baptisms. Hence, besides technical and organizational disruptions to proven rice-growing practices, the new varieties involve a greater dependence on extrabarrio institutions, thereby reducing village autonomy. These varieties also offend against deeply felt religious and aesthetic needs. For these reasons, it is not difficult to see why farmers can simultaneously adjust to a new crop like tobacco or cotton while continuing to depend on traditional rice varieties. In other words, farmers in Zamora display instrumental rationality in their approach to cash crops. But a more complex notion of rationality is needed to describe their attitude to a subsistence crop like rice. For a subsistence crop such as rice, normative and aesthetic factors are as important in determining its rational acceptability as are technical and instrumental goals.

Barrio life has an apparent urban cultural orientation. Villagers often refer to town-life as culturally superior to barrio-life, even if they prefer to live in the barrio. Everyday life in the village is seen as monotonous and uneventful; it is contrasted with everyday life in towns and cities where one finds a variety of activities.

These town activities, however, are also seen as directly related to a highly monetized economy. Barrio life is, on the other hand, seen as relatively nonmonetized. Village culture revolves around annual events such as feasts and other communal occasions as well as the regular performance of life-crises rituals. These activities vary: from major performances of traditional plays like the *comedia* to private occasions like the celebration of a child's new name. The *comedia* involves scores of actors and musicians and can last for several days; the ritual of renaming a child, on the other hand, involves only a few participants. In between are events like school graduations, public dances, religious feasts (e.g., Christmas, New Year, All Souls' Day) and private but large gatherings at weddings, baptisms, funerals, and death anniversaries. Most of these occasions are marked by traditional dancing, singing and storytelling, oratory, competitive games, and feasting. While strong urban influences are present in many of these activities, their primary orientation arises out of well-established barrio practices.

Children who perform the latest dance styles during school programs to display their urbanity illustrate the modernizing influence of schooling. But in another context, such as a public dance or at a wedding, modern dancing is strongly disapproved and is interpreted as offensive to barrio mores. In other words, urban cultural influences are recontextualized to prevent their permeation into important aspects of village life. Adolescents in Zamora, as in the rest of the Philippines, strive to learn the tune and words of the latest pop songs, which they perform before their suitably impressed audiences. Yet these same adolescents, in their behavior if not in their songs, are also expected to conform to the exigencies of village courtship which are often diametrically opposed to the romantic sentiments of their songs.

As in other areas of peasant society, the effects of urban cultural influences on village life are not always predictable. Acceptance of a cultural trait at one level does not guarantee its incorporation at another. Village culture has its own imperatives and rationales, and whenever these coincide with urban influences, their assimilation and acceptance into village life is unproblematic. Often the precise paths of acculturation are unpredictable and not systematically intended. One of the major influences of schooling in Zamora since the war, for example, has been the rapid spread of the practice of superincision among adolescent boys. It was introduced by Manila-educated male teachers who, over the last couple of decades, have informed their students of this Tagalog practice. Nothing in the indigenous culture was particularly adverse to superincision while several elements associated with the symbolic creation of adolescent sexuality supported its acceptance.

Change affecting cultural, political, and economic aspects of village society is variable. Some areas of barrio life quickly respond to outside forces; others are stubbornly resistant.

Moral economists argued that the moral basis of peasant culture arises out of adaptations guaranteeing minimum subsistence rather than maximum efficiency. This explains why peasants are reluctant to enter a cash economy. While peasants see the advantages of a cash economy they do not want to rely on a market whose forces are beyond their technical and normative control. Peasant values are rational solutions to the particular exigencies of village life. If at times these values stress continuity and passivity, they may nevertheless be quickly transformed into radical protest under the appropriate conditions. The normative homogeneity of peasant society obviously varies, but internal factors tend to increase rather than diminish it. The political economists also assumed the rationality of peasants but saw its manifestation primarily in instrumental and strategic terms rather than in the normative sense. They pointed out the inevitable divisions of peasant society and argued that a cash economy may benefit the lower echelons of the peasantry. Village life generates its own impetus for change and whatever stability is present is due as much to the lack of alternatives and the oppression by its more powerful members as it is to a presumed desire to maintain generally shared norms and values.

This apparent disagreement between moral and political economists results from their failure to locate the appropriate order of rationality. The moral economists stressed the rationality of peasant normative systems while the political economists underlined the strategic concerns of peasant behavior. But these two distinct orders of rationality coexist in peasant society as they do in most other societies. The point is to identify the conditions in which one order is dominant over the other and the constraints that these conditions exercise over peasant behavior. Then one could ask under what conditions do normative values prevent strategic choices from generating structures that challenge traditional norms, e.g., the pursuit of market opportunities may contradict normative expectations of reciprocity (Keyes 1983).

This extension of the recognized rationality of peasant behavior to encompass the normative, the instrumental and strategic dimensions is revealing. But Habermas's notion of communicative rationality adds to our further understanding of the basis of peasant actions. Communicative rationality aims to achieve maximum understanding and is feasible only under conditions of unrestricted discourse. The response to change is often determined by the attempt to preserve the conditions for unrestricted discourse. Patterns of religious conversion and practice in Zamora represent such an attempt: in an initial resistance to Christianity; in the subsequent acceptance of Protestantism; and in the confining of Catholic practice to some areas of life and retaining traditional control over others. Similar attempts may be seen in resorting to customary forms of adjudication or settling disputes. The inexplicability, unpredictability, and expense of formal court proceedings are replaced by a procedure that ensures the active participation of all parties under conditions of discourse which are more likely to arrive at a mutually satisfactory understanding. While much formal political discourse is characterized by rhetoric, its practice is often limited to achieving strategic gains. In contrast, informal political forums are occasions for genuine and unbounded speech where normative as well as constative claims are exhaustively verified. However, such informal political forums do not extend beyond the barrio and hence whenever extrabarrio political links are established, strategic rather than communicative interests predominate.

The Zamora economy exemplifies high adaptive capacities for both technical and strategic action. This is best illustrated in the cases of Virginia tobacco and of cotton. But in the case of rice, noneconomic elements enter into the final decision; hence, while technical and strategic interests are present, normative and aesthetic factors must also be considered.

Finally, in the cultural realm as in other aspects of Zamora society, outside forces are incorporated within a preexisting structure of meaning and signification. The existing cultural system is neither exhaustive nor totally consistent; hence, new elements are easily assimilated. Their effects are often difficult to predict and in many cases, the behavior is recontextualized or situationally bounded. The analysis pursued in this study suggests that the concept of communicative action is as central to society and culture as are technical and strategic actions. Peasant societies are no exception and in some instances, these societies exemplify communicative action more fully than technologically advanced Western societies. This feature is undoubtedly related to the structures of power in relatively small communities that have maintained some autonomy from centralized states. The attempt by such communities to preserve that enlarged communicative rationality, or to resist its diminution may underlie many contemporary struggles over the transformation of peasant life. Such struggles are often portrayed as reactionary responses to change or as romantic attachments to the past. In reality they represent attempts to control conditions of discourse that allow the articulation of an alternative stance, making possible the conditions of resistance.

Some readers may object that the use of a culturally specific construct such as communicative rationality as developed by Habermas is inapplicable in other contexts and particularly in cultures lacking a developed and explicit philosophical discourse. Moreover, the societies that anthropologists traditionally study (Zamora is no exception) are not generally characterized by the differentiation of cognitive structures from social relationships or by a decentered view of the world that permits the structural or institutional separation of normative claims from technical or expressive ones (e.g., Evans-Pritchard's paraphrase of Mauss 1969). According to Habermas, "the spell that the cultural tradition casts on an intersubjectivity free of force and based on rationally motivated conviction cannot be broken" (1979:203) unless one is able to distinguish conceptually and structurally the normative order from the technical and expressive orders. In the quoted passage, Habemas reveals his Eurocentric bias. He assumes, like many anthropologically unaware social theorists, that culture and social structure impose themselves on their subjects so comprehensively and with such a force that only a philosophically sustained rational critique can expose their conventional nature. While reflective criticism is undoubtedly necessary in a culture such as ours, with its solid and enduring power structures, it may not be necessary in more loosely structured societies such as the Mbuti (Turnbull 1961) or the Subanun (Frake 1969). In these latter cases, an awareness of the conventional and agreed-upon nature of culture and social structure may result simply because the distribution of power is so diffuse that the maintenance and reproduction of culture and social structure require regular and conscious cooperation rather than simple coercion. In such circumstances, while we would not expect the Mbuti or the

Subanun to offer us a philosophically adequate critique of their societies in Habermas's sense, their conditions of free and unrestricted discourse could well lead to a perception of the conventional nature of the social order.

In Zamora, as in many other societies, the attainment of special know-ledge and power is associated with the temporary and voluntary withdrawal from society. This often involves contravening major norms and enduring ordeals in order to achieve a more comprehensive view of the world, society and the self. While this example does not satisfy Weber's and Habermas's criteria of rational action, it indicates a conscious scepticism of the natural and social orders and how to undermine them. Many of the practices of Hinduism and Buddhism are directed toward the same ends (i.e., the systematic undermining or unveiling of commonsense reality).

Zamora social structure is more enduring and complex than that of the Mbuti or Subanun. It includes several ethnic communities whose members enjoy a certain autonomy but who are ultimately affected by Ilocano provincial and Filipino national structures. Within such constraints, people in Zamora attempt to exploit and defend the areas permitting the exercise of choice. Its exercise takes place with the knowledge that Zamoran society is a part of a wider world which, while alluring, is less amenable to Zamoran control than is local society. In the local community, normative expectations are generally known or may be discursively redeemed. Technical knowledge is relatively accessible and claims to authenticity may be objectively assessed. Thus, the conditions for reaching an understanding are more likely to be present than they are in extravillage forums. This is shown by the eagerness that villagers display for certain forms of disputation. It is not uncommon for doctrinal debates to be actively pursued by the adherents of the different Christian denominations in Zamora. These occasions attract large crowds who evidently enjoy listening to the arcane theological de-bates. Disputes of a more serious nature such as adultery, theft or malicious harm are equally interesting to the majority of villagers. Adjudicators clearly distinguish objective conditions from normative expectations and authentic intentions. An example concerned a case of adultery whose deliberations lasted a week, including visits to neighboring districts to ascertain the facts, extensive discussions of the duties and rights of marriage, and a rigorous examination of motives and good faith. The strategic interests of the litigants and their kin were deliberately excluded while the case was being heard by the village elders, but these were later included within the pragmatic resolution of the dispute. While many of these discursive occa-sions are used for rhetorical purposes, there is a genuine attempt to articulate and explore the prevailing state of affairs and its implication for normative expectations. In other words, the conventional basis of Zamoran society is raised and tested against technical and expressive demands. What is lacking in Zamora, as in other societies studied by anthropologists, is a theoretical elaboration of the perception regarding the conventional nature of society by a class of intellectuals. Intellectuals as individuals (i.e., people who take considerable pleasure, and who spend a significant amount of time, in reflecting on the basis of society) exist in Zamora, as I would suggest they do in most societies (Radin 1957). But the division of labor and the institutionalization of social life have not generated a class whose major activity is systematic reflection. This activity (overlooking for the moment the presence in Zamora of schoolteachers, religious ministers and a handful of professionals) is only possible for seniors or elders whose economic position gives them ample time for reflection and whose status ensures that their ideas receive the community's attention.

However, the absence of a class of intellectuals and the lack of an explicitly philosophical discourse has not prevented people in Zamora from reflecting, albeit in a practical manner, on the nature of their society. Their right to this discourse is guarded jealously and is reflected in the variable response to the exogenous forces acting on their society.

Once we accept that peasants act purposive-rationally and value-rationally (even without having a philosophical account of rationality), we can expect them to seek conditions that allow them the full extent of possible choices. This involves maximizing the conditions for reaching an understanding, since only then would the technical knowledge, normative expectations and expressive orientations become available as possible bases for action. While a theoretical account of rationality such as that provided by Habermas may itself become a basis for rational action, its concrete practice depends on existing constraints, including the possibility of free discourse. Social theorists have so far given much attention to the cognitive and philosophical bases for rationality. They have, however, neglected to examine the structural bases for its exercise. The practice of reason can only take place within specific structural configurations, where assent or refusal are equally possible and the informational basis for choice is readily available. These structural conditions are often absent in societies which nevertheless possess the philosophical conceptions for its practice. Hence, a philosophical account of rationality must be complemented by an anthropological description of its practice. We might then be closer in understanding why it is that contemporary Western civilization is characterized both by an expanding rationalism and an eclipse of reason.

Through reference to the peasants' goal of preserving locally defined conditions of discourse, one can in the case of the Philippines more readily appreciate the following features: the persistence of animist practices and beliefs after the imposition of Spanish Catholicism in the sixteenth century; the strong attempts to secularize and indigenize the Catholic clergy and its theology from the eighteenth to the twentieth centuries; and, finally, the continued presence of religiopolitical movements in contemporary times despite the introduction of liberal American reforms and political independence. Attempts to understand these phenomena have usually stressed their so-called irrational character (Sturtevant 1976). The argument developed in this study is able to explain and confront such views within a more inclusive paradigm of social action without resorting to derogatory or exotic cognitive categories. It is precisely by taking advantage of discontinuities in the structure that peasants are able to exercise rational choice. Their attempts to preserve such discontinuities should be seen as a defense of the role of reason.

APPENDIX 1: Kinship Terminology

Cognates

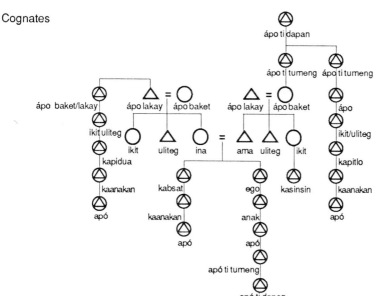

Reference/address for members of ego's generation extended to cousins

- manang/manong or kaka
- ego
- ading or innudi

Affines

- katugangan
- abirat
- hipag/kayong
- ego
- asawa
- kayong
- abirat
- hipag
- abirat
- abalayan
- manugang

Step Kin

- anakaina ama
- ina panakaama
- kabsat ti ama
- ego asawa
- kabsat ti ina
- anak siuman

(5) Ritual Kin

- compadre
- compadre
- ama/ina ti casar/buniag
- anak ti casar/buniag
- kabsat ti casar/buniag

casar (marriage)
buniag (baptism)

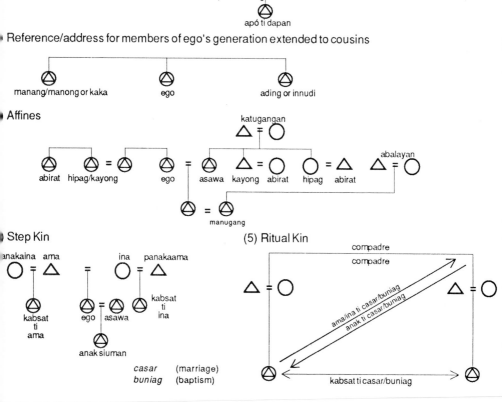

APPENDIX 2: **Members of Catholic Organizations**

Office Bearers of the Parish Pastoral Assembly 1975-1976

Position	Name (Occupation or rank)	Barrio of Origin
President	Mayor B. Velasco	Ambugat
Vice-Presidents	Miss S. Demala (school principal)	Ambugat
	Mr. L. Cuna (affluent professional)	Lucaban
Secretary	Mrs. G. Filio (school principal)	Luna
Assistant Secretary	Councilor Peralta	Bato
Treasurer	Miss. L. Tria (landowner)	Luna
Assistant Treasurer	Mr. L. Este (farmer)	Cabcaburao
First Auditor	Miss I. Este (school principal)	Cabcaburao
Second Auditor	Judge B. Primero	Masingit
Third Auditor	Former Vice-Mayor S. Sabado	Dayanki
Business Managers	Councilor A. Dalit	Balugang
	Councilor T. Doydan	Subadi
	Councilor E. Gamo	Manobok
	Councilor S. Goro	Lesseb
	Vice-Mayor T. Paraiso	Luna
	Former Councilor B. Tales	Padayao
	Former Councilor A. Reyna	Bangbangar
	Mr. M. Dizon (businessman)	Bato
	Mr. B. Demenden (insurance agent)	Luna
	Mr. E. Reola (chief of police)	Macaoayan
Business Managers	Mr. F. Mansang (surveyor)	Lucaban
	Mr. T. Daproda (farmer)	Dayanki

Note: Only 14 out of 26 barrios are represented: northern faction (11), and southern faction (11).

Members of the Knights of Columbus 1975-1976

Position	Name (Occupation or rank)	Barrio of Origin
President	Mayor B. Velasco	Ambugat
Advocate	Judge B. Primero	Masingit
Vice-President	Mr. L. Cuna (affluent professional)	Lucaban
Secretary	Councilor C. Peralta	Bato
Treasurer	Mr. J. Gatan (businessman)	Bato
Assistant Treasurer	Mr. E. Barcia (municipal treasurer)	Dayanki
Auditor	Mr. A. Brillantes (municipal secretary)	Macaoayan
Auditor	Mr. L. Filio (development officer)	Luna
Members	Mr. R. Temporada (businessman)	Luna
	Mr. B. Demenden (insurance agent)	Luna
	Councilor E. Gamo	Manobok
	Former Councilor A. Reyna	Bangbangar
	Mr. I. Liboso (businessman)	Dayanki
	Mr. J. Liboso (policeman)	Bangbangar

197

Mr. F. Mansang (surveyor)	Lucaban
Mr. E. Reola (police chief)	Macaoayan
Mr. A. Maoa (businessman)	Macaoayan
Councilor S. Goro	Lesseb
Mr. F. Mine (farmer)	Taliao
Mr. L. Velasco (postman)	Bato
Mr. E. Ventiso (teacher)	Lucaban
Councilor T. Doydan	Subadi
Mr. C. Peralta (professional employee)	Ambugat
Mr. J. Demala (teacher)	Ambugat
Mr. S. Yanka (professional employee)	Lucaban

Note: Only 13 barrios represented: northern faction (19); and southern faction (6).

Women's Associations 1975-1976

A. **Organizations stressing a public Catholic lifestyle**
   1. *Catholic Women's League*
      President: Mrs. E. Velasco (schoolteacher and mayor's wife; Ambugat)
      Vice-President: Miss S. Demala (school principal and mayor's cousin; Ambugat)
      Secretary: Mrs. G. Filio (school principal; Luna)
      Treasurer: Miss V. Principe (rich spinster; Luna)
      Business Manager: Mrs. T. Paraiso (vice-mayor's wife; Luna)
   2. *Legion of Mary*
      President: Mrs. G. Filio (school principal; Luna)
      Vice-President: Miss L. Recto (rich spinster; Luna)
      Secretary: Miss A. Belix (schoolteacher; Luna)
      Treasurer: Miss V. Tolian (rich spinster; Luna)

B. **Associations stressing private piety**
   1. *Society of Our Mother of Perpetual Help*
      President: Miss I. Este (school principal; Cabcaburao)
      Vice-President: Mrs. R. Temporada (businesswoman; Luna)
      Secretary-Treasurer: Mrs. A. Taneda (schoolteacher; Balugang)
   2. *Apostolados Y Apostoladas de la Oracion*
      President: Mr. L. Este (farmer; Cabcaburao) ⎫ effeminate men
      Vice-President: Mr. R. Guzan (farmer; Luna) ⎭
      Secretary: Mrs. L. Lentino (schoolteacher; Luna)
      Treasurer: Mrs. A Demenden (sister of municipal treasurer; Luna)
   3. *Society of St. Joseph*
      President: Mrs. J. Gatan (wealthy businesswoman; Bato)
      Vice-President: Mrs. A. Maoa (nutritionist, bus operator; Macaoayan)
      Secretary: Mrs. L. Dizon (head teacher; Bato)
      Treasurer: Mrs. B. Primero (judge's wife; Masingit)
   4. *Society of St. Anthony*
      President: Mrs. A. Ilante (wealthy landowner; Mambog)
      Vice-President: Miss B. Tilan (schoolteacher; Mambog)
      Treasurer: Mrs. T. Caba (businesswoman; Cadacad)
      Secretary: Miss C. Reyes (wealthy spinster; Mambog)

References Cited

ACHUTEGUI, P. and BERNAD, M. 1961. *Religious Revolution in the Philippines*. Manila: Ateneo de Manila Press.

AGPALO, R. 1972. *The Political Elite and the People*. Quezon City: University of the Philippines.

————. 1973. *The Organic-Hierarchical Paradigm*. Quezon City: University of the Philippines.

ALONSO, I. et al. 1968. *The Catholic Church in the Philippines Today*. Manila: Historical Conservation Society.

ANDERSON, A. 1966. The Modernization of Education. *Modernization: The Dynamics of Growth*. Edited by M. Weiner. Washington: Voice of America Forum Series.

ANDERSON, E. 1976. "Traditions in Conflict: Filipino Responses to Spanish Colonialism, 1565-1665." Ph.D. dissertation, University of Sydney.

ARCE, W. 1973. The Structural Bases of Compadre Characteristics. *Philippine Sociological Review* 21:35-50.

BANTON, M. (ed.). 1966. *Anthropological Approaches to the Study of Religion*. A.S.A. No. 3. Tavistock, London.

BARNETT, M. 1967. Subsistence and Transition of Agricultural Development Among the Ibaloi. *Studies in Philippine Anthropology*. Edited by M. Zamora. Quezon City.

BARTH, F. 1975. *Ritual and Knowledge among the Baktaman of New Guinea*. New Haven: Yale University Press.

BARTON, R. 1946. *Ifugao Religion*. Washington: American Anthropological Association, Memoir 65.

————. 1969 (1919). *Ifugao Law*. Berkeley, California: University of California Press.

————. 1973. *The Kalingas — their Institutions and Custom Law*. Chicago: University of Chicago Press.

BELLO, M. 1972. *Kankanai Social Organization and Culture Change*. Quezon City: University of the Philippines Press.

BERGER, P. 1973. *The Social Reality of Religion*. Harmondsworth: Penguin.

BERNSTEIN, B. 1973. *Class, Codes and Control*. London: Paladin.

BLOCH, M. 1974. Symbols, Song, Dance and Features of Articulation. *Archives Europeenes de Sociologie* 15(1):55-81.

————. 1977. The Past and the Present in the Present. *Man* (N.S.) Vol. 12:272-92.

BOCK, P. (ed.). 1969. *Peasants in the Modern World*. Albuquerque: University of New Mexico.

BOISSEVAIN, J. 1974. *When the Saints Go Marching Out*. Amsterdam: European Mediterranean Study Group.

BOURDIEU, P. 1977. *Outline of a Theory of Practice*. New York: Cambridge University Press.

————. 1979. The economics of linguistic exchanges. *Social Science Information* 16 (6):645-68.

BULATAO, J. and GOROSPE, V. 1966. *Split Level Christianity*. Quezon City: Ateneo de Manila University Press.

BRAGANZA, J. 1965. *The Encounter*. Cebu: University of San Carlos.

CARROLL, J. (ed.). 1970. *Philippine Institutions*. Manila: Solidaridad.

CHAYANOV, A. 1967. *The Theory of Peasant Economy*. U.S.A.: Thormer, Kerblay and Smith.

CLASTRES, P. 1977. *Society Against the State*. Translated by R. Hurley. New York: Mole Editions.

CLAVER, F. 1973. "Sharing the Wealth and the Power." Ph.D. dissertation, University of Colorado.
————, et al. 1973. *Bukidnon Politics and Religion*. I.P.C. Papers 11. Quezon City: Ateneo de Manila University.
COLE, F.C. 1915. *Traditions of the Tingguian*. Field Museum Series, University of California.
————. 1922. *The Tingguian*. Field Museum Series, University of California.
————. 1945. *The Peoples of Malaysia*. New York: Simon and Schuster.
COVAR, P. 1975. "The Iglesia Watawat ng Lahi: A Sociological Study of a Social Movement in the Philippines." Ph.D. dissertation, University of Arizona.
DOUGLAS, M. 1966. *Purity and Danger*. London: Routledge and Kegan Paul.
————. 1973. *Natural Symbols*. Harmondsworth: Pelican Books.
DURKHEIM, E. 1965 (1915). *The Elementary Forms of the Religious Life*. Translated by J. Swain. New York: Free Press.
EDER, J. 1974. "The Origin, Maintenance and Perpetuation of Social Inequality in a Philippine Community." Ph.D. dissertation, University of California, Santa Barbara.
————. 1975. Naming Practices and the definition of affines among the Batak of Palawan, *Ethnology* 14:59-70.
EGGAN, F. 1960. The Sagada Igorots of Northern Luzon. *Social Structure in Southeast Asia*. Edited by G. Murdock. Chicago: Tavistock.
EGGAN, F. and SCOTT, W.H. 1965. Ritual Life of the Igorots of Sagada. *Ethnology* 44:77-112.
EISENSTADT, S.N. (ed.). 1968. *The Protestant Ethic and Modernization*. New York: Basic Books.
ELLWOOD, D. 1968. *Churches and Sects in the Philippines*. Dumaguete City: Silliman University.
————. 1969. Varieties of Christianity. *Studies in Philippine Church History*. Edited by G. Anderson. Ithaca: Cornell University Press.
ENGELS, F. 1972. *The Origin of the Family, Private Property and the State*. Moscow: Progress.
FEGAN, B. 1982. Land Reform and Technical Change in Central Luzon: The Rice Industry under Martial Law. ASAA Fourth National Conference, Monash University.
FORONDA, M. and FORONDA, E. 1974. *Samtoy: Essays in Iloko History and Culture*. Manila: De La Salle College.
FORTES, M. 1969. *Kinship and the Social Order*. Chicago: Chicago University Press.
FOX, R. 1956. Ritual Co-parenthood. In *Area Handbook on the Philippines*. Human Relations Area Files, Chicago University.
FOX, R. and FLORY, E. 1974. *The Filipino People: Differentiation and Distribution Based on Linguistic, Cultural, and Racial Criteria*. Manila: National Museum of the Philippines.
FRAKE, C. 1969. A Structural Description of Subanun Religious Behavior. In *Readings in Cognitive Anthropology*. Edited by S. Tyler. New York: Holt, Rinehart and Winston.
FÜRER-HAIMENDORF von, C. 1969. *Morals and Merit*. London: Weidenfeld Goldbacks.
GALANTER, M. 1966. The Modernization of Law. *Modernization: the Dynamics of Growth*. Edited by M. Weiner. Washington: Voice of America Forum Series.
GALESKI, B. 1972. *Basic Concepts of Rural Sociology*. Translated by H. Stevens. Manchester: Manchester University Press.
GEERTZ, C. 1960. *The Religion of Java*. Glencoe: Free Press.
————. 1973. Religion as a Cultural System. *Anthropological Approaches to the Study of Religion*. Edited by M. Banton. London: Tavistock.
GEERTZ, H. 1961. *Javanese Family: A Study of Kinship and Socialization*. New York: Free Press.

GENNEP van, A. 1960. *The Rites of Passage*. Translated by M.B. Vizedom and G.L. Cafee. London: Routledge and Kegan Paul.

GIDDENS, A. 1973. *The Class Structure of Advanced Societies*. London: Hutchinson.

──────. 1976. *New Rules of Sociological Method*. London: Hutchinson.

GLUCKMAN, M. 1968. The utility of the equilibrium in the study of social change. *American Anthropologist* 70.

GLUCKMAN, M. 1971. *Analysis of a Social Situation in Zululand*. Manchester: Manchester University Press.

GODELIER, M. 1977. *Perspectives in Marxist Anthropology*. Translated by R. Bain. Cambridge: Cambridge University Press.

GONZALEZ, M. 1985. "The Edge of Structures: A Study of Rizalista Religious Ideology and Filipino Culture." M.A. thesis, University of Sydney.

GUERRERO, M. 1977. "Luzon at War: Contradictions in Philippine Society 1898-1902." Ph.D. dissertation, University of Michigan.

HABERMAS, J. 1979. Aspects of the Rationality of Action. *Rationality Today*. Edited by T. Geraets. Ottawa: Ottawa University Press.

──────. 1984. *The Theory of Communicative Action* 1: *Reason and the Rationalization of Society*. Translated by T. McCarthy. Boston: Beacon Press.

HART, D. 1955. *Philippine Plaza Complex: A Focal Point in Cultural Change*. New Haven: Yale University.

HEIDEGGER, M. 1962. *Being and Time*. Translated by J. Macquarie and E.S. Robinson. New York: Harper and Row.

HERTZ, R. 1960. *Death and the Right Hand*. Translated by R. Needham and C. Needham. New York: Free Press.

HINDESS, B. and HIRST, P. 1975. *Pre-Capitalist Modes of Production*. London: Routledge and Kegan Paul.

HOLLNSTEINER, M.R. 1963. *Dynamics of Power in a Philippine Municipality*. Quezon City: U.P. Community Development Research Council.

ILETO, R. 1975. "Pasion and the Intepretation of Change in Tagalog Society (1840-1912)." Ph.D. dissertation, Cornell University.

ILOCOS REVIEW. 1971. *Christian Beginnings in Ilocandia*. *Ilocos Review* 111, 1 and 2. Major Seminary, Vigan.

JAYAWARDENA, C. 1977. Women and Kinship in Acheh Besar. *Ethnology* 21 (5):21-38.

JASPERS, K. 1933. *Man in the Modern Age*. Translated by E. Paul and C. Paul. New York: Humanities.

JOCANO, L. 1968. *Sulod Society*. Quezon City: University of the Philippines Press.

──────. 1971. Conversion and the Patterning of Christian Experience in Malitbog. Central Panay. *Acculturation in the Philippines*, edited by P. Gowing and W.H. Scott. Quezon City: New Day Publishers.

──────. 1973. *Folk Medicine in a Philippine Municipality*. Manila: National Museum.

KEYES, C. 1983. Peasant Strategies in Asian Societies: Moral and Rational Economic Approaches - A Symposium. *Journal of Asian Studies* 41:753-68.

KEESING, F. 1962. *The Ethnohistory of Northern Luzon*. Stanford: Stanford University Press.

LANDE, C. 1964. *Leaders, factions and parties*. Southeast Asian Studies. Yale University.

LEACH, E. 1961. *Rethinking Anthropology*. London: London School of Economics.

LENIN, V. 1960. The Development of Capitalism in Russia. *Collected Works*, vol. 3. Moscow: Progress Publishers.

LENSKI, G. 1963. *The Religious Factor*. New York: Anchor Books.

LEWIS, H. 1971. *Ilocano Rice Farmers*. Honolulu, University of Hawaii.

LEWIS, I.M. 1971. *Ecstatic Religion*. Harmondsworth: Penguin.

LOVE, R. 1977. "The Samahan of Papa God, Tradition and Conversion in a Tagalog Peasant Religious Movement." Ph.D. dissertation, Cornell University.

LUCKMAN, T. 1967. *The Invisible Religion*. New York: Macmillan.

LYNCH, F. 1959. *Social Class in a Bicol Town*. Philippine Studies Program, University of Chicago.

————. 1965. *Trends Report of Studies in Social Stratification and Social Mobility in the Philippines*. East Asian Cultural Series 4, 163-91.

LYNCH, F. (ed.). 1972. View from the Paddy. *Philippine Sociological Review* 20 (1-2).

————. 1975. Religion. In *Society, Culture and the Filipino*. Edited by M. Hollnsteiner. Ateneo de Manila: Institute of Philippine Culture.

LYNCH, F. and MAKIL, P. 1971. The BRAC 1967 Filipino Family Survey. In *Acculturation in the Philippines*. Edited by P. Gowing and W.H. Scott. Quezon City: New Day Publishers.

McCLELLAND, D. 1966. The Impulse to Modernization. *Modernization: the Dynamics of Growth*, ed. M. Weiner. Washington: Voice of America Forum Series.

McCOY, A. 1977. "Ylo-ilo: Factional Conflict in a Colonial Economy Iloilo Province, Philippines, 1937-1955." Ph.D. dissertation, Yale University.

————. 1982. Baylan-Animist Religion and Philippine Peasant Ideology. *Philippine Quarterly of Science and Culture* 10 (3):141-94.

MAGANNON, E. 1972. *Religion in a Kalinga Village*. Quezon City: University of the Philippines Press.

MAJUL, C. 1967. *The Political and Constitutional Ideas of the Philippine Revolution*. Quezon City: University of the Philippines Press.

————. 1973. *Muslims in the Philippines*. Quezon City: University of the Philippines.

MARX, K. 1906. *Capital: A Critique of political economy* vol. 1 - 3. Chicago: C.H. Kerr and Company.

————. 1977. *The 18th Brumaire of Louis Bonaparte*. Moscow: Progress Publishers.

MARX, K. and ENGELS, F. 1975. On *Religion*. Moscow: Progress Publishers.

MAUSS, M. 1969. *The Gift*. Translated by I. Cunnison. London: Cohen and West.

MERCADO, L. et al. 1970. The Ilocano way of death and liturgical adaptation. In *Ilocos Review* 2, 1:42-89.

MILLER, M. 1904. *Report on Investigations in Northern Luzon*. Otley Beyer Collection Bey 16/2, National Library, Canberra.

MOSS, C. 1920. *Kankanay Rituals and Ceremonies*. Berkeley: University of California.

MUIZENBERG van den, O. 1973. Political Mobilization and Violence in Central Luzon. In *Modern Asian Studies* 7, 4:691-705.

————. 1975. Involution or evolution in Central Luzon? *Cultural Anthropology in the Netherlands*, eds. P. Kloos and J.M. Klaessen. Rotterdam.

NATIONAL CENSUS OF POPULATION AND HOUSING. 1970.

NAVARRO, I. 1974. *Las Hermandades Andaluzas*. Sevilla: Universidad de Sevilla.

NYDEGGER, W. and NYDEGGER, C. 1963. *Tarong: An Ilocos Barrio*. Ithaca: Cornell University Press.

OWEN, N. 1978. Textile Displacement and the Status of Women in Southeast Asia. *Michigan Occasional Papers in Women's Studies* 17. University of Michigan.

PERTIERRA, R. 1976. The Comedia: an example of conflict and authority in a Philippine Municipality. In *Asian Studies*, April, pp. 73-82.

————. 1978. Notions of Community and the Resolution of Disputes in a Philippine Municipality. *Customary Law Journal* 2:21-40. Sydney University.

————. 1979. "Rationale of religious belief among Philippine Catholics: an Ilocano example." Ph.D. dissertation, Macquarie University.

————. 1981. Religion and Politics in a Philippine Municipality. *Cultures et developpement* 13:123-60.

————. 1983a. Levy-Bruhl and Modes of Thought: A Reappraisal. *Mankind* 14, 2:112-26.

————. 1983b. Religion as the Idiom of Political Discourse in the Philippines: A Sociological View. In *Philippine Social Sciences and Humanities Review* 47, (1-4):219-42.

————. 1988. An Anthropological Perspective on Philippine Politics. In *The Philippines under Aquino*. Edited by Peter Krinks. Canberra: The Australian Development Studies Network. Pp. 115-34.

PHELAN, J. 1964. *The Hispanization of the Philippines*. London: Wisconsin University Press.

PIRON, G. 1965. The Church in the Philippines Today. *Dialogue* 2 (1):10-12.

POPKIN, S. 1979. *The Rational Peasant*. Berkeley: University of California.

RADIN, P. 1957. *Primitive Man as Philosopher*. New York: Dover Book.

RAEDT de, J. 1964. Religious Representation in Northern Luzon. *Saint Louis Quarterly* 2, 3:1-245.

————. 1969. Some notes on Buwaya society. *Saint Louis Quarterly* 7, 1:7-112.

REINANTE-DILEM, C. and DILEM-REINANTE, C. 1976. *Genealogy of the Dilem-Reinante Family*. Burgos.

REYES de los, F. and VIDAL, C. 1965. *Character Education and Good Manners and Right Conduct*. Manila: Abiva Publishing.

REYNOLDS, H. and GRANT, F. (eds.). 1973. *The Isneg of the Northern Philippines*. Dumaguete City: Silliman University Press.

RICE PRODUCTION MANUAL. 1970. Revised edition. Quezon City: University of the Philippines.

ROSALDO, M. 1980. *Knowledge and Passion*. New York: Cambridge University Press.

ROTH, D.M. 1977. *The Friar Estates of the Philippines*. Albuquerque: University of New Mexico Press.

ROUTLEDGE, D. 1979. *Diego Silang*. Quezon City: University of the Philippines.

RUTTEN, R. 1983. Women Workers of Hacienda Milagros. *Antropologisch-Sociologisch Centrum*. No. 30, Amsterdam: University of Amsterdam.

SCHAFF, A. 1973. *Ensayos sobre Filosofia del Lenguaje*. Barcelona: Ariel.

SCHEANS, D. 1963. Suban Society. In *Philippine Sociological Review*, July, pp. 21-35.

————. 1966. Anak ti Digos. In *Philippine Sociological Review*, April, pp. 56-57.

SCHLEGEL, S. 1970. *Tiruray Justice*. Berkeley: University of California Press.

SCHMITZ, J. 1971. *The Abra Mission in Northern Luzon Philippines 1598-1955*. Cebu City: University of San Carlos Press.

SCOTT, J. 1976. *The Moral Economy of the Peasant*. New Haven: Yale University Press.

SCOTT, W.H. 1974a. *The Discovery of the Igorots*. Quezon City: New Day Publishers.

————. (ed.). 1974b. *Philippine Sociological Review* 22. Also issued as Sagada Social Studies Special issue, nos. 1-4.

SHANIN, T. (ed.). 1971. *Peasants and Peasant Societies*. Harmondsworth: Penguin.

SHOESMITH, D. 1978. "Church and Revolution in the Philippines 1896-1904." Ph.D. dissertation, Australian National University.

SMART, J. 1970. The Manolay Cult: the Genesis and Dissolution of Millenarian Sentiments among the Itneg of Northern Luzon. *Asian Studies*, vol. 8, 1:53-93.

SOUTHWOLD, M. 1971. Meanings of Kinship. In *Rethinking Kinship and Marriage*, ed. R. Needham. A.S.A. 11. London: Tavistock.

STA. ROMANA, J. 1955. "Iglesia ni Kristo". M.A. thesis, University of Manila.

STEINBERG, D. 1967. *Philippine Collaboration in World War II*. Manila: Solidaridad.

STURTEVANT, D. 1958. "Philippine Social Structure and its Relation to Agrarian Unrest." Ph.D. dissertation, Stanford.

————. 1976. *Popular Uprisings in the Philippines*. Ithaca: Cornell University Press.

TENAZAS, R. 1965. *The Santo Nino of Cebu*. Cebu City: San Carlos University.

TERRAY, E. 1972. *Marxism and Primitive Societies*. Translated by M. Klopper. New York: Monthly Review Press.

THOMAS, W. and ZNANIECKI, F. 1919. *The Polish Peasant in Europe and America*. New York: Gotham.

TORRES, P. 1982. *Philippine Virginia Tobacco: 30 years of increasing dependency*. University of the Philippines: Third World Studies Center.

TOURAINE, A. 1973. *Production de la societe*. Paris: Hachette.

TURNBULL, C. 1961. *The Forest People*. London: Picador.

TURNER, M. 1978. Interpretations of Class and Status in the Philippines: A Critical Evaluation. *Cultures et developpement* 10, 2:265-96.

TURNER, V. 1967. *The Forest of Symbols*. Ithaca, New York: Cornell University Press.

—————. 1974. *The Ritual Process*. Harmondsworth: Pelican Books.

VANOVERBERGH, M. 1955. Isneg Tales: Folklore Studies. In *Journal of Far Eastern Folklore* 14:1-148.

WARD, B. 1963. *Women in the New Asia*. Paris: UNESCO.

WEBER, M. 1970. *From Max Weber*. Edited by H. Gerth and C.W. Mills. London: Routledge and Kegan Paul.

—————. 1971. *The Sociology of Religion*. Translated by E. Fischoff. London: Methuen and Co.

WEINER, M. (ed.). 1966. *Modernization: The Dynamics of Growth*. Washington: Voice of America Forum Series.

WERNSTEDT, F. and SPENCER, J. 1967. *The Philippine Island World*. Berkeley: University of California Press.

WILD, R. 1975. *Bradstow*. Brisbane: Angus and Robertson.

WILSON, M. 1971. *Religion and the Transformation of Society*. New York: Cambridge University Press.

WOLF, E. 1966. *Peasants*. New Jersey: Prentice Hall.

WOLFF, L. 1960. *Little Brown Brothers*. Manila: Erehwon Press.

WOLTERS, W. 1983. *Politics, Patronage and Class Conflict in Central Luzon*. Institute of Social Studies, no. 14. The Hague.

Index